Books by Dr. Barnhouse

Genesis: A Devotional Commentary
The Invisible War
Revelation: An Expositional Commentary
Thessalonians: An Expositional Commentary
Acts: An Expositional Commentary

THE PANORAMA OF THE CONTINUING CONFLICT BETWEEN GOOD & EVIL

DONALD GREY BARNHOUSE

ZONDERVAN™

GRAND RAPIDS, MICHIGAN 49530

ZONDERVAN™

Preface

T wo features of the ministry of the late Dr. Donald Grey Barnhouse made his witness unique: his tremendous insight into Scripture, and his remarkable ability to bring the truths he gleaned from his study to the Christian layman in such a way as to make the Bible come alive. Those who have heard Dr. Barnhouse teach, and those who have read his writings, can testify that this is true.

In this series of studies on *The Invisible War,* Dr. Barnhouse explored a theme rarely touched upon by students of the Bible: the great conflict which exists in the spirit realm. Although almost entirely unrecognized by mankind, this warfare affects, in one way or another, the life of every person on earth and especially the life of the child of God.

Dr. Barnhouse traces the vast spiritual conflict back to the period before the beginning of Time and, step-by-step, follows its unfolding to the final battle of wills at the end of Time. In these pages, questions that have long troubled thinking people concerning the trials, sufferings and difficulties of life, are clearly answered. Here also are practical suggestions for facing life's obstacles. Here are sane, sensible explanations for the continued existence of good and evil on earth in what appears to be a never-ending tug of war. In a brilliant manner, the author has stretched out the panorama of Time and focused upon it the illuminating light of Eternity.

It was my privilege to sit under the teaching ministry of Dr. Barnhouse for some ten years and, later, to be associated with him in his work during the closing years of his abruptly shortened life. Many of the ideas and concepts to be found in these pages came to me with real force and blessing as he gave them orally in his church and Bible classes and, later, in the pages of *Eternity,* the monthly magazine he .founded.

Therefore, I am delighted to be able to write this preface for the superb study of a Bible teacher whose ministry had such a lasting effect on my own life and the lives of so many Christian people around the world. I am certain that this book will take its place as one of the greatest Dr. Barnhouse wrote during his lifetime, unfolding as it does an entirely new area of Biblical truth for many readers who have never before contemplated this invisible battle involving God, Satan, angels, demons and mankind. Indeed, I know of no other available book today which offers so comprehensive a treatment of so complex a subject.

HERBERT HENRY EHRENSTEIN
Director of Biblical Studies
Evangelical Foundation, Inc.

Table of Contents

1 : *The Great Interval*

A N Easterner who was motoring in the great southwestern area of our country studied a map to plot his itinerary. He decided that he wanted to see the Grand Canyon of the Colorado River and then proceed north into Utah for a glimpse of some of the other natural wonders of the West. The route he sketched on the map called for a straight trip north, crossing the Grand Canyon from the southern to the northern rim. However, it took several minutes on the part of a friend who knew the country to bring him to the realization that the tiny fifteen-mile gap, which hardly showed on a small map, was not bridged by any road; and that, in order to get from El Tovar on the south to Bright Angel on the north, it was necessary to drive for hours over desert roads. To the casual observer, it seemed incredible that there was not some way to link the two great highways that come so close to each other. But, when the tourist stood on the south rim of the Canyon and saw the mile-deep chasm of twisted and tortured earth, he realized why his friend had told him to put an extra full day's driving in his itinerary. There was a gap that could not be bridged, but which had to be circled on a wide range.

A GREAT GULF FIXED

We are reminded of this as we read the first two verses in the Bible. Probably one of the commonest errors in Biblical interpretation is the thought that the first verse of Genesis and the second verse are closely connected in time. This error leads many readers to believe that God had originally created the earth in chaotic form. Their minds are driven to the rim of the first verse, "In the beginning God created the heavens and the earth," and they too readily suppose it possible to go right on into the next verse, "And the earth was without form and void, and darkness covered the face of the deep."

Yet there is no doubt that between the two there is a great gulf fixed. I say "no doubt," for the matter is amply demonstrated by the

9

Scriptures themselves. Following the close of the passage, the punctuation after the first verse of the Bible is a mighty period, or, even better, what the English grammarians call a "full stop." In the beginning God created the heavens and the earth. Period. There is the divine prelude to the symphony of the Scriptures. That verse takes us back, back, back into the edges of a past eternity in which God, the Father, Son and Spirit, lived in that entirely sufficient majesty of being which encompasses Deity. If this had been recorded in the book of Psalms, there might well have been written here the word *Selah* — pause. Stop and consider. You are on the edge of an abyss. Something happened to the heavens and the earth which God had created. Millions of years may have run their course during that first creation, and other millions may have elapsed in the interval between the two verses. We do not know. But there was an interval, and we can be absolutely certain that it was a great one.

How to Read the Bible

Our certainty rests upon the Word of God and upon some of its statements about how we are to read its pages. An illustration is, perhaps, the best way to come to the heart of the method. Some years ago I entered the playroom of our home one evening, and found my two boys at work on a large picture puzzle which had been given one of the members of the family at Christmas. It was a finely made puzzle, on three-ply wood, beautifully cut, and among its hundreds of pieces a score or more were designed in the shape of common things. The little sister, three years old, too young to match the intricately cut edges of the pieces, had been allowed to pick out those pieces which resembled articles she knew and arrange them in rows at the edge of the table. She was eager to show me what she had done. Here was a piece in the shape of a clover leaf; here was an apple, a wheelbarrow, the letter S, the figure four, an umbrella, a violin and a bird. To her mind those and the other shaped pieces were the most important things in the puzzle. To see them, and to identify something that was in her world, made it all very interesting. To her older brothers, however, the shape of individual pieces was merely incidental. They knew that the violin would become part of a cloud, that the umbrella would be lost in the pattern of a lady's dress, and that the other figures would melt into flower garden and trees.

Each Verse Has Its Place

This illustration is almost perfect for the student of the Word of God. The unfortunate person who takes some text by itself and attempts to build a doctrine on it will be in utter confusion before he has gone very far. Only with this wrong type of Bible reading can anyone ever come to the absurd conclusion so often expressed, "You can prove anything by the Bible."

When, however, the shape of the individual verse is fitted into the whole divine plan of the revelation of God, the full-rounded, eternal purpose begins to be seen; and the whole of the Word of God becomes something so stupendous, so eternal, so mightily divine, that every rising doubt is checked immediately. There comes, then, a knowledge of the finality of God's revelation which becomes as much a part of the believer as his breathing, or his sense of being alive. Any other possibility cannot be entertained even for a moment. The believer knows that the Bible is the Word of God, even more surely than he knows that he is alive.

If we are going to understand the Word of God, we must have a spiritual attitude toward it. The Lord said that "the natural man receiveth not the things of the Spirit of God: for they are foolishness unto him: neither can he know them, because they are spiritually discerned" (I Corinthians 2:14). God refuses to reveal Himself to just any casual passer-by. The Lord indicated this when He said in the Sermon on the Mount: "Give not that which is holy unto the dogs, neither cast ye your pearls before swine, lest they trample them under their feet, and turn again and rend you" (Matthew 7:6). This same thought must have been in His mind when He prayed, saying, "I thank thee, O Father, Lord of heaven and earth, because thou hast hid these things from the wise and prudent, and hast revealed them unto babes. Even so, Father: for so it seemed good in thy sight" (Matthew 11:25, 26). The fact that one must have a spiritual attitude that comes from spiritual life in order to understand the deep things of the Word of God is also the true meaning of the great verse which we quote in paraphrase: "For whosoever hath [new life in Christ], to him shall be given [knowledge of the divine plan and revelation], and he shall have more abundance: but whosoever hath not [the new life in Christ], from him shall be taken away even that [common sense and deep learning that might make him one of the world's leaders of the world's thinking] he hath" (Matthew 13:12).

PUTTING THE PUZZLE TOGETHER

The proper method of Bible study, then, is analogous to the putting together of the puzzle. For any given doctrinal subject, read the entire volume, selecting every verse that bears on the truth under study. Put all of these passages together, and the synthesis of the result is the true Bible doctrine on the question with which you are concerned.

A verse from Moses, and one from Ezekiel, and one from Paul, put side by side, each illuminating the others, fit into the perfect pattern of the whole design and give the whole light which God has been pleased to reveal on that particular theme. Taken one by one, the verses may be no more than mere shapes, meaningless as far as the over-all purpose of the inspired revelation is concerned. This is why the Lord says that one of the first principles of Bible study is that no Scripture is of "private interpretation" (II Peter 1:20). The exegesis of the Greek shows that this verse should not be interpreted to restrict the right of the private individual to read and understand the Bible for himself.

The Lord says that the anointing by the Spirit renders us capable of understanding, so that we do not need to have any one teach us (I John 2:27). The existence of teachers by divine order and arrangement is like the original institution of divorce, not because it was God's first choice, but because of the hardness of the hearts of men (Matthew 19:8). The responsibility for reading and knowing the Word and will of God is upon every individual, who must find out for himself, conclude what he believes and be ready to give an answer for the hope that is within him, knowing that he will be answerable to the Lord for the content of his faith, and that he will not be permitted to present the excuse that he believed what some church or group of clergy interpreted for him. All this to show what the passage does not teach. Positively, what it does teach is that no passage of Scripture is to be taken by itself, but that Scripture must be read in the light of the rest of the Bible.

Many heresies arise from a false interpretation of a single verse of Scripture, and the matter is even sadder when we realize that the interpretation would have been corrected if the heretic had taken time to collate all of the passages covering the subject on which he erred. The one sure method of continuing in the path of truth is to have before you all that the Bible reveals on any possible point of discussion. Obviously, for any one man to know all truth would mean that he had compacted the whole of the Scripture, like a pyramid, and made it stand upon its apex with its full weight upon a single passage. Then the whole process would have to be begun over again and continued through all the thousands of topics which could be discussed from the Bible. Time is too short for any one man to do this. That is why no individual has ever been able to write a satisfactory commentary upon the whole of the Bible. Men who have spent their lives on a single book have produced the great commentaries on those individual books.

THE DOCTRINE OF THE TRINITY

Although it has utterly failed to push it to its proper and warranted conclusions, the Church throughout the ages has recognized this principle in the most obvious instances. Everyone knows that every Christian creed, Eastern, Roman or Protestant, acknowledges the doctrine of the Trinity. How did the Church arrive at that doctrine? There is no essay, treatise or even single passage in the Bible that teaches the truth. The Trinity — the word itself — is not found in the Bible, though the Church has rightly found the fact and the doctrine there. Even a Unitarian, if he be an honest Unitarian and has studied the Bible, would be forced to confess that there are passages in the Scriptures which attribute the creation of the universe to each of the three members of the Godhead. In Genesis, it is the Father who is the Creator: "In the beginning God created the heavens and the earth" (Genesis 1:1). In the New Testament, it is the Lord Jesus Christ who is the Creator: "All things were made by him: and without him was not any thing made that was made" (John 1:3). In the book of Job, it is the Holy Spirit who is designated as the Creator: "By his spirit he hath garnished the heavens" (Job 26:13).

The Church, from the beginning, has taken such scattered passages, and many others that carry similar thought, and has put them together, boldly and correctly, forming the doctrine of the Trinity as it is found in the creeds and theologies of widely varying sects. The fathers and reformers never found it strange to take a verse out of Genesis and fit it to a verse in John, and to bring a verse from Job alongside to cast yet more light on a doctrine. Such a method, which would be outrageous in any other work, is a necessity in the study of the Bible. You may not take a paragraph from astronomy, one from psychology and one from apiculture and fit them together to draw a conclusion about the balance of centrifugal and centripetal force. But a line from the prophetic vision of Ezekiel, one from the Mosaic writings and one from the poetry of the Psalms may well be put together to show us some truth about God and His heaven and His will for man.

THE LAMB THAT WAS SLAIN

As the application of this method which we are about to make may startle some readers, it may be well to amplify this discussion of method by bringing one more example that has become commonly known throughout Christendom by its use in the universal Church. It would be impossible to know the Biblical doctrine that surrounds the familiar symbol of the Lamb without taking the account of the sacrifice of Abel, that of Abraham offering Isaac, that of Moses and the Passover, and putting them together with the order of the day of atonement, to form the foundation of the doctrine of the Lamb, as the atoning sacrifice for sin. Only then we can understand the continuing development of the doctrine throughout the rest of the Scriptures. In Isaiah, we discover the first hint that the Lamb is to be a man (53:5, 6). In the fourth gospel, we see John the Baptist pointing to Jesus as the One who is God's Lamb, come to bear away the sin of the world (1:29). In the epistles, we learn that Christ, our passover, has been sacrificed for us (I Corinthians 5:7); and by the time we reach the Revelation we are ready to join with the myriads to sing: "Worthy is the Lamb that was slain to receive power, and riches, and wisdom, and strength, and honour, and glory, and blessing" (Revelation 5:12).

GOD BREATHED THE MESSAGE

It would be a simple matter to multiply illustrations of this method of setting forth the doctrines of the Word of God. These we have mentioned will suffice. We should not pass on, however, without realizing the implications of this method of study. The fact that many men of varying backgrounds, writing over a period of sixteen hundred years, could produce a work in which every part may be fitted perfectly into every other part, with not one verse too many and not one verse too few, demonstrates that behind the human authors there was God who breathed through them the message He wished to have recorded at the time and in the manner and form that suited His purpose.

It is objected by some that the marks of human personality upon the writings of the various human authors indicate that the Bible is a human book. We would answer this with an analogy. The angel who announced to Mary that she would become the mother of the Messiah, heard the Virgin ask, "How shall this be, seeing that I know not a man?" The answer came: "The Holy Spirit shall come upon thee, and the power of the Highest shall overshadow thee; therefore also that holy thing which shall be born of thee shall be called the Son of God" (Luke 1:35). So the baby was born. He was the second Person of the Trinity, the Son of God. But He was not a Chinese baby, nor a Negro baby, nor a Nordic Aryan; He was a Jewish baby. The greatest glory of Israel was this: "of whom as concerning the flesh Christ came, who is over all, God blessed for ever" (Romans 9:5).

Just as the Holy Spirit came upon the womb of Mary, so He came upon the brain of a Moses, a David, an Isaiah, a Paul, a John, and the rest of the writers of the divine library. The power of the Highest overshadowed them, therefore that holy thing which was born of their minds is called the Holy Bible, the Word of God. The writings of Luke will, of course, have the vocabulary of Luke, and the works of Paul will bear the stamp of Paul's mind. However, this is only in the same manner that the Lord Jesus Christ might have had eyes like His mother's, or hair that was the same color and texture as hers. He did not inherit her sins, because the Holy Spirit had come upon her. If we ask how this could be, the answer is that God says so. And the writings of the men of the Book did not inherit the errors of their carnal minds, because the writings were conceived by the Holy Spirit and born out of their personalities without partaking of their fallen nature. If we ask how this could be, again the answer is that God says so.

For all these reasons, therefore, because of the nature of the divine revelation and the manner in which it was unfolded progressively, from heart to heart and from century to century, we must follow the method of bringing texts from all parts of Scripture and putting them together to form one coherent entity of doctrine. Furthermore, this method of Bible study is set forth in the second chapter of First Corinthians. Here the writer insists on the supreme importance of the very words of the Biblical vocabulary, as opposed to human, philosophical terms: "And my speech and my preaching was not with enticing words of man's wisdom, but in demonstration of the Spirit and of power . . ." And writing of the things revealed by God, he continues: "Which things also we speak, not in the words which man's wisdom teacheth, but which the Holy Spirit teacheth; comparing spiritual things with spiritual" (I Corinthians 2:4, 13). To give the full force of the Greek would be to translate it, "comparing spiritual things with the spiritual words."

It is this method of Bible study which we purpose to apply to the first verse of the Bible. Just as the lamb of Isaiah 53 explains the lamb of Exodus, so the details of creation given by Isaiah, Jeremiah and Ezekiel shed their revealing light on the first verses of the Bible.

II

On the one side of the abyss stands the phrase, "In the beginning God created the heavens and the earth." We come to the other side and read the second verse as it is found in the King James Version: "And the earth was without form and void, and darkness covered the face of the deep." The revisers in both the English and American revisions, not satisfied with the terms "without form and void," have given us the better translation, "waste and void," though the RSV has gone back to the King James rendering. Still another translator interprets the Hebrew as "a wreck and a ruin." In French there is a common expression which translates our idea of *topsy-turvy:* it is *tohu-bohu* — an expression transliterated from the Hebrew of this second verse of Genesis. These are the words which various translators have rendered "without form," "void," "waste," "desolate," "empty," "wreck," "ruin."

Just here the importance of the comparative method of Bible study is seen. In Isaiah 45:18, we read that God did not create the world as it is found in the second verse of Genesis: "For thus saith the Lord that created the heavens; God himself that formed the earth and made it; he hath established it, *he created it not tohu . . ."* Here is the same Hebrew word as in the second verse of the Bible. It is a formal statement: God did not create the earth as it is portrayed in the description that has commonly been called chaos. The great French Catholic translator, Abbé Crampon, boldly renders it thus: "He hath established it Himself and did not make it as a chaos [Qui l'a fondée Luimeme et qui n'en a pas fait un chaos]." It is noteworthy that the Revised Standard Version has adopted this reading. "He did not create it a chaos."

This categorical statement is sufficient to prove beyond any shadow of doubt that the first and second verses are separated by an interval. We might read the two verses from Genesis and the one from Isaiah as follows: "In the beginning God created the heavens and the earth. And the earth – though God most certainly did not create it that way – became a wreck and a ruin, and darkness covered the face of the deep."

That we have every right to translate the verb by the continuing form "became" is amply demonstrated by the fact that this precise form is thus translated in other parts of the Old Testament, as for example, "Lot's wife looked back and she *became a pillar of salt"* (Genesis 19:26).

So far, this is very satisfying to the heart. If a perfect God should create a very imperfect world, chaotic, waste and desolate, a wreck and a ruin, it would be a violation of one of the great spiritual principles, stated by the Holy Spirit Himself: A fountain cannot send forth sweet water and bitter (James 3:11). And if "a good man out of the good treasure of the heart bringeth forth good things: and an evil man out of the evil treasure bringeth forth evil things" (Matthew 12:35), how much more must a good and perfect God bring forth a good and perfect creation? Mrs. Mary Baker Eddy saw this dilemma and sought to resolve it by saying that God had created everything perfect, and that, therefore, everything is perfect, and that any impression to the contrary is but an error of mortal mind. What she failed to realize was that the invisible war had broken out against the background of a perfect creation, and that God, for His own purposes, which we shall study in detail, put forth His Word to turn that perfect creation into a wreck and a ruin. So our hearts rest quietly in the truth set forth by the Psalmist, "As for God, his way is perfect . . ." (Psalm 18:30).

One objection has been imagined which we will do well to meet and set aside at once. It is argued that the passage in the Ten Commandments concerning the seventh day contradicts what we have been saying. We read the following: "For in six days the Lord made heaven and earth, the sea and all that in them is, and rested the seventh day" (Exodus 20:11). The answer is that there is a vast difference between the original creation of the heavens and the earth, and the subsequent formation, fashioning and restoration of that same earth which had been turned into chaos.

The careful reader of the first chapter of Genesis will note that the word *create* is found in the first verse and appears no more in the account until the introduction of life, in the fifth and sixth days of the restoration. God was not seeking mere literary effect when He used the several verbs in Isaiah, "Thus saith the Lord that *created* the heavens; God himself that *formed* the earth and made it; he hath *established* it, he *created* it *not* a chaos, he *formed* it to be inhabited: I am the Lord; and there is none else" (Isaiah 45:18).

To create, as the great linguist Rabbi Naskman put it, is "to produce out of nothing." It is to call into being some material thing without the aid of any existing material. It is the materialization of a thought of God. The discoveries of the atomic age, centering in the recently acquired knowledge that mass and energy are the same thing in different form, give powerful significance to the Bible teaching that the material universe is the tangible expression of the Word of God going forth in the command of His desire. "By the word of the Lord were the heavens made: and all the host of them by the breath of his mouth . . . he spake and it was . . ." (Psalm 33:6, 9).

We are not told in Scripture how God created the heavens and the earth. We do not know whether it happened in an instant, as He most surely could have caused it to appear had He thus desired; or whether the process of creation covered a period of long ages. God could have done it any way He liked. He has revealed only the quantity of truth that seemed best to Him for His purpose. There is not a line in the Bible which is placed there for mere rhetorical effect, or for the gratification of curiosity. To satisfy the carnal mind was not one of God's purposes; of that we may be sure. What we have in the Book is all relevant to His main purpose. He is giving us the story of the eternal plan, with special emphasis on man's complete ruin in sin, and His own perfect remedy in Christ.

The other verbs which are used to describe the work of the six days, such as *made, divide,* and *set,* are used elsewhere of work done with existing materials, as when a woman prepares a meal or a man builds a boat. The original creation was before the forming and fashioning.

That something tremendous and terrible happened to the first, perfect creation is certain. We know that later the earth which had become waste and empty was re-formed and refashioned in the six days and peopled by the newly created beings, Adam and his wife; and that this renewed and restored earth, of which it is stated six times that God saw that it was good (1:4, 10, 12, 18, 21, 25) and once that it was very good (1:31), was later cursed on account of man's sin. We have every right to argue from analogy that the original creation, long before Adam's remade world was cursed because of earlier sin, fell into chaos because of the righteous judgment of God upon some outbreak of rebellion. We believe that there is sufficient light in the Word of God to give us more than a few details. Somewhere back before the chaos of the second verse of Genesis there was a great tragedy and a terrible catastrophe.

It should be pointed out, perhaps, that the knowledge of this explanation of the Scripture is nothing new. It is well over a hundred years since Dr. Thomas Chalmers of Scotland observed that there must be a considerable interval of time between the first two verses of Genesis. And we read in the notes of Crampon, who is perhaps the greatest Biblical scholar produced by the Roman Church in modern times and who works in the shadow of all the church fathers, the following: "Verse two refers to the indefinite interval of time which separates the primordial creation from the organization of the terrestrial globe as the author is about to describe it. This interval gives every latitude for explaining the transformations which matter has undergone according to the diverse scientific hypotheses." If the Church had followed these great students, Protestant and Catholic, there would not have been so great a furor concerning the modern theories of science, and it would have been much easier to winnow the wheat of truth from the theories and to throw out the chaff of speculative hypothesis.

As we have said we do not know anything of the time element involved. God may well have first created the earth over the course of millions or billions of years; or He may have done it in the flash of a second and then allowed it to go on in its perfect form for untold millions of years. We do not know. Again, after the earth was blasted in judgment and had become a wreck and a ruin, it may have remained in that state for another period of ages. We do not know. There is not a line in the Bible on that subject. All we know is that there are two unknown periods to be accounted for — 2x to express it mathematically — and if some scientist wants to argue that the age of the earth is 2x to the nth degree, it makes no difference whatsoever to the child of true faith. We know that our God spoke the original word of creation, and materialized the original thought of the divine idea which became the heavens and the earth. We know that it was the hand of a holy God which struck the earth into ruin because of a great outbreak of rebellion, and we know that it was the hand of our Lord which moved, all in His own time, to bring the earth out of that chaos. This was the same hand that was later pierced with nails for the salvation of the sinner. We know, too, that it was the voice of our God which spoke the great *fiat,* "Let there be light . . ." We know that that same voice is calling unto hearts to return to Him for rest, and that that same light is ready to shine into darkened hearts to reveal the light of the knowledge of the glory of God in the face of Jesus Christ (II Corinthians 4:6). We know, also, that the other verbs in the account of earth's history — God made, God formed, God fashioned, God said — are all within the power of the omnipotent God who said, "For my thoughts are not your thoughts, neither are your ways my ways . . . For as the heavens are higher than the earth, so are my ways higher than your ways, and my thoughts than your thoughts" (Isaiah 55:8,9).

For one more illustration let us go back to the Grand Canyon in Arizona. Some time ago, I took my family back to my boyhood home in California. Upon our return, we drove down from southern Utah to see what is certainly among the greatest of all the scenic wonders of this earth's surface. We arrived at our cabins just as darkness was falling, and it was night before we were able to go to the rim of the canyon. At our feet lay a blackness as deep as the night above. My children stood beside me as I told them what lay at their feet. I described the vast chaos that was between us and the pinpoints of lights, fifteen miles away on the southern rim. It could not be seen in the darkness of the night, and all that I told them had to be taken on faith. But next morning we returned for the sunrise. First of all we could see the outline of far peaks, towering high above the canyon. They were visible while the pit beneath was still in darkness. As the moments passed, we began to see the rough outlines of the canyon rim, though the bottom still lay invisible in the darkness. It was only when the sun had lighted the peaks fully and the canyon's rim was bathed in light that the scene below became visible. So it is with the study of the Word of God.

The light of God comes to the human heart progressively. "He that cometh to God must believe that he is, and that he is the rewarder of them that diligently seek him" (Hebrews 11:6). Then the peaks light up. We see Sinai and tremble at the law, realizing our death in sin. Then Mt. Calvary shines forth and we see the Saviour dying in our stead. We believe and are saved. Then light grows clearer, and we begin to know more about ourselves and our daily walk. Then we begin to see the light of God fall into the great deeps of His eternal plan; and only then can we hope to have the answer to the great questions of the past and the future which rise out of the fact that there is an invisible war which is being fought furiously and in which we have a greater strategic role than we might imagine.

2 : Lucifer

IN the normal course of reading the book of Genesis, we would come, in the third chapter, to the introduction of a new character, a malignant being who is immediately revealed as the bitter enemy of both God and the newly formed and created man. Who is this being and from whence did he come? Are we to believe in the eternal duality of good and evil? We shall see the revelation of the origin of evil in such a way that this duality is proved to be false. But if, as some would have it, the Lord created the heavens and the earth in the six days and saw that all was good, whence did this enemy creep in? There is no place in such a theory for the origin of evil and the beginning of rebellion against the Creator. When we see, however, that "In the beginning God created the heavens and the earth," and that "He created them not a chaos," but that they became that way as a result of judgment, we have the truth, and are both instructed and satisfied.

In this third chapter of Genesis, there is a being subtle and full of hate, who is clearly identified from many passages of Scripture under various names. Many shades of his horrible character will become more distinct as we study the whole subject. At the outset he is described as a serpent, and lest there should be any doubt as to the identity of the animating mind behind the voice that speaks, we have the clear identification at the other end of the Bible, where we read of "The great dragon . . . that old serpent, called the Devil, and Satan" (Revelation 12:9). We are about to consider his origin and thus to find the answer to the great question of the origin of sin. The knowledge of this fact will enable us to orient our thinking in a world of problems, economic and political, and will bring us to a clearer picture of the future which is overcast with so many clouds of war and menace, and it will give us a more simple knowledge of the struggles which touch us personally, as life with all its change, brings us face to face with sickness, sorrow, adversity and death.

21

There are two ways of approaching our study. It would be possible to take various portions of Scripture and, bit by bit, build up an outline from which we could draw certain conclusions. But there would be some, unfamiliar with such studies as this, who, not knowing the direction of our aim, would be confused. We intend, therefore, to adopt the method which is used in courts of law. At the beginning of a trial the prosecuting attorney outlines his case, tells the court and the jury what he purposes to prove, and then proceeds to bring forth the witnesses, one by one, to substantiate the picture which he has sketched.

In our first chapter, we have seen that there is a great interval between the first and second verses of Genesis. In the beginning there was a perfect creation. How long this creation lasted, we do not know. But we do know that in charge of much of it, if not all, God placed a mighty and magnificent being to rule and govern in His name. We shall show that God created this being with more power and beauty than He ever gave to any other. This spirit being was named Lucifer the "Son of the morning." He ruled for God as prophet, priest and king. How long this righteous government in full obedience to the single will of God endured, again we do not know.

INDEPENDENT RULE

There came a time when this being, filled with pride because of his own power and attainments, entertained the thought in his heart that he could govern independently of God. He therefore proclaimed that he would set up an independent rule, whereupon a multitude of the angelic beings of heaven decided to follow his rule and join him in his rebellion against God. These form the company of the fallen angels and probably the demons. As a result of this proud revolt against the will of God, the Lord God Almighty blasted the material universe in a curse of temporary judgment and the earth became without form and void, a wreck and a ruin, a chaos, and darkness was upon the face of the deep. Much later, on the occasion of the creation of Adam, God moved to re-form, to refashion, this earth.

The drama we have just outlined took place in that interval between the first two verses of Genesis, but it is necessary to go to other portions of the revelation of God in order to find the details of the origin of this great rebellion.

In the twenty-eighth chapter of Ezekiel, there is a revelation of truth which can, and indeed must, be fitted into the great interval between the opening verses of Genesis. The first part of the chapter is a lamentation against one who is called the prince of Tyre. We have no reason for doubting that this portion of the chapter is addressed by the Holy Spirit to the reigning prince of Tyre, a contemporary of the prophet. He is one of many men throughout ancient and modern history who have been lifted up with such pride that they imagined themselves to partake of deity.

In the eleventh verse, however, there is a transition of thought. We read: "Moreover the word of the Lord came unto me, saying, Son of man, take up a lamentation upon the king of Tyrus . . ." So far as we know from secular history there was no king of Tyre, only the prince spoken of in the first part of the chapter. Who is this king of Tyre? Everything that is spoken to the prince could be said without difficulty of an earthly ruler. But in the judgment that is addressed to the one who is styled king of Tyre, it is immediately apparent that a being above and beyond the sphere of human life is in view. Nor should this astonish us. The Lord, on several occasions, addressed Satan indirectly, and we hope to establish that the power behind the earthly ruler of Tyre is Lucifer who became Satan.

SATANIC POWER

It should be remembered that the first time in the Bible where Satan is addressed he is spoken to through the intermediacy of the serpent (Genesis 3:15) who was his mouthpiece. We remember again that in the gospels the Lord spoke to Satan through Peter. When Peter permitted the enemy to get control of his lips for a time, the Lord turned on His disciple, saying: "Get thee behind me, Satan" (Matthew 16:22, 23). There are other instances of indirect address of Satan in the Bible which we will mention as we proceed. It is not extraordinary, therefore, that God should speak to Satan here in Ezekiel through the intermediacy of an earthly ruler. Many things in history will become clearer to the student of the Bible who is also a student of history when it is realized that behind every earthly power there is a satanic power lurking, seeking to control and dominate for the glory of the rebel who declared war against God. We are not to be misled by the assertion that "The powers that be are ordained by God" (Romans 13:1). All that Satan has done or is doing or will do is by the permissive will of God, who, since the Lord Jehovah is both omniscient and omnipotent, was certainly never astonished by the outbreak of Satan. It will become increasingly clear that Satan is working within the limits of the eternal plan of God.

The first statement in this judgment is a recognition of the high position which Satan had occupied in the government of God before his fall. "Thus saith the Lord God; Thou sealest up the sum, full of wisdom, and perfect in beauty . . ." (Ezekiel 28:12). There is evidence to the effect that God created the beings of the spirit world in ranks and orders. Like an army which has privates, non-commissioned officers, field officers, staff officers and a commander-in-chief, the spirit beings seem to be in similar ranks; the angels, the archangels, principalities, powers, the seraphs, the cherubs. Of all these orders of creation, Lucifer was the climax in gifts, power and beauty. So great was his rank and power that even after his fall, Michael, the archangel, one of God's greatest messengers, "dared not bring against him a railing accusation, but said, The Lord rebuke thee" (Jude 9). Let this teach us, in passing, that the common attitude of the worldling, speaking about the devil as "his satanic majesty," or "old Nick," certainly has no foundation in Scripture. We should have toward him that healthy respect which realizes that we are safest when we entrust our keeping to the power of our Redeemer, the Saviour Christ, and recognize the truth of that line from the hymn:

> The arm of flesh will fail you,
> Ye dare not trust your own.

It should be noted that we have refrained as much as possible from the use of the word "angel" and have used instead the term "spirit being." The reason for this comes out of the real meaning of the Greek word *angelos* which has been transliterated to form our English word, *angel*. The Greek word had a very simple meaning — a messenger, and the good news brought by the messenger became the ev-angel. The man who ran across the hills from Marathon to Athens with the news of the Greek victory was an "angel" to the Greeks, and the news he brought was the "evangel." When this fact is understood it leaves no possibility for the gross error into which the group of people known as "Jehovah's Witnesses" have fallen. They take hold of some of the Bible passages where Jesus Christ is clearly presented as an "angel" and conclude that He was, therefore, less than God, no more than a creature, though they present Him as the highest of all creatures. They fail to see that anyone, from a demon to a man, to a spirit being, to the Son of God Himself, can be a messenger for the Lord. I can send my son on an errand, and I can send a servant on an errand, but that does not make my son a servant, nor does it make the servant my son. In the second and third chapters of Revelation there are men who are presented as "angels." All of the Old Testament references to "the angel of Jehovah" may be seen clearly to speak of the Lord Himself. A large majority of the passages where the word "angel" is used refer to the spirit beings who are sent to minister to them who shall be heirs of salvation (Hebrews 1:14).

In the Garden

Plainly, our passage in Ezekiel teaches that Lucifer, upon his creation, took his place as the highest, most beautiful, most powerful and wisest of the creatures of God.

The next phrase of Scripture concerning the nature of this being is: "Thou hast been in Eden, the garden of God . . ." We know, of course, from the third of Genesis, that Lucifer, in his fallen state, was in the Eden of Adam and Eve, but he was not there in his unfallen state. The Eden pictured by Ezekiel is not the Eden in which Adam walked, for that Eden was described as a garden of trees and vegetable growth. This Eden in Ezekiel is a place of rare mineral beauty. The statement is this: "Every precious stone was thy covering, the sardius, topaz, and the diamond, the beryl, the onyx and the jasper, the sapphire, the emerald, and the carbuncle, and gold . . ." There are two other passages in the Scripture which shed light on the meaning of this verse. The one is almost a parallel passage. In the Apocalypse there is a description of the New Jerusalem, whose foundations are described in terms not unlike those of our verse (Revelation 21:19, 20). A wealth of precious stones forms the foundation of this city which is to be the dwelling place of the Lord Jesus and His saints in their rule over the earth. The other passage ties these two together. The jeweled city of the past is to be replaced by the jeweled city of the future. There will be a splendid New Jerusalem, abode of the saints, because there was the splendor of the dwelling place of the first governor of the earth. The rule of Christ and His redeemed will occur in the times of restoration of all things (Acts 3:21). We can look in the future for an analogy of all that is revealed in the past, and we can look in the past for an analogy for all that is revealed of the future.

It is not necessary, of course, to conceive of these as literal jewels, although they could be if God wanted them that way. They are symbols. C. S. Lewis has an excellent paragraph on the nature of symbols in his *Christian Behaviour*. He says, "There is no need to be worried by facetious people who try to make the Christian hope of 'heaven' ridiculous by saying that they don't want 'to spend eternity playing harps.' The answer to such people is that if they cannot understand books written for grown-ups, they should not talk about them. All the Scriptural imagery (harps, crowns, gold, etc.) is, of course, a merely symbolical attempt to express the inexpressible. Musical instruments are mentioned because for many people (not all) music is the thing known in the present life which most strongly suggests ecstasy and infinity. Crowns are mentioned to suggest the fact that those who are united with God in eternity share His splendor and power and joy. Gold is mentioned to suggest the timelessness of heaven (gold does not rust) and the preciousness of it. People who take these symbols literally might as well think that when Christ told us to be like doves, He meant that we were to lay eggs!"

God's perfect Prophet, Priest and King, with all the host of the saints chosen to reign with Him, will see on this same earth, which was the scene of the first sin of the universe, all things restored as they were before sin forced their crushing destruction. The fact that Lucifer was sheltered by such magnificence of precious stones is an additional indication of his rank and position in the first earth.

The exalted state of this mighty prince is further shown by the description of the accompaniments of music which surrounded him from the very first moment of his existence. We read, "The workmanship of thy tabrets and of thy pipes was prepared for thee in the day that thou wast created." There are two important lessons here. First we see that Lucifer was created. This ends the argument about the eternal duality of good and evil. Satan and evil had definite beginnings. They shall also have a definite end. Lucifer was a creation of God. The creature is subject to the Creator. The other fact of importance is that which shows Lucifer's magnificence from the moment of his creation. He awoke in the first moment of his existence in the full-orbed beauty and power of his exalted position; surrounded by all the magnificence which God gave him. He never had known a lesser moment. He saw himself as above all the hosts in power, wisdom and beauty. Only at the throne of God itself did he see more than he himself possessed, and it is possible that even that was in some sense not fully visible to the eyes of the creature. Certainly there was no outward evidence that would show him the futility of opposing a second will to that of God. There was no example of sin in the universe. This does not excuse his rebellion, but when we come to the account of his outbreak we can, perhaps, in spite of our sinful minds, understand a little better how the insurgence came about.

The chief of all created beings was set in the government of God as ruler over the creation of God. This is to be seen not only by the royal environment in which he was placed, but also by the express statement that God placed him in power, for this is the significance of the phrase in verse fourteen: "I had placed thee and thou wast upon the holy mountain of God" (Segond). (The Authorized Version renders the line, "And I have set thee *so*," as though it referred to the preceding phrase and with the last word in italics to show that it is not in the Hebrew.) We prefer to follow Segond, as above, or the Revised

Version which reads, "I have set thee *so that* thou wast upon the holy mountain of God." A reference to the concordance will bring out the fact that the mountain of God is a symbol for the government of God.

Herein we see the confirmation of a word spoken by Satan to the Lord Jesus Christ in the temptation. In Luke's account we read that the devil showed our Lord the kingdoms of this world and said unto Him, "All this power will I give thee, and the glory of them: for that is delivered unto me; and to whomsoever I will I give it" (Luke 4:6). In this the father of lies was not lying. God had placed him in the position of ruler and given to him the authority which he exercised and which he later wished to initiate from himself. Before his fall he may be said to have occupied the role of prime minister for God, ruling possibly over the universe but certainly over this world. The scene of Satan's government, therefore, becomes the theater of the entire invisible war. Here, where the fall took place, the Lord Jesus Christ glorified the Father (John 17:4). Here Satan has been the chief prince and here he still rules as prince. We shall see that this office has not yet been taken from him, for he shall reign until he is put under the feet of Christ. The earth will be the scene of the final triumph of Christ and His Church and the scene of Satan's final defeat. It is the dust of this earth which shall season Satan's diet for ever and ever.

3 : *Lucifer*
(CONTINUED)

THE priesthood of Satan is the next of his offices to be considered. We read, "Thou art the anointed cherub that covereth" (Ezekiel 28: 14). The idea expressed in the word *covereth* has been widely interpreted by the commentators, but we find the most satisfactory idea not in a commentary but in the French translation of Segond: "Thou wast the protecting cherub with spread-out wings." Here we begin to see him in his priestly function, associated with the cherubim who, even now, lead the worship of heaven (Revelation 4:9, 10; 5:11-14), and who were near the throne of God. The wings of the cherub are outspread as in the case of the cherubim whose images were placed on top of the ark of the covenant.

A further reference to his priesthood comes out in another verse in the same context. We read, "Thou hast defiled thy sanctuaries by the multitude of thine iniquities" (verse 18). The fact that Lucifer had sanctuaries indicates both worship and priesthood. It would appear that he received the worship of the universe beneath him and offered it to the Creator above him. This is intimated also in the statement that he had access to the highest realms of heaven, into the very presence of God, for we read, "Thou wast upon the holy mountain of God; thou hast walked up and down in the midst of the stones of fire" (verse 14).

One commentator, Pember, has explained this verse as follows: "The mountain of God is the place of His presence in visible glory, where His High Priest would, of course, stand before Him to minister. The stones of fire may, perhaps, be explained as follows. We know that the station of the cherubim is just beneath the glory at the footstool of the throne (Ezekiel 1:26). Now when Moses took Aaron, Nadab, Abihu and the seventy of the elders of Israel up the mountain of Sinai to see the God of Israel, 'There was under his feet as it were a paved work of a sapphire stone, and as it were the body of heaven in his clearness . . . And the sight of the glory of the Lord was like

28

devouring fire on the top of the mount' (Exodus 24:10, 17). This paved work of sapphire glowing with devouring fire is, perhaps, the same as the stones of fire; and if so, Satan's presence in the midst of them would indicate his enjoyment of the full cherubic privilege of nearness to the throne of God."

ONLY ONE WILL

We thus see that he stood between God and the creation. All of his authority was derived from God and God worked through him. Here, in the presence of God, Lucifer brought the worship of a universe of creatures and received those commands from the Almighty which, as the prophet of God, he transmitted to the worshiping creation. All was order, all was harmony. There was only one will in the universe and that was the will of God. Only one will. That fact constitutes the difference between eternity and time. In eternity there is none but the will of God; in time there is more than one will.

The writer gave the content of this chapter as a lecture in a certain city and afterward received a letter from a Christian brother concerning the difference between eternity and time, with some thought-provoking sentences that deserve the highest consideration, and with which we are in hearty accord. "Any definition of time is doubtless open to the charge of artificiality, since Scripture takes little notice of a distinction between it and eternity. However, if we attempt to distinguish one from the other, we can hardly conceive of time without a starting point. From then until the future eternity begins, we are aware of time through the sequence of events which can be established by reference to an initial point. Since God never began, we would properly take the oldest landmark as our point of reference." Our correspondent gives good reasons for beginning with the creation of the heavens and the earth, and ending with the creation of the new heavens and the new earth. He further writes, "From the standpoint of Scripture, as distinguished from the speculations of philosophy, I should say that time is that part of all eternity during which God brings to fruition His counsels of grace. In the past eternity we have His counsels; in the coming eternity we have the abiding consequences of those counsels wrought out in time . . . The fall of Satan is incontestably a notable event. Yet it does not represent God's first step toward carrying out His purposes. We can appreciate that the rebellion of one of the highest created beings would be a most inappropriate way to commemorate a beginning. To do so enhances the stature of Satan as an opponent rather than a rebellious subordinate . . ."

SATAN'S SIN

We agree with all this, and we shall show that Satan's sin of the heart and mind preceded his sin of the will. Most certainly we must not think of God as a mere opponent in the invisible war. Rather than allow such a thought to go forth we would have named this work *The Invisible Rebellion,* but we judged that the facets of the problem which most urgently claim our attention are those which reflect light on the conflict in which we are soldiers in a battle that was won before we ever had to begin fighting it.

It is important, also, that we realize that the condition of existence with but a single will in the universe prevailed until comparatively recently. Because we have already pointed out that unnumbered ages may lie between the time of the earth's judgment, when it was first made waste and empty, and the time, a few thousand years ago, when God moved to re-form the earth during the six days, it is not to be supposed that we have contradicted ourselves. For we must not forget that God is eternal, and that before the time of Lucifer's fall God, the Father, Son and Holy Spirit, had existed together in mutual joy and satisfaction, for ever and ever in the past. It was on this ground that Augustine argued the necessity of the Trinity, for since God is love, and love must have an object, there was the Father to originate love, the Son as the object of love and the eternal Spirit of love between them. It is only when we look at time through the Word that we realize that back of the very great past there is an infinite past during which there was the perfection of the single will of God.

ORIGIN OF EVIL

The next verse in Ezekiel's account gives us the key to the origin of evil in this universe. "Thou was perfect in thy ways from the day that thou wast created, till iniquity was found in thee" (verse 15). What this iniquity was is revealed to us in some detail in the prophecy of Isaiah, but there are already interesting indications in our passage that we may not pass by. The fact given here is that iniquity came by what we might term spontaneous generation in the heart of this being in whom such magnificence of power and beauty had been combined and to whom such authority and privilege had been given. Here is the beginning of sin. Iniquity was found in the heart of Lucifer. So far as we know, here is the only verse in the Bible which states clearly the exact origin of sin. Other passages only amplify this one; for instance, the passage we will consider later when we come to the nature of man's sin and what we might call the rules under which sin is practiced

(Isaiah 45:7). But the passage before us is the stark declaration by God that sin originated in the heart of Lucifer.

We have one more phrase in Ezekiel's account to consider closely. The Authorized Version reads: "By the multitude of thy merchandise they have filled the midst of thee with violence, and thou hast sinned" (verse 16). We shall see this whole picture much more sharply if we realize that each word is like a lens that needs to be finely focused to give a clearly etched image. First of all, we must not be led aside by our common use of the word *merchandise*, indicating things bought and sold. In Ezekiel's usage it means anything that passes through the hands. For example, we would say, in common speech, that a judge who used his high position for personal profit had made merchandise of justice. We knew of a distinguished musician who used his great talent, acknowledged throughout the world, to make himself the immoral master of the lives of some of his pupils. His merchandise was personality and artistic ability.

Lifted Up With Pride

So Satan, passing through his hands the merchandise of authority from God above to the creation below, and returning the merchandise of worship from the world of spirit beings to God above, decided, that, since he was wise and beautiful to such a degree, he could retain some of the worship for himself, and that he could originate some of the authority in himself. Thus he filled his heart with the violence of rebellion. He had been entrusted with God's government, priesthood and spokesmanship, but he wanted to act independently of God. He who was prophet — could he not give orders under his own authority instead of being utterly dependent upon the invisible God? He who found himself, as he was in truth, so magnificent, so beautiful, so filled with power, sealing up the sum — could he not take some of the worship of the multitudes for himself? Was there not some worthiness in himself that should be acknowledged? Here is the origin of sin.

There is a New Testament passage which sheds great light upon this phase of the truth. The Holy Spirit is speaking of the characteristics which must be possessed by one who is to be an overseer in spiritual things (I Timothy 3:1-6). We must understand that the spiritual principle involved is applicable to every Christian. For *overseer* the word *bishop* is used, but we must understand the meaning of the word. The Greek root *episkopos* from which *bishop* is derived, and which also gives our word *episcopal,* is a compound word. Part of it is the root that has given us *scope* and *telescope*. This part means "to view." The preposition *epi* means *on* or *over*. An *epi scopos* is simply an overseer. When Peter counsels the elders to take the "oversight" of the flock of God (I Peter 5:1), he is calling them to exercise a proper bishopric. The heavy-lipped Latins dropped the *e* and spoke of *ebiscopus* and then *biscopus*.

The heavier-lipped Germans and Anglo-Saxons altered it in a dozen ways, including *biscop, biscof* and *biscob,* and ultimately it settled down in England as *bishop*. So, in one sense, a bishop is a mispronunciation of a mispronunciation of a mispronunciation. That may be tolerated when the mistranslation is only linguistic, but if it becomes theological the error is satanic. Thus in this passage the Holy Spirit compares the actions of some overseers to that of Satan and says that a young convert should never be put into a place of spiritual responsibility, "lest being lifted up with pride he fall into the condemnation of the devil" (I Timothy 3:6). What a window to let light in on our passage on the fall of Satan!

An overseer, no matter what he or she is called must take the greatest care to avoid the pitfall of spiritual pride. There is a long list of qualifications for the man who would take a place of authority in the church, whether his oversight be that of minister, elder, deacon, trustee, vestryman, steward, Sunday school teacher or any of the other terms that men have derived from Scripture or devised for themselves. The list includes matters of right and wrong: the man must be blameless, no bigamist, vigilant, sober, of good behavior, given to hospitality, apt to teach, not given to wine, no striker (that is, not contentious), not greedy of filthy lucre, patient, not a brawler, nor covetous, one who ruleth well his own house having his children in subjection in all gravity. We know of churches which take these qualifications seriously. They will not elect to places of authority a man who has a son that is a drunkard, or a daughter who has consented to be married in the Roman Church to bring up her children in the blasphemy of the mass. For, says the Word of God, if a man know not how to rule his own house, how shall he take care of the Church of God?

But the principal pitfall is expressed in the words, "not a novice." A young convert should never, never be put in front in a place of prominence. How often Christians err against this provision. Some young man makes a decision for Christ, and there are those who urge him to get up the next night and begin preaching. It is totally contrary to the Word of God.

We have seen young men ruined by being pushed forward too rapidly. A young convert, when the Holy Spirit opens his mouth, may well testify that he has trusted in Jesus Christ as his Saviour. As time passes he may even witness briefly in a public meeting. But he must be seasoned and sound in the faith before he stands in a place of government or teaching in the Church of Jesus Christ. For if he is brought forth too soon, he will have the great temptations which come to one who sees himself standing before others who listen quietly while he does the talking. When a man feels this influence over an audience, and when he realizes that a congregation is often prone to take everything spoken from the pulpit as final and authoritative, he is tempted to speak in his own authority instead of in the authority of God. As a result he falls into the condemnation of the devil.

There are two examples from literature worth citing. Sinclair Lewis, winner of the Nobel prize in literature, depicts a minister in one of his novels who uses his place of power at the sacred desk to get hold of the affections of the women of his congregation; "for of this sort are they which creep into houses, and lead captive silly women laden with sins, led away with divers lusts" (II Timothy 3:6). And Milton, in his great poem *Lycidas,* describes those bishops who are "blind mouths." This may seem to be a mixed metaphor of the first category, but Milton knew the meaning of words. What is the highest function of a bishop? To be an over-seer. What would be the most un-bishop-like characteristic possible? To be blind. What is the function of a pastor? He is a shepherd, and his function is to feed. What is the most unpastoral characteristic a pastor can have? To want to be fed, that is, to be a mouth. So the combination of the most unbishoplike, unpastoral characteristics would make a man a "blind mouth." And as Milton goes on to say, in another magnificent play on words, the congregation is "swollen with wind." The image comes from the fact that the Greek word for "wind" is the same used for the "Spirit" throughout the New Testament. The "blind mouths" blow their foul breath of mere human philosophies instead of letting the sweet wind of the Holy Spirit come through to give life to the listeners. And as the principal outward symptom of starvation is a swollen belly, which would seem to indicate that the victim is fat and well fed, so the people who sit in the congregation under preaching that proceeds from man's lungs instead of from God's heart, are starvelings, who deceive themselves with the vain thought that they are truly fed instead of swollen with starvation.

The minister is thus tempted in the same way that Lucifer was originally tempted. The minister receives blessing from God in order to feed the people with the Word of God. When the people are blessed they give thanks and praise to God, and they often give it to and through the minister. There is a terrible temptation to take a commission from this worship and to stand in the presence of the people as "lords over God's heritage," to use the phrase of the Apostle Peter (I Peter 5:3). Only the man — and he may well be a young man, though not a young convert — who is seasoned with the grace of God can take of the things of God and minister them to the people without presuming to speak from himself instead of from God; and only such a man can lead the worship of the people to God without presumptuously assuming for himself a part of the worship which belongs only and entirely to God.

One last illustration of this principle of taking a commission for self comes to us from the writings of Hosea in the Old Testament. The people of Israel had become so accustomed to being the recipients of God's blessings and the channel of His power that they had begun to think that they had a patent and copyright on God. Round about them the Gentile nations were dying because Israel had not obeyed the injunction implicit in God's promise to Abraham, that in him [Abraham] should all the families of the earth be blessed. So, through Hosea, God spoke to the people and said: "My people are destroyed for lack of knowledge; because thou hast rejected knowledge, I will also reject thee, that thou shalt be no priest to me . . . As they were increased, so they sinned against me; therefore will I change their glory into shame" (Hosea 4:6, 7). Here is a perfect miniature of the sin of Satan. The merchandise of the worship of God had passed through his hands, and theirs, and they both had kept some for themselves.

The next verse of Hosea's account continues: "They eat up the sin of my people, and they set their heart on their iniquity." This is a picture of the priests who lived by the fact that people sinned and, in accordance with the law, brought beasts to the altars that their blood should be shed as a symbol of the remission of sins. The priests took the good cuts of meat from these offerings. The idea involved in the verse is that the priests were not too much concerned by the fact that the people kept on sinning, since that kept the food on their tables, and the sale of the superfluous animals kept them in luxuries. When they saw a poor sinner coming toward the altar with a bullock, they no longer said, with weeping: "Oh, God, a poor brother has sinned." Rather did they say, "Oh, brother, here is roast beef for dinner."

The passage in Hosea is thus seen to be almost a parallel statement with that of Ezekiel concerning the fall of Lucifer. "By the multitude of thy merchandise they have filled the midst of thee with violence, and thou hast sinned; therefore I will cast thee as profane out of the mountain of God" (Ezekiel 28:16). In many passages throughout the Bible, the term "mountain" is used as a symbol of government. Here then, is the announcement that Satan is cast out of the government of God. By his sin he lost, of necessity, the office of prophet since God no longer could use this unholy one as the mouthpiece for divine decrees. By his sin he lost the office of priest because he stole the worship which was due to God alone and kept it for himself. Now we see that by his sin he has lost the right of governing for God, who says: "I will destroy thee, O governing cherub, from the midst of the stones of fire." The sentence has been passed but is not yet executed. Satan still retains his power over this earth because God did not snatch it from him. He retains it, however, as a rebel, thinking that he can yet do something to bring order and peace within the borders of his chaotic realm. Satan is destined to frustration and eternal doom. God permits him to exercise that rebel power for only a moment more. The Lord, who makes the wrath of men to praise Him will ultimately make the warfare of Satan praise Him even more.

4 : Two Wills

THERE has been much theological argument and philosophical specu-
lation concerning the origin of sin. Even a child knows that all is not
right with this world. The adult can see that there are wars, catastrophes, death. The child can feel pain, sorrow and tears. When either,
the adult or the child, is told that there is an absolutely perfect God,
who has never made a mistake, in whom there could be no shade of
unrighteousness, there arises a question which will not be drowned.

WHY DOES GOD PERMIT SIN?

Some time ago, in the midst of World War II, the writer preached
a sermon in which the omnipotence of God was brought forth. The
Lord Jesus Christ was quoted, saying, "With God all things are possible"
(Matthew 19:26). At the close of the meeting a high school boy
came up with a question. With some little embarrassment, he asked:
"Please tell me this. If God can do absolutely anything, why doesn't
He smack Hitler down?" That same question in a thousand forms has
possessed the minds of men throughout the centuries. Why does God
permit sin? Why did God create the devil? Why does God allow wars
and calamities? We dare to say that we have the certain answer, and
that it is not a very difficult one.

Let us look at the same question as put by a world figure. Some
time ago the problem was stated by one of the greatest literary per-
sonages of this generation, Thomas Mann, the noted German exile.
In an essay written in German and published in the *Quarterly Review*
of the University of Virginia, Mann recounts that the great earthquake,
which destroyed Lisbon in the eighteenth century, took several hundred
thousand lives, most of them professing Christians whose death had
come to them in church buildings to which they had fled for sanctuary.
Throughout Europe the catastrophe was used as an argument against
the goodness of God in such a way that multitudes of people left the

shadow of the Church to become freethinkers. He then concludes that the late war, with all its aftermath, was an infinitely greater catastrophe and will have a similar effect but on a much wider scale, and he sees the end of religion in the masses, even as the Lisbon catastrophe ended religion among the thinkers. Whether or not Mann's conclusion is historically accurate is beside the point. Here are two people, a high school boy and a world-famed writer wondering about the supposed difficulty arising from the concept of a perfect God of love and the state of sorrow in which the world is plunged.

DIVIDED ALLEGIANCE

Yet we say that we have the answer to this problem, and that it is simple and satisfying. The answer is that there is now more than one will in the universe. When there was only one will in the universe, back in eternity past, there was peace and joy. When there shall be but one will again, all of the problems of the world will be settled. The difficulty in which the world finds itself today is not the problem of capital and labor, or the problem of production and distribution, or the problem of racial differences, or any of the other problems which bother the sociologists, the planners and the philosophers. Man's greatest problem today, whether he recognizes it or not, is how to push aside every other allegiance but the eternal one.

In Luke's account of the temptation, there is an interesting sequence of words which reveals clearly the nature of Satan's bid for our wills. The rebel prince, taking our Lord "up into a high mountain, shewed unto him all the *kingdoms* of the world in a moment of time. And the devil said unto him, All this *power* will I give thee, and the *glory* of them: for that is delivered unto me; and to whomsoever I will I give it. If thou therefore wilt worship me, all shall be thine" (Luke 4:5-7). A careful reading of these verses in which Satan is speaking will show that, in the three words we have italicized, they say, flatly: "Mine is the kingdom, the power and the glory." This is, of course, a flagrant challenge by Satan of the right of Christ to enter into the principality which Satan, from the day that he was first created, had held in fief, and over which he now claimed suzerainty by right of possession. Whatever else he had lost in his fall, his kingdom had never been taken from him. He claims it. He is like a squatter with a shack on the corner of a great estate who says to the Lord of the manor: "What are you doing in my yard?"

GOD'S KINGDOM, POWER AND GLORY

Christ replied to Satan with a verse from Scripture which brought things back to their proper perspective: "And Jesus answered and said unto him, Get thee behind me, Satan: for it is written, Thou shalt worship the Lord thy God, and him only shalt thou serve" (v. 8). In this verse, Christ rebukes Satan, announces the superiority and worth of God, and spurns utterly the proffered compromise. But perhaps even more significant is the action of the Lord, for immediately after the temptation He gathers His disciples on the mount and in the famous sermon teaches them what should be known as the disciples' prayer (Matthew 6:9-13). In it they are told to approach God as Father, to recognize His holiness, to desire His kingdom and the doing of His will. They are to pray for their daily bread and for forgiveness of their sins. They are to ask to be kept from testing and to be delivered from the evil one. Then, echoing the same order of words that Satan had used in pressing his preposterous claim, the disciples are taught to ascribe the kingdom, the power and the glory to God alone. How many millions of millions of Christians have prayed this prayer from the heart, thereby saying: "As for me and my house we will serve the Lord"! (It is interesting to note in passing that the Roman Church uses the shorter form of the prayer, as found in Luke, and does not say, "For thine is the kingdom, and the power and the glory.")

The world cannot solve any of its own problems because it is subject to the one who is the god of this age (II Corinthians 4:4), who blinds the minds of them who believe not, lest the light of the glorious Gospel of Christ, who is the image of God, should shine unto them. The great problems that leave the world in misery can, therefore, be solved by God alone. This is the lesson that God must teach by man's repeated failures throughout all the ages of his history. Time must continue until it has been thoroughly demonstrated that there is no health or hope apart from God. Though it will mean the final chaos of all that man holds dear in his civilization, the total bankruptcy of ability of both Satan and men to do anything for man must be thoroughly and conclusively demonstrated.

THE PURPOSE OF HISTORY

When we understand that God is continuing in patience with man until this lesson is fully set forth before the universe, we can understand the real purpose of history. Every thought and device conceivable to the mind of Satan and man must be explored and found wanting. Here is the essence of a relativity which is more important than that set forth by Einstein. One of the most visible differences between eternity and time is the difference between one will and more than one will. There are some beings who can begin to live life with the quality of eternity even in the midst of time. These are those who are born again, and who thus on earth begin to live eternal life. The Christian should reject decisively the thought that eternal life is to begin when this physical life is over. We read on a tombstone that a man "entered into eternal life" on the day of his death, but the Bible teaches that for ʳ Christian eternal life begins, not on the day a man enters heaven, but on the day eternal life enters into the man through the new birth. Eternal life for the one who becomes a child of God through faith in Jesus Christ begins at the moment of the new birth. The true believer learns to say, even now: "Thy kingdom come; Thy will be done – in me – as it is in heaven."

This is, indeed, the goal of the Christian life while on earth. This is the reason why we are left upon earth after we have been prepared for heaven by the atonement provided by Christ and the implantation of His life through which we are made partakers of the divine nature.

We do not control the earth of Russia or Britain or the United States, or even of our garden where weeds war against us, and cannot therefore bring it into subjection to the will of God. We have no power over alien lands to see that God's will is done in them. But we do control that bit of earth of which we are made and, like Paul, we are to keep our body under and bring it into subjection (I Corinthians 9:27), and every thought into captivity unto the obedience of Christ (II Corinthians 10:5). Only then, when we have given this portion of fallen dust over to the control and power of the risen Lord, shall eternity have control over our life in time, and the problem of the wills shall begin to be solved.

Having considered the fact of Satan's original perfection and fall, we now proceed to study further the consequences of that rebellion – the entrance of the second will – so that we may have a basis for the answer to the problem of continuing evil and the present force of sin in the world.

It is necessary to consider, for a moment, a certain method which some of the prophets used in setting forth their prophecies. It is frequently evident in certain cases that the writer begins to relate some happening, contemporaneous with his ministry, and suddenly, without a pause, the text skips over whole ages and speaks of events which are hundreds or thousands of years in the future or of other events which were similarly distant in the past.

One of the more obvious of such cases is that of the fortieth chapter of Isaiah. Here the prophet speaks of the comfort which had come to Israel because some local warfare of that time had been concluded. But, hardly pausing for breath, the prophet continues with the words which identify John the Baptist and his ministry. These, in turn, are seen to be the announcement of the forerunner of the kingdom of peace that shall be brought by the Messiah, when every valley shall be exalted and every mountain shall be brought low. Thus, in the course of four or five verses, we are projected from Isaiah's time to the time of John the Baptist, and thence to the return of the Lord Jesus Christ.

The fourteenth chapter of Isaiah, very important for our subject, contains an even more remarkable example of this double or triple application of a given passage. The prophet first writes of one who is called the king of Babylon (Isaiah 14:4), which may have primary reference to the contemporary ruler of Babylon. We remember that Ezekiel's vision began concerning an earthly ruler and then continued with a great revelation concerning the power behind that earthly throne. The Lord uses the same literary method in Isaiah where the more significant allusion is to the sinister power who uses earthly monarchs. We soon see that the Lord, who spoke indirectly to Satan through the serpent in Genesis (3:16), through Peter in the gospels (Matthew 16:17), and through the king of Tyre in Ezekiel (28:12), is here speaking to Satan through the king of Babylon. The scene is laid at the time of the end, when Satan shall be bound and his power broken. To the peoples who have known so much grief, the Lord says: "And it shall come to pass in the day that the Lord shall give thee rest from thy sorrow, and from thy fear, and from the hard bondage wherein thou wast made to serve, that thou shalt take up this proverb against the king of Babylon, and say, How hath the oppressor ceased! the golden city ceased! The Lord hath broken the staff of the wicked, and the sceptre of the rulers. He who smote the people in wrath with a continual stroke, he that ruled the nations in anger, is persecuted, and none hindereth . . ." (Isaiah 14:3-6). As a result of the binding of Satan, "the whole earth is at rest, and is quiet; they break forth into singing" (verse 7). The rulers of all ages who have preceded Satan in punishment see him arriving in the bottomless pit (cf. Revelation 20:3), and the scene is described as follows: "Hell from beneath is moved for thee to meet thee at thy coming: it stirreth up the dead for thee, even all the chief ones [Hebrew, great goats!] of the earth; it hath raised up from their thrones all the kings of the nations. All they shall speak and say unto thee, Art thou also become weak as we? art thou become like unto us? Thy pomp is brought down to the grave, and the noise of thy viols; the worm is spread under thee, and the worms cover thee" (Isaiah 14:9-11). And to make the identity sure, Satan is directly addressed. "How art thou fallen from heaven, O Lucifer [day star], son of the morning! how art thou cut down to the ground, which didst weaken the nations!" (verse 12).

Then the scene is turned back to the beginning of Lucifer's fall. His original high position is brought into sharp relief, and the words of his declaration of independence are presented to us. "For thou hast said in thine heart, I will ascend into heaven, I will exalt my throne above the stars of God; I will sit also upon the mount of the congregation, in the sides of the north: I will ascend above the heights of the clouds; I will be like the most High" (verses 13, 14). Comparing this passage with the one in Ezekiel, it is evident that the origin of sin in the pride of Satan was soon followed by the outward manifestation of a rebellion of his will against the will of God.

It is of extreme importance that we catch the transition which comes with the introduction of this second will. It is now manifest that eternity has taken on a new aspect, or, to put it otherwise, that time is fully under way. The quality of eternity is the fact that there is but one will — the will of God. Then all was holy, all was righteous: there was no evil whatsoever. The quality of time is that there is more than one will. There came into the universe a second will, rising from the heart of Lucifer, the highest and most wonderful of all the created beings in the universe. In addition to the voice of God, there was now a second voice saying: "I will . . ." There was rebellion; but, more important, back of the rebellion, there were two wills. That means conflict. It is possible to say that the shortest definition of sin is simply "I will . . ." It makes no difference who speaks the words. The will of God is a line of truth and goodness that is unbending. It moves straight and with certainty across the universe of space, time and thought. Any variation from that will of God, be it only in the slightest fraction of a degree, causes a tangent of separation and deviation — and that is sin. In the future the universe will get back to eternity; there shall be no more time, because there shall be no more deviation from the will of God. Christ shall put down all rule and all authority and power. For He must reign until He hath put all enemies under His feet (I Corinthians 15:24, 25). Those of us in whom God plants eternal life are made partakers of the divine nature, having escaped the corruption that is in the world through wanting one's own way (II Peter 1:4, Greek). We then are able to say from the heart that which no man who is not born again can say, namely, "Thy will be done . . ."

When the second will appeared in the universe, God dealt with it immediately and with finality. We must admit at once that God could have destroyed the power of Satan in the very first moment of his rebellion had He so desired. To hold any other thought would be the denial of the omnipotence of God. Why then did God not strike down Satan's rebellion with one great stroke, thus preventing the miseries and the catastrophes which have come out of that rebellion like hot lava out of a volcano, burning and destroying all in its path?

In order to get the answer it is necessary to get God's point of view. In the capital of the United States there is an obelisk more than five hundred feet high in memory of the first president. If someone placed you with your face six inches from the monument and told you to look at it, you would get an impression of a wall of stone, but little more. As you were led from it to obtain a proper perspective, the soaring needle point would take on quite different proportions in your mind and eye. So it is with the problem of Satan's sin and rebellion. There are some scenes which demand distance and angle if we are to appreciate their scope and grandeur. Satan recognized this principle for you will remember that he took the Lord Jesus Christ up into a high mountain, and showed unto Him all the kingdoms of the world in a moment of time (Luke 4:5). Every man must look at this problem either from the place of Satan's choice or from that of God's. If you are standing on the mountain of Satan's choice, your view is clouded by the mists and fogs which he causes to rise to hide those portions which are displeasing to him. If you are willing to be subjected to God Almighty, the Author of the universe, He will set your feet on the summit from which you can see the whole of His tremendous plan, and there will not be the slightest shadow to dim the vision.

But be absolutely assured that the vantage point which God offers for the survey of the eternal plan cannot be reached except on God's terms. It is totally impossible to comprehend spiritual things until you have been given a new spirit in the regeneration that God provides on the basis of the atoning death of Christ. If you will accept the divine verdict as to your own rebellious position and condition, and if you will accept the divine verdict that God is eternally satisfied with that which Jesus Christ accomplished in dying upon the cross as a substitute for you, bearing the stroke of wrath which was your due, then God will plant within you a new life and you will find that Christ Jesus is made unto you wisdom and righteousness (I Corinthians 1:30). The man who has thus trusted in Christ will be able to be lifted into the very mountain of God to see the plan of God. The man who rejects the Lord Jesus Christ as his personal Saviour is "dead in trespasses and sins" (Ephesians 2:1). It is also true that the Christian who has been made a "partaker of the divine nature" (II Peter 1:4), and who walks in his own will instead of in surrender to the will of God, is said to possess a spiritual astigmatism which makes him "blind," so that "he cannot see afar off" (II Peter 1:9).

From the mountain of God, however, we are able to see divine truth. He "hath raised us up together [with Christ] and made us sit together in heavenly places in Christ Jesus" (Ephesians 2:10). From this vantage point we can see and understand.

We now look upon this question from the point of view of heaven and from the outlook of eternity. Time shrinks into an insignificant moment between two eternities. We look back and realize that there was "a forever and forever and ever" before God created Lucifer. We look into the future and we see that there will be another "forever and forever and ever," after God, the Lord Jesus Christ, has "put down all rule and all authority and power. For he must reign, till he hath put all enemies under his feet" (I Corinthians 15:24, 25).

What appears to us from our worm's eye view of earth to be vast stretches of time, covering all the generations of man's history and the ages of the earth, shrinks into a single moment between two eternities during which God is permitting evil to prevail for a brief space and out of which He shall bring a multitude of sons capable of sharing His glory and of ruling the universe from a position higher than that of Lucifer before his fall. Though these sons shall have a dignity and a glory far above that which Lucifer knew, and though they shall exercise powers and hold prerogatives far higher than those given to the first governor of the universe, there shall never rise in any heart the thought of rebellion against the authority of God. If we are asked why we thus *conclude,* there are several answers. First, the old nature of Adam with its rebellious heart was judged at the cross of Christ; and at our death or at the transforming appearance of Christ it ceases forever to have a place within us. Second, the new creation (II Corinthians 5:17), which made us partakers of the divine nature (II Peter 1:4), is a nature which cannot sin (I John 3:9) for His seed remains in us. Lastly, if sin were ever to break out again it would demand another atonement and the Scripture tells us that Christ having been raised from the dead, dieth no more, death has no more dominion over Him (Romans 6:9).

Moreover, no son brought from the miry clay and made to stand upon the high rock, will ever wish to take any glory to himself, but will realize that all worship belongs to the Godhead. No son, with the indelible memory that he was lifted from the pit of sin, will ever wish to arrogate to himself an authority which he knows belongs to the Creator alone. Thus God shall have with Him an infinite company of sons, ruling the universe for Him and giving all of the glory to Him.

5 : *Two Wills*
(CONTINUED)

T HERE were at least two courses open to God when Lucifer sinned. He could, in His omnipotence, have destroyed Lucifer with a stroke. Had He done this, He could never have created another being as high and wonderful as Lucifer, seated as prime minister of the universe, possessing the gift of will and of choice, without seeing the same rebellion occur again and again We may be thankful that God did not strike Lucifer down and so make of eternity a series of high creations, willful rebellions and powerful outbursts of judgment and suppression.

However, the evidence of Scripture and history shows that God chose rather to give the rebel a full opportunity of exploiting every avenue of his power and wisdom so that it might be demonstrated that nothing good could ever come to the creation apart from that which originates in God Himself. The full significance of this is better understood after we have considered the details of Satan's willful claims. When Satan conceived a will that was contrary to God, he formulated a plan of attack which is set forth in the five "I wills" of Isaiah's account.

REBELLION BEGAN ON EARTH

The first, "I will ascend into heaven," is the announcement of his general objective and includes the very important fact that *the rebellion began on this earth*. Milton, in *Paradise Lost,* has Lucifer beginning in heaven, and cast out when he gathers a host of angels to fight against God. Thrust out with their leader, they all fall to hell where they lie

> Thick as autumnal leaves that strow the brooks
> In Vallombrosa.

After a consultation in Satan's palace, which they have built in hell and named Pandemonium, it is recounted that a rumor has been current in heaven to the effect that God was planning to create a new world and govern it by a new creature to be called man. It is decided, therefore, that their best policy is to investigate the rumor and, if it is verified, to turn their attention to man, so that, seducing him, they might frus-

44

trate the plans of God. The poem goes on to show the carrying out of this plan, the consequent sin of man and the loss of Paradise. Where there is a partial mitigation of error through the presentation of the fact that redemption is through Christ untold numbers of students, reading the poem in class, get the idea that the above doctrinal outline is Biblical. This is far from the truth, Satan's rebellion began on this earth and proceeded toward heaven and the throne of God.

GOD'S THRONE THE CENTER

Men have long argued the question of the center of the universe. Some, through tradition, taught that the earth was the center of all things. This was a purely human, if not satanic, point of view. When Copernicus brought out his astronomical system, there were those who opposed it on the ground that it could not be true since they supposed the Bible depicts a geocentric universe — a universe that is a circle or globe of which the earth is the center. But, of course, the Bible nowhere teaches any such thing. It goes without saying that the heaven of God's throne is the center of all things, but the material universe, in the sovereign plan of God, was created as a vast theater to declare the glory of God (Psalm 19:1). Now, where is the center of a theater? Is it on the floor at the intersection of the diameters of its auditorium? Is it midway between floor and ceiling above the intersection of its diameters? Or, is it the stage on which the play is enacted? The answer is obvious. In this theater of the universe, the earth is the stage on which the whole drama of rebellion, ruin, fall, judgment, redemption, salvation and the triumph and ultimate vindication of God's wisdom and righteousness is being unrolled in the amazing spectacle of the invisible war. It is in this light we must understand the words of Christ as He came to the end of His earthly life and faced the cross: "I have glorified thee *on the earth* . . ." He said this to the Father, as though announcing that the very dust which had seen the original rebellion had now seen the greater obedience out of which should come the final banishment of sin from the universe.

THE HEAVENLY TERRITORY

Let us now consider the heavenly territory which Satan proposed to conquer. The Bible uses the word or idea of heaven in four different senses: that of the immediate atmosphere of earth, including the clouds; that of our solar system and the heaven of the stars; that of the lower heavens, presently occupied by the forces of Satan and the scene of his spiritual activity; and that of the far above heavens of the throne of God. We make no attempt to go into detail about a subject so wonderful that when Paul speaks of a man caught up into the third heaven, he describes him as having heard words that are "not lawful for a man to utter" (II Corinthians 12:4). But we do know that Moses was strictly admonished to make every detail of the tabernacle and its worship serve "unto the example and shadow of heavenly things" (Exodus 25: 40; Hebrews 8:5) and the New Testament tells us that the tabernacle was itself the pattern of things in the heavens (Hebrews 9:23). When we read that the tabernacle contained a holy place and the holiest of all (Hebrews 9:2, 3), we are to understand that there is a similar plan in the heavenlies. Thus, we read that Christ in His Ascension entered into the holy place (Hebrews 9:12), higher than the heavens (Hebrews 7:26); or, as it is stated in Ephesians, He was raised to the right hand of the Father in the heavens far above all principality, and power, and might, and dominion, and every name that is named (Ephesians 1: 20, 21).

We have already seen that Satan's palace was on the primal earth, in Eden, the garden of God (Ezekiel 28:13) which antedated the first rebellion. We have noted that one of Satan's main titles concerns itself with his principality over this particular world (John 14:30; 16:11). Now, it is most important that we determine *where Satan was at the moment of his rebellion.* Most commentators have assumed that he was somewhere in heaven, that his fall took place there, and that he was cast down to earth. However, we find no evidence for such a position. Rather do we find the Bible specifically teaching that his rebellion took place on earth and that its first manifestation was a bold statement from Lucifer that he would ascend into heaven.

THE PROPHETIC PAST

Perhaps this difficulty has arisen for some commentators through a misreading of a prophecy made by Christ concerning Satan's future ejection from heaven: "I beheld Satan as lightning fall from heaven" (Luke 10:18). We shall establish that, although it is in the past tense, this phrase is assuredly a prophecy of something that has not yet taken place. Since its ultimate occurrence is a part of the plan of God, it can be expressed as something done and accomplished. Many future events are thus set forth in the Bible in what is known as the prophetic past tense.

Perhaps the most thrilling example of this usage is the statement concerning ourselves that we are already glorified and in heaven: "whom he did foreknow he also did predestinate to be conformed to the image of his Son [past tense for a past event]. Moreover whom he did predestinate them he also called [past tense for a past event]; and whom he called them he also justified [past tense for an event that was once future for believers and is now past, but which is yet future for those who shall be saved in days to come]; and whom he justified them he also glorified [past tense for an event that is wholly future]" (Romans 8:29, 30). There are many similar usages of the past tense in the Word of God.

This is surely the principle to be applied to the passage in question. The seventy who had been sent forth to preach returned to the Lord in exultation because even the demons were subject to them. Looking for a moment beyond His disciples and seeing that glorious day when Satan and all his forces should be swept out of heaven, the Lord answered: "I beheld Satan as lightning fall from heaven."

Much later the Lord spoke again of this removal of Satan from the heavenly sphere, saying: "Now is the judgment of this world: now shall the prince of this world be cast out" (John 12:31). Here again we must understand it as prophecy, as a proclamation of the moral ground upon which God will deal with sin. Christ, about to die, is saying: "Now is the cross coming to pass, and it is the basis of the judgment of this present world system. Now is the cross coming to pass, and it assures the doom of Satan."

In view of these passages therefore, we believe the career of Satan should be outlined thus: He began on earth as its prince. He entered into heaven carrying the worship of his principality into the presence of God, even into the very throne room. So great was the power that he saw himself exercising on earth, greater than the power of lesser creatures stationed on various levels in the heavens, that he determined to move into heaven and take possession of its government. This is the heart meaning of the Isaiah passage with its series of "I wills." They are five cries of progressive desire for more and more power. They reflect the inner mind of Lucifer where his imagination had already moved him from his own throne on earth to the throne of God in heaven. Each succeeding declaration is one step beyond the last. The first, "I will ascend into heaven," is the demand that the sphere of his rule be lifted from earth to the heavens. Seeing himself as more glorious than the creatures used by God in the administration of the sanctuaries of heaven, he sets forth his extravagant claims that he will go up, up, up, even until he has displaced the Most High God on the throne of the universe.

His second pretension, "I will exalt my throne above the stars of God," is not a mere literary repetition of the previous clause. In order to understand this phrase it is necessary for us to comprehend some things that the Bible teaches about the stars. If we examine every verse in the Bible where there is mention of the stars, we will see, immediately, that the passages fall into two groups. There are those verses which refer to the stars which we see in the sky, the study of which falls in the realm of astronomy. But there are other verses which clearly speak of stars which are not to be seen in the skies, but which are messengers of God. Nor should we stumble at such a differentiation. Anyone receiving a letter from a traveler in Southern California telling that he had seen many stars would have to discover from the context whether he had been at one of the astronomical observatories on the mountains back of Los Angeles or at a movie in Hollywood! Just as surely there is a double usage of the word "stars" in the Word of God.

The best known reference to the messenger-stars is in John's vision of Christ in the Revelation, where the Lord is seen holding the seven stars in His hand, and these are declared to be His messengers to the churches (Revelation 1:16, 20). Another well-known passage occurs in the words spoken by Jehovah to Job, asking where he was when God laid the foundations of the earth: "Whereupon are the foundations thereof fastened? or who laid the corner stone thereof; when the morning stars sang together and all the sons of God shouted for joy?" (Job 38:6, 7). The careful Bible student will find other references which indicate that other angelic servants of God bear this title. The believers in Christ are told that "they that be wise shall shine as the brightness of the firmament; and they that turn many to righteousness as the stars forever and ever" (Daniel 12:3). There is evidently in heaven a great company, which, for want of a better vocabulary of heavenly things, we shall call starry angels, all of whom are conformed to the will of God and have a place in heaven. It is above them that Satan desired to exalt his throne.

Indeed, he wanted to go even higher. He said in his heart, "I will sit upon the mount of the congregation, in the sides of the north." Just as the Bible passages containing references to the stars may be divided into astronomical and spiritual references, so a close study of the word *congregation* in the Bible will reveal a series of references to earthly companies, such as the children of Israel, and other references which apply to a glorious company in heaven. Some of the latter may even have followed Satan in his fall, for we read: "God standeth in the congregation of the mighty; he judgeth among the gods . . ." (Psalm 82:1). These are the rebel powers which still usurp the functions of deity in their following of Satan. How illuminating such a passage as the eighty-ninth Psalm becomes when seen in this connection. "And the heavens shall praise thy wonders, O Lord; thy faithfulness also in the congregation of the holy ones. For who in the heaven can be compared unto the Lord? who among the sons of the mighty can be likened unto the Lord? God is greatly to be feared in the assembly of the holy ones, and to be had in reverence of all them that are about him" (Psalm 89:5-7). In other words, Satan desired to have the position of government over the angelic hosts that were administering heaven.

This scene of government is "in the sides of the north." We leave the reader the delight of studying all the passages in the Bible which refer to heaven as being in the north. To a concordance list of such passages, we must not forget to add the word from the Psalms: "Promotion cometh neither from the east, nor from the west, nor from the south, but God is the judge" (Psalm 75:6, 7).

We next read that Lucifer declared, "I will ascend above the heights of the clouds." There is by now a pattern for understanding the meaning of these passages. Just as there are stars and stars, just as there is an earthly and a heavenly congregation, so there are clouds and clouds in the Bible. Just as modern writers took the word *cloud* to describe the wonder that accompanies an atomic explosion, though it is not a cloud, so the word has the spiritual meaning also. There are passages which speak of clouds of the kind we know, which are blown across the sky before a summer wind, or catch the glories of the sun at the end of the day. But there are also clouds in the Bible which speak of the glory of God, having no connection with what meteorologists would classify as cirrus or cumulus clouds. We remember the pillar of fire by night and the cloud by day which led the children of Israel in the way (Exodus 13:21). It was from this cloud that the Lord protected the Israelites from the Egyptian host (Exodus 14:19, 20). Again, when the tabernacle was set up, the cloud was sent to cover the holy place, and it was there that the Lord appeared to His people (Exodus 40:28-34). We remember, too, that this same cloud was seen returning to heaven at the time of Ezekiel's vision (Ezekiel 9:3; 10:4; etc.). It is of this cloud we read in the New Testament, when, at the birth of Christ, the "glory" of the Lord shone round about the angels (Luke 2:9). Christ ascended into heaven and a cloud received Him out of the sight of the apostles (Acts 1:9). When He comes again for His saints He shall take them from this earth into that cloud of glory (I Thessalonians 4:17). He announced to the High Priest at the time of His trial and death that He would return to earth "coming in the clouds of heaven" (Matthew 26:64; Revelation 14:14-16). These clouds are not what we see in the sky, but are the visible marks of a glory far transcending human thought and for which there is no word which could evoke any image in our thinking. This is the symbol of the glory of God and the very throne of heaven. Above this Satan desired to climb.

To introduce Satan's last defiant cry, let me tell a story. I believe it would be possible to get a fairly accurate idea of the life and character of a man simply by setting down in order the names, nicknames, pet-names, titles and epithets applied him throughout his life. I suggest the following: Male, John Smith; precious baby; Junior; Skinny; Butch; Red; Smitty; Yeah-Touchdown — Smith; John B. Smith, B.A.; sweet-heart; corporal; sergeant; lieutenant; D.S.O.; John Smith, M.A.; the Reverend John Smith, D.D.; darling; daddy; beloved pastor; fearless preacher; nosey parson; saint; interfering meddler; orator; author; trav-eler; grandfather; Mr. Chairman; our venerable leader; cantankerous opponent; pastor emeritus; the late Reverend John Smith, D.D., LL.D.; Christian gentleman; scholar; a man after God's own heart.

If we thus can follow the course of a man's life, from his birth to his grave, by means of his names and titles, then surely the names of the Lord God Almighty recorded in His Word are revealing. However, our illustration falls down. The names and titles given to man touch no more than the externals; but the names of God reveal the innermost nature of His character and being. Thus "the name of the Lord is a strong tower; the righteous runneth into it and is safe" (Proverbs 18:10). There are nearly four hundred names for God in the Bible.

In his last arrogant thrust at God, why did Satan cry: "I will be like the Most High"? From all the possible names of God, why did Satan choose "the Most High"? Why did he not say, I will be like the Creator? Why did he not aspire to be like God in His names of Saviour, Redeemer, Comforter? Why did he not desire to be like the Eternal Word, the Shepherd, the I AM, the Light, the Way, the Life, the Truth, or any of the other names by which we may know our God? The an-swer is found in the meaning of the title, "the Most High," as indicated in its first usage in the Scriptures.

Back in the story of Abram we have the record of an incident re-vealing the inwardness of the name "the Most High." Abram was re-turning home after the battle with the kings and the deliverance of Lot. We read that "Melchizedek, king of Salem, brought forth bread and wine [the communion element]; and he was the priest of the most high God. And he blessed him, and said, Blessed be Abram of the most high God, possessor of heaven and earth . . ." (Genesis 14:18, 19). Here is the key to the pride of Satan. God is revealed as *El Elyon,* the Most High God, and in this character He is "the Possessor of heaven and earth." This is what Lucifer wanted to be. His rebellion was not a request for God to move over so that he might share God's throne. It was a thrust at God Himself. It was an attempt to put God out so that Satan might take His place as possessor of the heavens and the earth.

Another passage in which the name of the Most High appears explains many things in human history. Before his death, Moses sang a prophetic song in which we find the following: "Remember the days of old, consider the years of many generations; ask thy father, and he will shew thee; thy elders, and they will tell thee. When the most High divided to the nations their inheritance, when he separated the sons of Adam, he set the bounds of the people according to the number of the children of Israel" (Deuteronomy 32:7, 8). There is no authority for the reading "sons of God" as found in the Septuagint and the RSV. All other versions, Jewish, Protestant, Roman Catholic, English, French and German agree with the Hebrew and the KJV — "children of Israel."

The Most High set the bounds of the people. Yet we find the Assyrian king, type of Antichrist of the future, boasting: "I have removed the bounds of the people, and have robbed their treasures; and I have put down the inhabitants like a valiant man" (Isaiah 10:13). Is it any wonder that the Lord has Isaiah interrupt the boaster to say, "When the Lord hath performed his whole work upon mount Zion and on Jerusalem, I will punish the fruit of the stout heart of the king of Assyria, and the glory of his high looks" (verse 12).

We can see that the thrust of tyrants and the domination of peoples by dictators is a Satanic thing, a direct rebellion against the fixed decrees of God.

War has been declared. The great, governing cherub had become the malignant enemy. Our God was neither surprised nor astonished, for, of course, He knew before it happened that it would happen, and He had His perfect plan ready to be put into effect. Although the Lord had the power to destroy Satan with a breath, He did not do so. It was as though an edict had been proclaimed in heaven: "We shall give this rebellion a thorough trial. We shall permit it to run its full course. The universe shall see what a creature, though he be the highest creature ever to spring from God's Word, can do apart from Him. We shall watch this experiment, and permit the universe of creatures to watch it, during this brief interlude between eternity past and eternity future called time. In it the spirit of independence shall be allowed to expand to the utmost. And the wreck and ruin which shall result will demonstrate to the universe, and forever, that there is no life, no joy, no peace apart from a complete dependence upon the Most High God, Possessor of heaven and earth."

6 : *The First Mouthful of Dust*

WHEN Satan rebelled and sin entered the universe, there were two courses of action open to God, since His nature would not allow Him to ignore it. The Almighty Jehovah, the most High, Possessor of heaven and earth, certainly had the power to strike down the creature whom He had brought into existence through His creative Word, and to annihilate him or put him in prison. There was no lack of power or opportunity. But if God had thus brought down the first enemy, He could never have created another mighty being like Lucifer with the freedom of choice, for there would always have been the possibility of another rebellion and the necessity for another repression. The history of heaven would then have been dotted with a series of disasters.

A COMPLETE TRIAL

The other alternative open to God was the one which we know from the Bible and from observation that He chose to follow. The claims of Satan to equality or superiority in power should have their complete trial. The universe should see, once and for all, if it were possible for any creature whatsoever, of any rank, however exalted, to live for even a moment independent of God the Creator. That full trial of the possibilities of a second will in government is the nature of the duration that we call time.

But there was one matter which had to be attended to immediately. A holy God could not permit a rebellion without showing His hatred of sin. Holiness had to be manifested. He must, unless He were to violate His character of holiness, blaze forth against sin. His attitude must be declared even though He were about to permit surprising latitude to the rebel for a definite period of time. God, therefore, spoke the Word of judgment and the material world — in fact, the whole domain of Satan — was blasted to chaos with a single breath from God. There are many substantiations of this fact in both science and the Bible.

This is the event which occurred between the first and the second verses of Genesis. The world, waste and empty, without form and void, was the result of this Word of judgment spoken by the Almighty God.

REVELATION OF THINGS PAST

While we are quite accustomed to revelations from God concerning the future, whether immediate or remote from the time of the inspired writer, we must not be startled by the thought of revelations from God concerning things in the past. Should it be thought strange that God, who knows and reveals the future, has also been pleased to reveal certain things which took place in the shadowy past — shadowy to us who are creatures, but containing no shadows for Him who is light and in whom dwelleth no darkness at all?

God makes a great accusation against men — against thinking men — because they will not believe what is revealed about the past history of this earth, although the evidence is set forth, not only in the Bible, but in the world beneath their feet. Through Peter, God says, "For this they willingly are ignorant of, that by the word of God the heavens were of old [i.e., in Genesis 1:1], and the earth standing out of the water and in the water: whereby the world that then was, being overflowed with water, perished [in Genesis 1:2]: but the heavens and the earth which are now [re-formed in Genesis 1:3 ff.], by the same word are kept in store, reserved unto fire against the day of judgment and perdition of ungodly men" (II Peter 3:5-7). Note carefully the distinction between the two worlds: "the world that then was" and "the heavens and the earth which are now." We put aside the superficial interpretation that the destruction mentioned in verse two refers to the time of the flood. The world did not perish then, but it did in the cataclysm of the earlier judgment.

Men postulate that all things have always been as they are now, and that there have been no great moments of divine intervention either to create, to reveal or to punish. All things continue as they were, modern science says. But the Bible says that men are willingly ignorant when they express this doctrine of continuity. All things do not continue as they were. They were begun in perfection and altered in judgment again and again. The world went on its disintegrating way, and God intervened at Calvary. He is about to intervene again in the doings of mankind. Of these things, God accuses men of being *willingly* ignorant. He has revealed them. They can be known, but men will not know them. The greatest charge that can be brought against a man who counts himself to be logical is that he is willingly ignorant. For, in bolder terms, it means he is dishonest.

Intellectual Unbelief

Dishonest skeptics do not wish to know the truth; they only wish for an excuse to hide themselves from the prodding of the Holy Spirit. Like the woman at the well, reminded of her adultery, they are willing to find refuge even in theological discussion in order to avoid the searching, probing finger of God in the putrifying wound of their sinful being. Answer one of their fancied objections, and they will grudgingly admit the validity of your argument and change the ground of their objection. Pursue them by the logic of eternal truth from position to position, and they will only, when they have exhausted all of the arguments known to them, start round the circle again. We do not expect to convince such by any setting forth of truth. Men love darkness rather than light because their deeds are evil (John 3:19).

But we recognize clearly that there are, for instance, in our university circles, an increasing number of people who have been brought up away from the Biblical background that was so common in the Victorian era. These are probably honest skeptics. They do not have the content of consciousness upon which the Spirit may do His work. Their minds, totally ignorant of what the Bible really teaches and, worse, filled with false ideas that they suppose it teaches, are concerned with philosophical questions about God, man, moral issues, etc. They are undoubtedly honestly seeking, even though blindly and in the wrong direction, for answers to life's problems. Many evangelical Christians, knowing God's flat statement that there is "none that seeketh after God" (Romans 3:11), have considered that these gropers might well be dismissed with merely a casual proof text. We have too frequently been as harmless as doves without being as wise as serpents. This has caused many hungry intellectuals to conclude that there are no answers in evangelical Christianity to the problems which they see. It has even probably — since nature abhors a vacuum — been no small factor in the conversion to Roman Catholicism of many who, looking for truth and having willingly suspended disbelief in Christianity, have accepted in the Roman Church a highly intellectualized development of what in reality is a false premise.

The Sword of the Spirit

Christians who would work with such people must have both a knowledge of the problems as they appear to the mind of the thinking unbeliever and a patient willingness to point out in the Word of God whatever of answer there is for the natural man. At the same time, we must remember that "the natural man receiveth not the things of the Spirit of God: for they are foolishness unto him: neither can he know them, because they are spiritually discerned" (I Corinthians 2:14). However, since we know that truth does not change and that God's method of dealing with souls is ever the same, we must be faithful in our wielding of the slaying sword of the Spirit. Thus only can we meet their real need. God never raised any soul to life through the Gospel without first slaying him with the law. With honest skeptics, for such often fall into this class, we should be firm and fearless while we speak the truth in love. Our burden should be: a holy God declares that all are less perfect than He, and therefore sinners; that the wages of sin is eternal death; but that He has provided a Sin-bearer in Christ who has fully met every demand of divine justice against the sinner. It is the entrance of such a word that gives light. No man has ever been argued into salvation; no man has ever been led to Christ through human wisdom. Only the flat presentation of human need and Christ's sufficiency will do it. "Not by might, nor by power, but by my Spirit, saith the Lord of hosts" (Zechariah 4:6).

However, whether or not the skepticism is honest, God's verdict remains the same: men are *willingly* ignorant in the matter of divine intervention. God has intervened and will yet again intervene. It was God's hand in creation, judgment, re-formation, further creation and judgment, incarnation and redemption. His hand will yet be seen in future judgment and in triumph. Men who reject divine intervention in favor of the theory of continuity are, says God, willingly ignorant of the truth.

Let us now consider some of the evidence substantiating the fact of God's intervention in creation to wreck it by a great catastrophe at the time Lucifer made his bold bid for power. Many details are to be found in various passages of the Old Testament which cannot be applied to any moment in time other than that described in the second verse in the Bible. In the book of Jeremiah, we read: "I beheld the earth, and, lo, it was without form and void; and the heavens, and they had no light. I beheld the mountains, and, lo, they trembled, and all the hills moved lightly. I beheld, and lo, there was no man, and all the birds of the heavens were fled. I beheld, and, lo, the fruitful place was a wilderness, and all the cities thereof were broken down at the presence of the Lord, and his fierce anger" (Jeremiah 4:23-26). By quoting in Jeremiah the second verse of Genesis, God has placed this passage in time for us. Jeremiah's vision is of the earth made waste and desolate; of the earth in the catastrophe that came in judgment and not in creation, since God states so exactly that He did not create the earth in chaos (Isaiah 45:18, R.S.V.).

The earth was without form and void, waste and empty, a wreck and a ruin. From the catastrophe which touched all the sidereal heavens, there were tremendous manifestations on the earth. An earthquake of such violent proportions took place that the mountains are said to have trembled, and the hills to have moved lightly. It should be noticed that lightly does not mean slightly. The hills moved with lightness, would be a more adequate translation. The RSV says the mountains were quaking and the hills moving to and fro. The description is comparable to that of another judgment where it is said that the mountains skipped like rams and the little hills like lambs (Psalm 114:4). It is a scene which, had there been an earthly onlooker to observe it, would have been described in terms of the most violent upheaval: mountain ranges were hurled across continents, hills following like scattered pebbles. This is the force of the Psalmist's phrase of hills skipping like lambs across a field. Nothing but an explanation like this will satisfy the facts of geology where the various strata of the earth's surface, sometimes vertical, sometimes horizontal, sometimes upside down, show how mountains were twisted and tortured until they lie in agonized heaps across the continents, like the cinders of a burnt out hell.

Halley, the great astronomer, most popularly known today by the comet which bears his name, was much interested in the effect that such a celestial body might have upon this earth if it came very close to it. One of his recorded observations is significant in this connection. He noted that the North Pole is a few degrees away from true north, and that our earth does not move around the sun in an orbit where its mass is constant in the vertical plane of its axis. Our change of seasons is based on this fact. At the equinoxes the earth is in the vertical position, but as the months go on it tilts, now to the north, now to the south, in its regular motion. Halley wondered if the earth had once been in the vertical position, and if a comet might have pulled it slightly from its original position. He wondered, further, what the effect of such a tilting would have been. So he set himself to calculate the volume, mass and weight of the oceans of the world, and drew the conclusion that such a change of balance in the spinning globe would have pulled the seas from their beds and sent them whirling round the earth, picking up the mountain ranges and tossing them onwards [like rams and lambs?] with the maximum in centrifugal force, until the equilibrium of the new polar axis had become established and the world settled down with the mountains lying broken in their new positions, and the seas set in their new boundaries.

We take such an hypothesis, very modern and quite legitimate in scientific circles, and are amazed to find the parallelisms with that which

God has revealed. In the ninth chapter of Job, we read: "If he [God] will contend with man, he cannot answer him one of a thousand. He is wise in heart, and mighty in strength, who hath hardened himself against him, and hath prospered?" (Job 9:3, 4). And at this point, thinking of the original hardening of Satan against God and the wreckage which had come because of that rebellion, Job goes on to describe the judgment which had come: "Which removeth the mountains, and they know not: which overturneth them in his anger. Which shaketh the earth out of her place, and the pillars [poles?] thereof tremble [are moved from the vertical?]. Which commandeth the sun, and it riseth not; and sealeth up the stars . . ." (Job 9:5-7).

In addition to the catastrophe on earth, it is plainly stated that there was a catastrophe in the visible heavens. Jeremiah declares that the heavens had no light (4:23), and Job says that the light of the sun and the stars was shut off from the earth. The changing of light in heavenly bodies here described in the Bible is not unknown today to modern astronomy. In the skies there are sometimes seen stars which flare up in a great explosion, and then sink back into darkness. These are called *novae*. A star of the tenth magnitude has been known to flare into third or fourth magnitude for just a few days, and then, after the brief period of great light, the star will sink back to twelfth magnitude, or will fade to even dimmer proportions. But even apart from facts visible to the human eye, the believer will recognize that an omnipotent God can do what He wishes with His creations, and can change with His Word that which He first created with His Word.

The shutting off of the light of the sun would have caused the precipitation of all moisture to the earth, and all of the waters of the earth would have been frozen. The geologists tell us that there are traces of glaciers across the whole surface of the earth, with marks of a great ice cap in the center of equatorial Africa.

In one of the Psalms, there is a further reference to God's intervention in catastrophic judgment: "Then the earth shook and trembled; the foundations also of the hills moved and were shaken, because He was wroth . . . he bowed the heavens also, and came down: and darkness was under his feet . . . . Then the channels of water were seen, and the foundations of the world were discovered at thy rebuke, O Lord, at the blast of the breath of thy nostrils" (Psalm 18:7-15).

At the end of Job's great testing the Lord appeared to him, vindicating him in the matter of charges brought against him by his "comforters." And in the divine revelation of the person and power of God to His suffering servant, whose body and soul had become a battlefield in the invisible war, God makes reference to the original creation, the catastrophe of judgment, and the re-formation that followed. "Where wast thou when I laid the foundations of the earth? declare, if thou hast understanding. Who hath laid the measures thereof, if thou knowest? or who hath stretched the line upon it? Whereupon are the foundaions thereof fastened? or who laid the corner stone thereof; When the morning stars sang together, and all the sons of God shouted for joy?" (Job 38:4-7). Then, in the next verse, after this description of the creation, we move on immediately to the scene of great judgment. "Or who shut up the sea with doors, when it brake forth, as if it had issued out of the womb? When I made the cloud the garment thereof, and thick darkness a swaddlingband for it, and brake up for it my decreed place, and set bars and doors, and said, Hitherto shalt thou come, but no further: and here shalt thy proud waves be stayed?" (Job 38: 8-11). After these two sections on the original creation and judgment, the Lord then proceeds to speak of the re-formation, reminding Job of the time when He had spoken on the first of the six days, commanding the morning and causing "the dayspring to know his place; that it might take hold of the ends of the earth, that the wicked might be shaken out of it?" (Job 38:12, 13).

Nor is such judgment upon sin out of keeping with the nature of God. In fact, there is a consistent revelation throughout the Bible of God's hatred for sin, and, except as limited by His patience and grace for purposes of His own, of His pouring out of wrath upon all ungodliness. The ground was cursed when Adam sinned (Genesis 3:17). The flood came when the race was about to be overcome with demon possession (Genesis 6:4-7). The Great Tribulation is announced for the ending of this present age (Matthew 24:21). The world itself, after all its sin, is to burn with fire at the end of time (II Peter 3:7-10), while the lake of fire is to embrace Satan (Revelation 20:10) and all who have persisted in following him (Matthew 25:41). In the light of all these, we can well understand the beginning of the series when God's judgment flamed against the domain of Satan at the first outbreak of willfulness. The curse of God had to issue forth against the creation which had been corrupted by sin.

Leaving the discussion of the physical aspects of the curse upon the realm of Satan, let us consider the judgment of the earth from a spiritual point of view. It was a judgment which was peculiarly fitting, for it revealed at one and the same time the power of God and the impotence of Satan. God had created the earth and the heavens by His Word. Lucifer had announced that he wished to take possession of them for himself. By the simple Word of God the heavens and the earth were toppled into judgment chaos. In that same moment Satan got his first mouthful of dust.

Dust in the mouth is a perfect figure for defeat and frustration. We remember, as a small child, being proffered what appeared to be a beautiful apple. Childlike, we took the largest bite possible, and broke into an imitation apple, made of cotton, and painted to represent a luscious fruit. The mouth had been ready for a delicacy and received dust instead. In Adam's time the Lord pronounced the curse upon the serpent because the latter had become the tool of Satan. He announced that "dust shalt thou eat all the days of thy life" (Genesis 3:14). In the future, with the one exception of the serpent's method of taking its food, the curse shall be removed from the earth. The wolf and the lamb shall feed together, the lion shall eat straw like the bullock, and even the poison shall be removed from the fangs of the serpent (Isaiah 11:8). Yet though the creation is thus restored, "dust shall be the serpent's meat" (Isaiah 65:25).

From the very moment when Lucifer in his pride, cried out, "I will . . . I will . . ." he was doomed to everlasting disappointment. The creature who thinks even for a moment that he can get along without God, that he can accomplish anything in his own power, is doomed to the sensation best described as "dust in the mouth." The first experience the fallen cherub knew was that of seeing his domain in waste and desolation without being able to do a thing about it. There must have come upon him with stunned surprise the knowledge that his beauty and wisdom were insufficient for the task which now lay before him. He had wanted to possess heaven and earth, but he discovered that it was a judged universe and that he had no power to set it right. There began to dawn in his darkened mind the fact that his wisdom was not omniscience, that his power was not omnipotence, that he was a creature and had no ability to create. He had lifted himself toward heaven in a surge of awful desire to be like God, and his mouth was now filled with dust. He had carried with him a group of angels and demons who had been willing to accept his authority, and they would learn that all of them with their combined intelligence and power would be unable to put the chaotic world together again.

A little later we see the Spirit of God brooding upon the face of the deep, with a brooding which was a thought of love, and which contained a plan of redemption. There must have been another brooding also, the brooding of Satan, dark and sinister. Pride was wounded and hatred was feeding and fattening upon itself. There is no picture more dreadful than that of Satan roaming in the midst of the destroyed creation, totally impotent. There was the appetite of desire to be, to act, to possess, and there was the fulfillment of a sense of emptiness, of inaction because of inability, and of the possession of a shell, a fragment, a waste and desolation. The mouth had watered for a delicacy, the grasping bite had filled tongue and teeth with dust. Here was the ultimate in absolute frustration. Satan may well have raved in the madness of that chaotic darkness. If he called out, "Let there be light," there was no answer save the empty echo of his cry ranging through dead sparks of former suns and the desolation of a ruined earth.

Let every man and woman who wishes to be independent of God in Christ know that the path of any creature who cuts loose from a surrendered dependence upon the Redeemer-God is in the path of Lucifer. Emptiness, inability, frustration, dust: these are the portion of the man who walks his own way. Satisfaction is not to be found outside of God as revealed in Jesus Christ, and obedience to His will. There is no other source of joy.

During the second World War, when the forces of Germany were at their farthest point of advance, a cartoon was published in the London *Star* which perfectly illustrates our point. It appeared at the moment when Hitler's armies were in the foothills of the Caucasus, and Rommel was standing within the borders of Egypt, boasting that he would be resting in Cairo within a week or two. Then, suddenly, the Russian power began to make itself felt, and the armies of Montgomery (who advanced with the Bible and *Pilgrim's Progress*), began their victorious march across Africa. The cartoon showed Hitler standing on tiptoe upon a heap of skulls, reaching into the sky where his fingers were just barely missing a cloud in the shape of the word "Victory." The title of the cartoon was, "It is always just out of reach." So it is for Satan, and so it shall be for all who follow in any path of rebellion against the one will of God.

7 : *The Stage Reset*

THE drama of the invisible war may be said to be in three acts, each divided into various scenes and with interludes of judgment. At times the actors look on and at times the audience plays a part. What we have seen in the earlier chapters comprises the first act ending with the black curtain of judgment falling on the final scene. Let us summarize in one paragraph:

A brilliantly lighted curtain was lifted disclosing a setting of great magnificence with multitudes of angelic hosts in view. The most splendid of all of those creatures, full of wisdom and perfect in beauty, stepped to the center of the scene. He spoke: "I will ascend . . . I will exalt . . . I will sit . . . I will ascend . . . I will be like the most High." Suddenly there was a crash of thunder. Every light went out. The whole scene was dark, and an even darker curtain enveloped the stage. The universal audience was gripped with horror. It awaited the next move with breathless tension.

THE CURTAIN OF DARKNESS

Thus the judgment of God on Satan's rebellion turned out the lights on this world. We do not know how long this period of judgment lasted. It may have been long ages. The geologists tell us of the scars of the travail of earlier years, and they believe that millions of years must have been necessary to have brought about some of the phenomena which are found in the earth. Let it be millions of years. Whatever the theory as to primeval time, it can be dropped into the vastness of Genesis. Does some theorist wish to claim that a billion years elapsed in bringing the ocean to its present degree of saltiness, or the land to its present eroding depths and emerging heights? Then put that billion years in between the judging blast of God and the fiat of light. Does another scientist advance a theory which seems to destroy this and set forth a hypothesis which would show that all natural phenomena can be explained on a basis of brevity? Then say

61

that the going forth of the command of light followed the devastation of judgment's wreckage by no more than the interval between one stroke of lightning and its thunder. At the moment, science holds a theory of length of ages. This does not contradict the Biblical facts, for the Bible furnishes only an outline enabling us to discern the sequence of events but not the time length in the details of the events.

In any event the curtain of darkness fell on the first act. The interval may be counted short from God's point of view, and yet long from the scientist's point of view. A child counts a year as a long time; an adult has learned differently. From the point of comparison with eternity, the intervals of time are but flashing instants.

It is therefore of no importance how men may theorize about the time length necessary to form some of the scars of judgment that are upon our world and upon the dead and the dying sun. Fallen man may be unwilling or unable to identify these scars with the marks of the wounds of sin and with the judgment of a holy God whose nature blazed forth to reveal both itself and its enemy. But it can scarcely be expected that men, who will not recognize similar wounds in their own hearts and who will not acknowledge their distance from their Creator, should see clearly into the spiritual nature of the judgments that once took place on this earth.

SATAN'S HELPLESSNESS

Whether the interval between the scenes is counted in man's moments or God's aeons, it finally came to an end, and the second act of this universal drama was ready to begin. At last the Spirit of God moved into the realm of Lucifer and began to brood upon the face of the black waters of earth. Without this divine activity the world would have remained forever in the murky night of divine judgment which shrouded its chaotic state. Not only was it impossible for the darkness of earth to transform itself into light, but Satan had no power to alter the chaos which pride had brought down upon his province.

A journalist has said that the idea of unscrambling an egg is the symbol of the impossible. When God wrecked Satan's realm He confronted the fallen cherub with just such a problem. Satan's ruined principality lay before him. As long as it was shrouded in the darkness of the judgment, it was hidden from the gaze of the angelic hosts. But light was to break upon the judged creation. The pretender who had claimed that he would be like the Possessor of heaven and earth was to be revealed as a braggart unable to dissipate a cloud or re-form a clod. He was to lie in naked impotence before all creation. It would now be seen that he who had the power to bring destruction had no power to create, and he who had called for followers to worship his wisdom was to see that wisdom proved powerless. He could not bring order to that which God had marred. How this must have accentuated the bitter gnawing in the heart of Satan.

We are not to think of a creature "perfect in all his ways" becoming in an instant "the dragon . . . that old serpent, called the Devil, and Satan, which deceiveth the whole world" (Revelation 12:9). Rather are we to note a developing malignancy in this depraved being which grew with his ever-increasing hatred of God and which fed upon itself and its frustrations. Milton in *Paradise Lost* saw the need for time in the development of such a degradation, and, while Milton's idea of precipitation from heaven to hell with a subsequent invasion of earth is totally unscriptural, his thought of Satan's gradual disintegration and decline from high nobility to base malignancy is in the line of truth. Certainly in the dark interlude between the judgment of the first creation and the going forth of light which was to preface its rehabilitation, we find place for such development.

GOD'S POWER

What Satan could not do even in ages, God could do in a single word. The whole of the Godhead was working in divine unity to reset the stage for the coming unfolding of the drama. Thus the Father did it, giving the command, "Let there be light." Thus the Holy Spirit did it, brooding upon the face of the deep. Thus the Son, the eternal Word did it, being Himself the Verb in the statement, "And God said . . ." Ten times in the first chapter of Genesis we find this phrase, and each time Christ is present in it.

Christ, indeed, is the principal protagonist in all of the scenes of the invisible war. "He is before all things, and by him all things consist" (Colossians 1:17). Though He has not yet appeared by name in the Genesis narrative, the book is inexplicable without Him, and one of the foremost purposes of the New Testament is to reveal Christ as present in every part of the Old. We are not turning aside, therefore, from the onward march of our history of the invisible war if we introduce some of the texts in the opening verses of the creation account which discover Him as the member of the Godhead who was actually performing the work. Thus the New Testament can say of Christ, "All things were made by him, and without him was not anything made that was made" (John 1:3). We might well translate the opening phrase of John's gospel, "In the beginning was the Verb, and the Verb was with God, and God was the Verb. All things were made by Him . . ."

So it was Christ who dispelled the darkness. "And God said, Let there be light, and there was light." The light which came over the chaotic universe was a light produced by the Word of God. "The entrance of thy words giveth light," the Psalmist says (Psalm 119:130). And the whole history of God's dealings manifests the power of the Word of God to bring light out of darkness, life out of death. This is our God, and there is none else besides. He alone can do this. *Fiat lux* — and there was light.

The shining of light into the waste and desolate creation must have brought Satan to instant attention. Although in the Genesis account Satan first appears on the sixth day when God made man, we may be sure that he had not been unconcerned during the previous days. From the very first moment when the Lord spoke the Word that brought light shining out of darkness, Satan was aware that God had intervened in what that fallen angel had come to look upon as being his own possession.

It is important to remember that Satan has always looked upon this world as his personal property. There is much that will remain incomprehensible if we overlook this fact. When Lucifer first awoke to consciousness, it was with the knowledge that he was ruler. When he was first placed in authority, it was by the edict of God who created him the cherub anointed for high purposes. God had said, "I have set thee so" (Ezekiel 28:14); and even in his fallen state Christ called him "the prince of this world" (John 14:30). When the Lord Jesus Christ met the blasphemy of the Pharisees who had suggested that His power was Satanic, He did it with an answer which recognized the principality of Satan: "Every kingdom divided against itself is brought to desolation; and a house divided against a house falleth. If Satan also be divided against himself, how shall his kingdom stand?" (Luke 11:17, 18). Where the Lord Himself recognized that Satan possessed a kingdom on earth, how can we imagine that Satan was without a supreme sense of his own lordship? True, Satan had failed in his first attempt to increase his power outside the earthly sphere where God had set him. Yet he still had his principality, and he would work tenaciously to hold it and would resist every attempt, even by God, to encroach upon it. If God should try to endow Adam, this intruder, with a lordship in Satan's domain, Satan would seek to alter the relationship and make Adam his own creature. Satan wanted power. It was sweet to him, and he would fight for it. Every user of power tends to entrench himself in his position and place of power, and tends to expand that power to its utmost in every possible direction. This is true of men today, whether individuals or groups, whether committees, branches of government, bureaus, legislatures, synods, presbyteries, pastors, shop foremen, office managers, policemen, husbands, wives or any person holding any authority whatsoever over another. This is one of the laws of human history, and it flows out of the nature of Satan and the nature of his rebellion against God.

GOD STILL ON THE THRONE

If the period of darkness and chaos was a prolonged one from the creature's point of view, the shock must have been all the greater when Satan discovered that God, after a long age of silence and inactivity in the realm of the darkened world, had not abandoned it to its governor, but still had an interest in it, still considered it as His province and under His sovereignty and evidently was now moving to work out some purpose of which Satan was in ignorance.

The divine command went forth and light streamed onto the stage which had known both the first act of creation with the music of the morning stars and the interlude of darkness which had followed. When the light pushed back the curtains of darkness, the stage was seen to be empty. No character walked the boards; no scenery was in place. Judgment lay illuminated before the eyes of the universe. Even those who had given their allegiance to Satan and who with him had not been able to pierce the veil of darkness were now forced to see the horror of a divine judgment on the material universe, illustrating the hatred of God against sin.

But now, in the succeeding days, God Himself began to shift the scenery upon that bare expanse, vacant and formless. There would be six days of sceneshifting and then the second act in the drama would be presented. A new character would be created around whom the greatest battles of the invisible war would be fought. Finally after six days of preparation, the new character stepped on the scene: it was man newly awakened to consciousness.

Since we are not presenting a detailed commentary on Genesis, we pass over the great riches to be found in the story of the six days to consider man himself. We merely sum up in passing, even as the phrase in the ten commandments does, the events of the six days. There we read: "For in six days the Lord made heaven and earth, the sea and all that in them is" (Exodus 20:11). Note well that it does not say that the Lord *created* these things in six days. The verb *create* is used for origination. The other verbs used in the story of the six days have no concept of creation in them. These new words have to do with the arranging and ordering of the existing materials into new forms. "God divided . . . God made . . . God gathered . . . God set . . ." These are the predicates of the account of the six days. They are words used of secondary work which has no thought of creation in it. Thus we may repudiate utterly the idea that the world was created in six days, and establish that the Bible, when taken in its utmost literalness, teaches that the perfect, created world was blasted to ruin and desolation after which it was re-formed and refashioned in the six days as the stage upon which the drama of sin and redemption was to take place.

This is the reason why God did not destroy the earth utterly. God had a plan for it. The very place which had been the scene of the challenge to the authority of the Most High God was to see His triumphant vindication. The day would come when God's Son, the Lord Jesus Christ, would bring His life on earth to a close and would pray in the garden of Gethsemane, "I have glorified thee *on the earth;* I have finished the work which thou gavest me to do" (John 17:4). Out of that fall of Lucifer and the subsequent fall of man, through the redemption provided in Christ, God would bring a mighty company of believers, children, sons, whom He could raise to the very throne of heaven without the remotest possibility that any one of them would ever claim any power in his own right. When these saints are in heaven and at work in the government of God, they will be the first to acknowledge, and will continually do so, that God is the one true God, that there is none like unto Him, that He is the source of life and power, and that to Him shall be ascribed all of the praise and the glory.

SATAN'S ATTACK ON GENESIS

Before coming to the entrance of man upon the scene, let us take notice of one of Satan's favorite stratagems in his war against God. Knowing that the account of his rebellion is detailed in the Scriptures, he does everything possible to discredit the Book. Knowing that Genesis sets forth the intervention of God in Satan's kingdom, he is especially bitter in his attacks upon these pages. Satan's hatred of the Scriptures is evident in many ways; every attack upon the Bible may be known to come from him. He will use any arm or instrument to belittle the veracity and authenticity of the Scriptures. At times the assaults are open and even virulent. At times they are hidden and subtle. But always he has but one real hatred, one enmity, and that is the hatred of the living and true God. If Satan can get men to disbelieve in the record of the first lines of the Bible, he can get them to disbelieve in the deity of the Lord Jesus Christ Himself. If Satan did not realize this fact before the incarnation of the Lord Jesus, he certainly has known it since; for Christ stated, as we have seen, that no man could ever believe in the Christ of the gospels if he did not believe in the writings of Moses, including of course these pages in Genesis (John 5:46, 47). The reason the Jews rejected Christ was because they had rejected Moses; it is impossible for any man to believe fully in the New Testament gospels if he has rejected the Pentateuch. It is not to be wondered at, therefore, that Satan brings his every force to bear against this portion of the Bible. Destroy this and he knows, for Christ has taught it, that man cannot believe in the Christ of God.

Among the most widely prevalent attacks upon the book of Genesis is the idea, universally taught by liberal theologians and, unfortunately, disseminated by many teachers who are merely the echoes of the echoes of the originators of the theory; that the first and second chapters of Genesis contain two different stories of creation, and that these two stories were patched together by a later editor to make the account which we possess today. This, of course, is not so. In the first place, we have shown that there is no detailed account of the original creation to be found anywhere in the Bible. There is not one line to tell us whether this original creation took place in the flash of a Word, or whether God was pleased to plant a perfect amoeba and let it split and re-split for ages and ages. We simply do not know. In the second place, these two chapters of Genesis do not even contain two different accounts of the refashioning or the restoration of the earth. What the Genesis account does do is first to give a general outline of the order of events. Then the author returns to select the most important item in the series that has been described and proceeds to amplify it because it is the basis of all that is to follow.

Let me illustrate this in a different realm. There is hardly a week goes by in which I do not write a letter which parallels very closely the structure of the first two chapters of Genesis. I may write thus to a friend or a loved one: "I left Philadelphia on Monday and preached in New York that evening. After the meeting, I took the train for Ohio and preached in Canton on Tuesday evening, Akron on Wednesday, Cleveland on Thursday. I returned east by train Thursday night, preaching in Lancaster on Friday, and reaching Philadelphia at midnight for my three days at home before starting out again on my circuit of teaching." After having given this outline of the whole week, I may well begin another paragraph, saying: "At Cleveland, on Thursday, I saw a most remarkable display of jewels in the store of a Christian friend who for years has been composing pictures with jewels arranged against black velvet. Using hundreds of stones, large and small, the diamond, the ruby, the topaz, the emerald, the sapphire, he arranges brilliant designs which attract hundreds of people to his show windows. I saw one of a peacock, with the multicolors of his plumage made up of hundreds of jewels placed against the velvet background." Is there anything extraordinary in the structure of such a letter? Yet there are men who have attacked the Bible because the first chapter gives a running account of all six days of restoration, while the second chapter takes up in detail the appearance of man on the sixth day.

ELOHIM AND JEHOVAH

As their argument against the structure falls down, so does that against the content of the narrative. They say that the stories differ because different names are used for God but when we remember what we have seen about the almost four hundred names of God and how God reveals Himself through those names the matter becomes clear. *Elohim* is the name of God used in matters of creation and power. *Jehovah* is the name that is used in connection with all of His acts that lead to redemption. Thus in the account of the flood it is *Elohim,* the Creator, who tells Noah to enter the ark with two of each kind of animal for the preservation of the species, and it is *Jehovah* who tells him to take seven of the clean animals for sacrifice, and who shuts him in so that he is safe.

That these pages are divinely inspired is a fact which is woven into every part of the writing. One commentator, who has devoted much thought and care to the narrative of the six days, writes of this first chapter: "The orderly manner in which God proceeded, the ease with which He accomplished His work, the excellency of that which was produced, and the simplicity of the narrative, at once impress the reader. Out of the chaos was brought the 'cosmos,' which signifies order, arrangement, beauty; out of the waters emerged the earth; a scene of desolation, darkness and death was transformed into one of light, life and fertility, so that at the end all was pronounced 'very good' . . . Genesis One is to be regarded not as a poem, still less as an allegory, but as a literal, historical statement of divine revelation . . . Marvelously concise is what is to be found here. A single verse suffices to speak of the original creation of the heaven and the earth. Another verse is all that is needed to describe the awful chaos into which the ruined earth was plunged. And less than thirty verses more tell of the six days' work, during which the Lord 'made heaven and earth, the sea, and all that in them is.' Not all the combined skill of the greatest literary artists, historians, poets, or philosophers this world has ever produced, could design a composition which would begin to equal the first of Genesis. For depth of theme, and yet simplicity of language: for comprehensiveness of scope, and yet terseness of expression; for scientific exactitude, and yet the avoidance of all technical terms: it is unrivaled, and nothing can be found in the whole realm of literature which can be compared with it for a moment. It stands by itself. The brevity of it evidences the divine wisdom of Him who inspired it. Contrast the labored formulae of the scientists, contrast the verbose writing of the poets, contrast the meaningless cosmogonies of the ancients and the foolish mythologies of the heathen, and the uniqueness of this divine account of creation and restoration will at once appear. Every line of this opening chapter of the Holy Scriptures has stamped across it the autograph of Deity."

THE PARADOX OF THE FORTUNATE FALL

When the whole of the revelation is seen in one panoramic view, it becomes evident that the creation of man was a deliberate move of divine strategy in the invisible war. Out of this creation and fall and out of the redemption which was to follow, there was to come the complete revelation of the depths of the wisdom and the knowledge of God (Romans 11:33). This has been called "the paradox of the fortunate fall."

The comprehension of much of the rest of the Bible depends upon the understanding of the place of man in the ranks of created beings. The angelic beings had been established in an orderly hierarchy. Lucifer was created as the highest of all; there was no creature superior to him. Beneath him were all the varied orders of the angelic creation: cherubs, seraphs, the archangels, principalities and powers, the lower angels, and those creatures who were the inhabitants of the pre-Adamite earth whose disembodied spirits, it has been suggested, became the demons when they followed Lucifer in his rebellion. All of these hosts, innumerable in their ranks and gradations of position and power, were before God as models of previous creations. In addition, there was the infinite creative imagination of God. But when the Almighty moved to create man, He did not use any of the angelic models before Him. Man was not given the power of Lucifer. He was not given the might of those who are called the principalities and powers. He was not given the speed of angels nor their freedom of movement throughout the air and the heavens. God created man below all of these angelic orders and tied him to earth with the law of gravity, limiting him in space, in time, in intelligence and in power. It was a principle of the divine strategy which will become more and more apparent as we proceed.

In the eighth Psalm, David sings, "O Lord, our Lord, how excellent is thy name in all the earth! who hast set thy glory above the heavens. Out of the mouth of babes and sucklings hast thou ordained strength because of thine enemies, that thou mightest still the enemy and the avenger. When I consider thy heavens, the work of thy fingers, the moon and the stars, which thou hast ordained; what is man, that thou art mindful of him? and the son of man, that thou visitest him? For thou hast made him a little lower than the angels, and hast crowned him with glory and honour. Thou madest him to have dominion over the works of thy hands; thou hast put all things under his feet: all sheep and oxen, yea, and the beasts of the field; the fowl of the air, and the fish of the sea, and whatsoever passeth through the paths of the seas. O Lord, our Lord, how excellent is thy name in all the earth!"

The key phrase in this passage is that which places man in the scheme of creation as being made "lower than the angels." Here is the divine strategy. Out of the lowest, God shall bring the highest. He shall even, Himself, condescend to be incarnate in this low level of creation. And out of that level, yes, even out of man fallen below the low level on which he was created, God shall bring a race of sons who shall be associated with Him forever in the government of the universe. Thus shall come the greatest glory to God, and the full victory in the invisible war. The second chapter of Hebrews is the divine commentary which establishes the text and reveals its spiritual meaning.

Although the unregenerate scientist would insist that man was not created, God declares that man is a creature. The unregenerate man is the natural man who "receiveth not the things of the Spirit of God: for they are foolishness unto him: neither can he know them, because they are spiritually discerned" (I Corinthians 2:14). If someone complains that we are not in agreement with modern science, we point to the fact that had the Bible in 1870 agreed with the science of 1870, the science of 1880 would have thrown the Bible into the discard, even as it threw out the science of the previous decade. The science of 1890 smiled complacently in turn at the science of 1880, while the science of 1900, which had now reached the Twentieth Century, was so up-to-date that little before that time could stand. So it has continued, decade after decade. Today in some fields the science of November has discarded the science of February. In the basements of our great libraries are past editions of the encyclopedias which reveal the shifting changes in man's opinions about science, but always the Word of God stands, unchanged. The early editions of the encyclopedias laugh at the Mosaic authorship of the Pentateuch on the ground that writing did not exist in the time of Moses. Today the archaeologists point to writing a thousand years before Moses and speak of the irony of the fact that there are evidences that some of this writing in the pre-Mosaic period was done in the very peninsula of Sinai where Moses lived and wrote.

We once had a man refer to an article in the fourteenth edition of the *Encyclopedia Britannica* as proof for the assertions he was making against the Bible. We asked him to take the first volume and look up the article under "Amazon." From this we noted the length of the great South American river and the area of its basin. We then asked him to turn to the article in a later volume on "Rivers." Here the length of the Amazon was given at a figure differing by more than a thousand kilometers and that of the area by about a million square kilometers. If the writers from one volume to another cannot agree on the length and area of an earthly river, how can they expect us to stake our faith in eternal verities on their guesses concerning the river of life?

Through all of the shifting of the hypotheses of men, the Bible stands alone in its unique position. As the pendulum swings from hypothesis to hypothesis, as theories are advanced and discarded, the little of true knowledge that is acquired once and for all, and which is being increased grain by grain, is always in line with the truths announced in the Word of God.

8 : *Satan's First Attack*

AFTER the first proud rebellion of Lucifer against God, and the judgment of God upon the province of the rebel prince, there is no evidence of any activity on the part of Satan. Whatever may have happened in the dark period while the earth was waste and desolate is mentioned nowhere in the Bible. We can understand this, for, as we have already mentioned, it is outside the scope of the Biblical revelation to lend itself merely to the satisfaction of man's curiosity.

Suddenly, however, at the spoken Word of God, "Let there be light," there came that profound change in the territories ruled by Satan which was the prelude to the subsequent work of God in re-forming the world. This movement of God after a seemingly long period of inaction was in preparation for the carrying out of His eternal decrees which included the whole plan of redemption and various phases of the invisible war. When the light of God shone upon the turning ball of earth, revealing its chaotic wastes, there must have been great rage of heart for Satan and those who had followed him, as they remembered its former glory and the splendors of their early habitations.

EARTH RE-FORMED

As day succeeded day in the work of God, Satan must have watched every act with a grim and growing interest which was all the more resentful because he was unable to do anything about it. Dry land appeared out of the waste of waters, and the seas began to bathe a thousand shores. Trees and flowers and grass appeared, and the soft green of vegetal beauty covered the world which had so lately lain in shrouded horror. Sun, moon and stars were once more visible on earth as the mists of judgment were dispelled. The sea began to swarm with its myriad creatures, and the air again knew the song of birds. Satan's pride stimulated his envy, but as yet he saw nothing to excite his jealousy, for all these birds and animals had body and life but no spirit,

72

and he knew that there was no creature here that could challenge the power and authority which he yet possessed in this domain.

But on the sixth day, God created man in His own image. In the fifth chapter of Genesis, we read a summary of all that took place in the creation of man. "In the day that God created man, in the likeness of God made he him; male and female created he them; and blessed them, and called their name Adam, in the day when they were created" (Genesis 5:1, 2). There must have been an almost instant awareness in the mind of Satan that here was his rival at last. For man awoke to find himself a creature of noble beauty and wisdom, and to be informed that he was to have dominion over the whole of the renewed earth, over all that he could see around him. We may be sure that Satan was not far distant when the Lord God said to the newly created couple, "Be fruitful, and multiply, and replenish the earth, and subdue it; and have dominion over the fish of the sea, and over the fowl of the air, and over every living thing that moveth upon the earth" (Genesis 1:28).

MAN'S CREATION

Although we are interested here in man only insofar as he is a part of the invisible war, he is such an important weapon in that war that it is necessary to understand the nature of his creation. God was choosing man as the arm which would defeat Satan, both in bringing him to naught and in replacing him in the scheme of the government of the universe. It was to be out of man that Christ would come, and it would be through certain chosen members of the human race that God would proclaim the defeat of Satan (Ephesians 3:10).

It is often possible to read the thoughts of a man by his actions. Watch a shoplifter in a store looking around him every way, moving furtively, slipping an article into his pocket before walking away casually, and you can read the thoughts of the man. Watch Satan moving into the garden of Eden, opening his attack on Eve, and you can deduce his thoughts when he saw the first man and woman placed on this earth. The earth was Satan's kingdom; God had set him in power over it (Ezekiel 28:14). Moreover, Satan had never been dispossessed by any edict of God. Satan's attack on man was a frontal attack on God Himself. The Almighty had placed an offensive force in the midst of the enemy-held territory. To proceed against this force was to proceed against the Power which had placed it there. However, the action would end, as all other satanic actions must end, with dust in the mouth for Satan. For the battle of the garden of Eden, though on the surface a victory for Satan, was in reality the beginning of his ultimate rout;

it contained the seed from which would develop the most shameful phases of his ultimate defeat.

LOWER THAN THE ANGELS

In order to understand these ramifications of the fall of man, we must recall the position in which God created man in relation to the scale of all other beings. We have noted that God did not create man after any of the models of angels, seraphs, cherubs or other existing orders of beings. God did not choose any of these beings, which, by their names and by other Biblical revelations concerning them, are seen to possess great might, rightfully called principalities and powers. God did a new thing; He brought forth a creature that would be tied to earth by gravity and that would be beneath the lowliest angel in power and rank. One of the great clues to the proper understanding of the invisible war, found in the Psalms, and brought out in sharp relief by the Holy Spirit in the epistle to the Hebrews, is the declaration, concerning the creation of man, "For Thou hast made him a little lower than the angels" (Psalm 8:5; Hebrews 2:6-8). The RSV translates the passage in the Psalms, "Thou hast made him little less than God," but the New Testament quotation of this passage, found in the second of Hebrews, is "Thou didst make him, for a little while, lower than the angels." The Hebrew word is one that is often rendered "God," but it is in usages where it must be translated, "the gods," or "the angels." It is unfortunate that the translators did not follow the hint given by the Holy Spirit, that is, of course, more than a hint, even a positive translation that should have been accepted without question, and that would have been accepted if the translators had believed in the inspiration of the words of Scripture. At all events, the New Testament quotation is sufficient to justify our teaching: in being made for a little while lower than the angels, he was, indeed, made lower than the angels.

ANGELIC OBSERVERS

There must have been many interested observers when God created man. All of heaven must have known that God was finally on the move against the rebellion of Satan. God had spoken light to the darkened cinders of our immediate universe, and Satan suddenly had been snapped out of his sullen brooding. There is a passage in the Scripture which indicates the great interest of the angel hosts in all of the events which concern the earth, men and the whole plan of God. Peter tells us that the Old Testament writers gave themselves to the study of their own writings in order to find out the meaning of the revelations of which they had been the channel (I Peter 1:10-12). The

Spirit of Christ had been in them for the communication of truth, but they were not sure of the time schedule and searched diligently in order to sort out the different revelations and place them in proper order. The passage closes with a statement, much stronger in Greek than in English, to the effect that the angels themselves were intensely occupied with this same study. We can readily understand, therefore, that the whole of the universe of angels, unfallen and fallen, must have been engrossed with the action that followed what we might call the Ten Commandments of the re-creation, God's "Let there be . . . Let there be . . ." At this divine fiat, there came into ordered being, light, a firmament, the waters, the dry land, the vegetal world, the stars of the heavens for signs and for the calendar, the moving creatures of earth, the higher animals, and, finally, man.

COMBAT RENEWED

Is not the fury of Satan's resentment reflected in his actions? Was he not saying in his heart: "Even though I could not dispel darkness, bring order out of chaos, or create new beings to follow me, does God think that He shall replace me with this puny creature, man? I, who am higher than all the angels, the archangel, the seraphs and the cherubs, shall I be dispossessed by one who is lower than the angels? God may well say to man that he is to have dominon over the fish of the sea, the fowl of the air, the cattle, and over all the earth, and every creeping thing that creepeth upon the earth (Genesis 1:26), but He will have to do better than Adam if He thinks He is going to oust me. I am wiser than Adam, and I shall now move to attack God by seducing Adam away from Him, and I shall attach him to me. Just as I got many of the angels to follow me in my rebellion, so I shall get man to leave God and give allegiance to me."

So, the war, which had remained in a quiet phase throughout the period when the earth had been a wreck and a ruin, was now renewed in great intensity. God moved a new combatant into the field, established a beachhead and Satan attacked. When we remember his objective, we understand the nature of his defeat. His was a dual purpose: he was moving, by the diplomacy of seductive temptation, to get man away from God, but more than this, he was seeking to get man to give his allegiance to himself.

The third chapter of Genesis has become one of the great battlegrounds of human thought. Satan must hate it more than any other page in the history of writing, with perhaps the one exception of the cry on the cross that announced the doom of Satan: "It is finished" (John 19:30). His efforts to destroy it and with it the memory of his defeat are paralleled many times in human relationships. There is a striking illustration in Hitler's attempts to nullify the disasters of World War I. Germany, defeated in 1918, was forced to sign the armistice capitulation in a railroad car on a siding in the Forest of Compiegne. It was on the crest of the movement to wipe out the memory of that defeat that Hitler came to power. When France fell before the Nazi forces twenty-two years later, instead of following his troops into Paris and dictating a peace at Versailles or at the Louvre, Hitler, remembering 1918, had his engineers lay railroad tracks to the military museum where the armistice car had been exhibited between the wars, and bring it back to Compiegne. It was on the exact spot where German might had yielded in 1918 that the French generals were forced to sign the capitulation of France in 1940. The pictures of that scene reveal a remarkable sight. The erratic, frustrated corporal of the first war, now master of Germany and France, actually danced in front of the armistice car as he came out. Totally unconscious of the clicking cameras, he slapped his thighs, grinned ecstatically, shook his head from side to side, and executed lively steps of glee. The memory of the defeat was to be eradicated by the surcharge of victory, superimposed at the very place of the humiliation.

Because Satan has sought to eradicate every trace of his curse and terrible defeat from the memory of man, and because man has been willing to aid and abet in this attempt since the fall is so shameful an epoch in the history of man himself, the third chapter of Genesis has been assaulted as few others in the Bible have been. We shall not make any attempt here to answer the arguments which have been brought forth against the fact of man's sin. We are aware of the ridicule which has been heaped upon the incident. We know of the subtle attack made upon the account of the creation and fall of man by the theory that man did not come from the creative hand of God but that he is the product of some developmental process and is on his way up to greater and greater heights. We have read the findings of paleontology and biology. We have heard the sneers of modernism against the Biblical account, and we have seen the awkward attempts of some theologians to account for the present sin of man without admitting the historicity of the fall. Bruner, for example, in *Der Mensch im Wiederspruch,* seeks to account for sin without the fall. The more recent work of Whale, the English theologian, follows in the same line. The latter, retreating from the untenable theory of the liberal theologian of the past, comes to the plain admission that man is a fallen creature though he does not admit the original fall. He writes: "The fall refers not to some datable aboriginal calamity in the historic past of humanity, but to a dimension of human experience which is always present — namely, that we who have been created for fellowship with God repudiate it continually; and that the whole of mankind does this thing along with us." Niebuhr has followed in the steps of these other theologians. So we have the new liberalism admitting the results of the fall without being willing to accept the fact. From this they go on to argue for a salvation from sin which is apart from God's gift of His Son as a vicarious, substitutionary Saviour, taking in Himself the wrath which was due from God's justice toward the sin of the rebels. We can see Satan, like the Hitler of the French armistice slapping his thighs and dancing his jig.

To return to the simplicity of the Biblical narrative: God made man lower than the angels, but He also endowed him with something called "the image of God." Of what did this image consist? Certainly we do not conceive of God as possessing head, hands, arms, feet and other physical features. The Bible does not present an anthropomorphic God. It is true that the Word of God describes the actions of God in behalf of man under some figures of speech that make use of the bodily characteristics of man: for instance, "The Lord's hand is not shortened, that it cannot save; neither his ear heavy, that it cannot hear" (Isaiah 59:1); and "The eyes of the Lord run to and fro throughout the whole earth . . ." (II Chronicles 16:9). But the Bible also says, "He shall cover thee with his feathers, and under his wings shalt thou trust" (Psalm 91:4). Such a verse does not mean that God is a bird. Anyone can understand that the latter quotation is a figure of speech. So are the former and all similar quotations. For "God is Spirit" (John 4:24); and "a spirit hath not flesh and bones" (Luke 24:39). Of what, then, does the image consist in which God created Adam?

It would be possible, theologically, to say that the eternal God, invisible Spirit, foreknew the physical image in which He would send His Son Jesus Christ, and created Adam in that physical image. For Christ "is the image of the invisible God, the firstborn of every creature" (Colossians 1:15). While there is probably much truth in that idea, it may be more nearly the truth that God created the human body to have physical functions which were expressions of invisible functions. Is not the eye, which gives to us the meaning of the reflections of light that falls on various objects within the field of our vision, a symbol of God's awareness of all things, for He is light and in Him is no darkness at all (I John 1:5)? Is not the arm, with its muscular structure controlling the hand and its intricate workings, a symbol of the power and strength of God and His ability to form all things as He would desire them? Thus, in an accommodated sense, it is possible to say that man, even in his fallen condition, contains the vestigial remnants of the original creation. And God prescribes the death penalty upon murderers because He made man in His image (Genesis 9:6).

But in all the more important meanings of the term, it is impossible to say that man, in his present fallen condition, still retains the image of God. The Bible controverts such a thought, teaching us that man lost the spiritual image of God in the fall, and that the true image is regained in our regeneration. Of the sons that proceeded from Adam and Eve we read, "And Adam lived . . . and begat a son in his own likeness, after his image" (Genesis 5:3). That fallen image of Adam in which likeness he begat his progeny, was far, far from the image of God in which the first human father had been created. The man that we see walking in the streets of our cities or in the jungles of our darker continents is the product of fallen Adam. It is only when an individual man is born again through faith in the redemptive work of Christ that he is created anew in the image of God, as we shall see in more detail. "The first man is of the earth, earthy; the second man is the Lord from heaven. As is the earthy, such are they that are earthy: and as is the heavenly, such are they also that are heavenly. And as we have borne the image of the earthy, we shall also bear the image of the heavenly" (I Corinthians 15:47-49).

Unregenerate man is not in the image of God. The image which is merely flesh and blood cannot inherit the kingdom of God (I Corinthians 15:50). The false idea that all men still retain the divine image is so entrenched in the thoughts of men that they are more than startled when the fresh winds of the Word of God would blow the mind clear of the heresy of man's natural goodness and divinity. In the eighteenth century, South, a famous London peacher, astounded the loose-thinking deists of his day with the declaration that man at his best was a low, fallen creature. In his famous sermon, "Man Created in God's Image," South wrote a line which was discussed even in the House of Commons: "An Aristotle was but the rubbish of an Adam, and Athens but the rudiments of Paradise." There have been those who have called this sentence "fantastic," but most certainly South is in agreement with the Word of God. Furthermore, the modern science of genetics is moving in that direction, for those in the laboratories of the world who are studying the problems of life have already reached conclusions concerning the divisions of the genes and chromosomes that make up an individual which would make any true scientist hesitate before denying that all of the gifts of humanity were once combined in one set of parents. Everything that has ever come out of mankind for good since the origin of the human species was contained in Adam and his bride. We must look upon that pair, then, as combining even more than the gifts and graces of a Shakespeare, a Plato, a Beethoven, a Michelangelo, an Isaac Newton and an Einstein, and as excelling in charity our tenderest philanthropists and in bravery our mightiest heroes.

Some time ago I chanced upon an item in the newspapers which contained a carefully prepared mathematical analysis of the possibility of holding any given series of cards in a hand of bridge. There are fifty-two cards in a pack, and a given player receives one-fourth of these, or thirteen. That he should receive thirteen of a given suit is a matter of millions and millions of deals of the cards. If there were a hundred cards instead of fifty-two, the chance would be one in billions of billions. We can understand, therefore, that the unnumbered multitudes of genes and chromosomes possessed by the original set of parents could come forth in the infinitely varied pattern of human gifts and personalities. Only once in thousands of years could the arrangement of a Shakespeare come to life, and history unites with the mathematical laws of chance to tell us that this is so.

More about the image of God in man may be learned from an examination of certain New Testament passages. The Bible teaches that fallen man is "dead in trespasses and sins" (Ephesians 2:1), and "not subject to the law of God, neither indeed can be" (Romans 8:7). But when a man is born again, there is a new creation (II Corinthians 5:17), and the individual becomes a partaker of the divine nature (II Peter 1:4). Of what does this divine nature consist?

There is an incident in the life of Jesus Christ which may well be the least known or preached about of all His wondrous acts. Even the artists have overlooked it in their countless delineations of His great deeds. In the galleries of the world may be found thousands of canvasses depicting the scenes surrounding the annunciation to the Virgin, the bringing forth of the newborn Babe in Bethlehem, His glorious miracles, and the death and Resurrection of our Lord. But who ever saw a canvas showing the Lord Jesus with His outstretched hand under the chin of one of His disciples in the act of breathing on him? We know of no such painting. Yet, on the first resurrection day, just such an incident took place. The disciples, frightened because of their fear of the Jews, were huddled away in an upper room, hiding from possible danger. The Shepherd had been slain and the sheep were in terror. Suddenly Jesus Christ appeared in the midst of them. He spoke peace to them, and then, the gospel says, Jesus "breathed on them," and said to them, "Receive ye the Holy Spirit . . ." (John 20:22). The spiritual mind will remember, of course, that on one other occasion in the Bible we find God leaning over man to breathe upon him. In the story of the creation we read: "The Lord God formed man of the dust of the ground, and breathed into his nostrils the breath of life; and man became a living soul" (Genesis 2:7). In the light of the Genesis passage, how significant the act of Christ becomes! The image of God had come upon Adam by the divine inbreathing of the breath of God. That image had been lost in the fall. The risen Lord Jesus Christ, who has just come out of death into the victory of life after accomplishing the redemption of a fallen man, begins His work among His disciples by breathing upon them once more.

This is all the more significant in the light of the meaning of the word "breath." We all know the Greek word for breath without knowing that we know it. We use it when we speak of the malady which strikes that organ of the body which draws in air, warms it, and sends out breath. We call this disease "pneumonia" because it is the disease which affects the *pneumon,* the lung, the breath box. The same word is found when we describe a tire that has air in it. We call it a "pneumatic" tire, and a drill which is driven by compressed air is a "pneumatic" drill. All of these words come from the common Greek word for breath, which is *pneuma,* and it is the word which we find in the Bible for the Holy Spirit, the Holy *Breath,* the Holy *Pneuma.* So when the Lord Jesus breathed on the disciples, He gave back to lost man the breath, the spirit, the image of God which had been lost in the fall. The unregenerate man does not have the image of God. The difference is invisible and spiritual. Paul, in Colossians, describes the believer in this respect as having "put on the new man, which is renewed in knowledge after the image of him that created him" (Colossians 3:10). The image, then, is a moral and intellectual likeness, and not physical. It is an image which was lost in the fall and which is renewed in the new creation at the moment the individual believes God's Word about the Lord Jesus Christ. In the Ephesian letter, the new man is described as being "created in righteousness and true holiness" (Ephesians 4:24).

When God created man, he possessed this moral and intellectual superiority which made it possible to speak of him as being "in the image of God." Sin was not then inherent in man as it is today. It is true that he had been created on a low plane, lower than the angels in power and might and beauty, but he had been created with a knowledge and a moral righteousness that were in the image of God. It was man's will that made it possible for him to depart from the plan of God, and it was against this will that Satan launched his attack. His primary strategy was dictated by his hatred of God, and not by his hatred of the creature whom he saw in the garden. He would seek to detach man from the will of God. His further strategy was prompted by his overweening pride. He would seek to increase the number of his own worshipers by attaching man to himself. In part Satan was successful. Man fell. But although man was detached from God he did not join Satan's forces. In the world today men seek not the will of Satan but their own will. They have become the "children of wrath" (Ephesians 2:3). Some few became children of the devil (John 8:44). An infinite company became "children of God" (Galatians 3:26). The children of wrath and the children of the devil unite as the "world" to oppose the course of the believers (John 15:18, 19). This conflict will be developed in a later chapter.

9 : Man, a Casualty

Wₕₑₙ we come to the third chapter of Genesis, there is a temptation to spend time in discussing the many doctrines which, in the chronological unfolding of Biblical truth, take their root here. Such teaching is necessary for the growth in knowledge of the student of the Bible. If he has any grasp of these doctrines, he will find that they clarify many other portions of the Scriptures. If he comes to the rest of the Book without this groundwork, he will be unsure in his conclusions. The very foundations of the Christian faith are laid here.

Doctrine in Embryo

Within this chapter almost all of the great doctrines which appear in the remaining portion of the Bible are to be found in embryo. One writer has summarized it as follows: "Here commences the great drama which is being enacted on the stage of human history, and which well-nigh six thousand years have not yet completed. Here we find the divine explanation of the present fallen and ruined condition of our race. Here we learn of the subtle devices of our enemy, the devil. Here we behold the utter powerlessness of man to walk in the path of righteousness when divine grace is withheld from him. Here we discover the spiritual effects of sin — man seeking to flee from God. Here we discern the attitude of God toward the guilty sinner. Here we mark the universal tendency of human nature to cover its own moral shame by a device of man's own handiwork. Here we are taught of the gracious provision which God has made to meet our great need. Here begins that marvelous stream of prophecy which runs all through the Holy Scripture. Here we learn that man cannot approach God except through a mediator." All of this and more is to be found in this wonderful chapter, and the student will do well to get all the light he can on these subjects. But we must not succumb to the temptation to diverge into byways, interesting as the prospect may be.

THE NATURE OF SATAN

Our subject is the rebellion of Satan and the consequent ramifications in the realm of angels and man, and the final putting down of all revolt and power that exalts itself against the knowledge of God. In this chapter we are particularly concerned with the fall of man.

As we proceed with the ordered reading of the Bible, we come now to the first mention of the devil. When he appears, he is already a malignant being, hateful and hating, manifesting himself as the seducer. This fact alone should have caused all thinking men to wonder at his nature and to search elsewhere in the Scriptures for knowledge of his origin and how he became what we here see him to be.

At this moment there were still but two wills in the universe. God's will and the devil's will. Man's will was yet in harmony with the will of the Creator. The plan of the serpent in the temptation was to get man to change sides in the conflict. He would thereby increase the number of his followers which he had obtained in his original rebellion against God, and would thus tighten his hold as possessor of the earth by having on his side those who were to replace (for this is the significance of "replenish" in Genesis 1:28) the inhabitants of the earth in its original state and who had been removed by the first judgment from their possession.

A TWOFOLD OBJECTIVE

So the enemy's objective in the battle of the garden of Eden was twofold. He wished to detach man from God, but he also wished to attach man to himself. Man is dependent upon God and if that dependence is destroyed something must take its place; the devil hoped that it would be a dependence upon himself. It may be wondered whether he had anticipated that man would not only desire independence of God, but that he would aspire to be self-sufficient. Even the angels who had followed him in the fall must, by now, have known many of the difficulties of independence. That man, created lower than the angels, should presume to rely upon himself alone, might not even have occurred to the lowest of the angels. Lucifer had underestimated the arrogance of willfulness, though he himself possessed it in its highest degree. Willfulness does not have the wingspread to carry the weight of a creature; nevertheless the creature would launch out from its high place no matter where the fall might take it.

The devil was to succeed in detaching man from God. But, although he led man away from the place of divine blessing, he did not lead him into his own camp either as a subject or ally. On the contrary, man was moved to the third point of a triangle, and the tensions that would be established along the lines between these opposing focal centers of will would ultimately set the stage for Satan's destruction. The Serpent led man away from God, but he led himself into a trap. Man away from God, but also away from Satan, was to be the channel of Satan's overthrow. Pyrrhus defeated the Romans at a cost so staggering to himself that his appraisal of the victory has become the standard measurement of certain costly defeats: "Another such victory and Pyrrhus will be destroyed." So at the very best, in Satan's accounting, the fall of man was a defeat for God's enemy.

DEFEAT IN VICTORY

It is very important that we note the nature of Lucifer's objective, for we shall be better able to judge the nature of his defeat. He grasped at one thing and missed it: the fact that he held something else for a moment was not victory. Missing what he had reached for in the first place contributed to his destruction. There are many parallels in history. One of the most notable, because its consequences were so vast, was Hitler's declaration of objective after he made war on Russia. He announced, during the course of the first autumn, that Germany was achieving the great objectives of the campaign: the occupation of Russian territory and resources and the destruction of the Russian armies. Most significantly, he said that though they won battle after battle and occupied area after area, their warfare would be a failure if they did not destroy the Russian armies. This had to be the supreme objective without which the seeming triumphs would be hollow victories indeed. How right he was came out in the years that followed. The Germans pushed all the way to the Volga. There were dozens of victories to be celebrated in Berlin, but failing to destroy the Russian armies they were themselves destroyed.

ADAM'S FALL

In seeking to accomplish his double objective of frustrating God and enhancing his own position, the devil attacked the first pair in the only way in which there could have been any possibility of success. We cannot judge his methods by our present experience because of the revolutionary change in human nature which became operative when man departed from God. Since the fall, man may be attacked from any one of three avenues: sin may approach him from the flesh, the world or the devil. In the garden of Eden, this was not the case. Man had not fallen, so did not yet have the flesh in its present evil form dwelling within his bosom to act as a fifth column in aiding Satan. The world of man — with a multitude of fallen natures reacting upon each other and competing for power and prominence – had not yet sprung up. The only way was for Satan to come with his own forces and to seek to detach man from dependence upon God and – this is very important – to get man attached to the cause of Satan. None of his minions was entrusted with the task. He deemed the matter of sufficient importance to undertake it personally.

The first point of enemy strategy was easily obtained: man fell. Satan would like man to believe that he succeeded in the second also, and that man is now a dependent of this evil master. But such is not the case. Adam did not sell his soul and that of the race to the devil. Satan by the fall did not become master of the human race. Such ideas are not Biblical in any way. There are many such notions which the masses of people hold by absorption from secular literature, but spiritual truth comes in quite another way, by divine revelation (I Corinthians 2:9-13). The idea of soul-selling is an ancient one and is part of Satanic theology which we will study more closely when we come to look more closely at what the Scripture calls his "devices."

THE SERPENT IN EDEN

When we read that Satan appeared as a serpent, we are inclined to think of the incident in terms of the reptiles which we know and which most people instinctively fear. We must erase this thought from our mind and project ourselves to the historical moment, considering this mouthpiece of Lucifer as Eve encountered him. The fear and dread of man had not yet come upon the animal world, for this was imposed by God as a part of the judgment at the time of the flood (Genesis 9:2). As Adam and Eve moved in their domain they were surrounded by the animals which Adam had previously named as God paraded each kind in his presence to see what he would call it (Genesis 2:19, 20). There is evidence that the serpent was the most wonderful of all the creatures. Our text says that it was more "subtil" than any beast of the field. This is the only place that this Hebrew word is translated "subtil"; elsewhere it is rendered "prudent" eight times and "crafty" twice.

The revealing factor in the analysis of the serpent's being is the name of the animal itself. In Hebrew *nachash* has been traced by scholars to two different roots: the one which means to hiss, to whisper, and which is used in the Bible for the whisperings of the soothsayers and the enchantments of the sorcerers; and the other which means to shine, and which has given the derivitives "brass" and "money" and, figuratively, "fetters" or "bonds" and also that which is "ignoble." It is quite a suggestive group of words to contemplate as coming from one source. When the possessed serpent approached Eve, it was the "shining one." We must think of it in terms of splendor and of the impression of beauty and awe that it made on Eve.

The link with Satanic power is found through two other words in the Scripture: seraph and Lucifer. The seraphim which Isaiah saw surrounding the throne of God are beings that transcend our experience and comprehension. However, we may gain some insight into the significance of their persons from the meaning of their name, "the burning ones." And the word *seraph* is the one used to describe the serpents, the *seraph nachash,* the fiery serpents, which plagued the people in the wilderness (Numbers 21:6). The serpent that met Eve was bright, shining, splendid, and the voice was the voice of one who bore a name that was precisely synonymous with the name of the serpent. *Nachash* and *Lucifer* are synonyms. The serpent is "the shining one" and Lucifer is "the shining star." The word *Lucifer* is, of course, Latin and comes from *lux* which means "light," and a suffix which means "to bear." The literal meaning of the word is "light-bearer." When we realize that the descriptive phrase, "son of the morning," is added to the name of the day-star, Lucifer, in the revelation to Isaiah (14:12) we have the fact that Lucifer, before his fall, bore the proud title, "The Bright Morning Star." This is one more in the list of names and titles borne imperfectly by men or by Satan which the Lord Jesus Christ took upon Himself, glorifying them forever by the perfections which He gave them. Thus He is the Witness, *par excellence,* and thus He was willing to be called a Servant. Thus He becomes Prophet, Priest and King. Thus He replaces Israel as the true Vine, and the fallen Adam by becoming the Last Adam.

Satan's tactics are easy to see in the account of the temptation and fall. He had to begin by a frontal attack on the Word of God and the goodness of God. It would have been impossible to reach man apart from the destruction of his confidence in the mind and heart of the Creator.

It was in the sphere of religious thought that Satan advanced in his projected seduction of the new race. He first attacked the Word of God: "Yea hath God said . . .?" (Genesis 3:1). A subtle question of doubt concerning the authenticity and validity of God's instructions to man is our introduction to this shining one in the book of Genesis. If we read the punctuation of the early chapters, we may note that the first interrogation of the Bible is in Satan's approach to the woman. It is true that what we call punctuation marks are not in the original language of Scripture, but there is a punctuation in the thought itself, and herein we find the first interrogation. Doubt and ignorance come from Satan and not from God who is the source of certainty and knowledge. A few verses farther along God calls to man, "Adam, where art thou?" The question was one designed to reveal to Adam where his sin had carried him. Naturally his presence was known to all-seeing God, for David will later exclaim, "Whither shall I go from thy presence? If I ascend up into heaven, thou art there: if I make my bed in hell, behold, thou art there" (Psalm 139:7, 8).

God, in placing man on the earth, gave him dominion over all the earth and its creatures. Only one very slender thread was put upon man to restrain him. He was commanded not to eat of the fruit of the tree of the knowledge of good and evil. Speculative religious writers have foolishly tried to explain the fruit which the woman ate and gave to Adam. There are those that wrongfully call the fruit an apple; there is no word to that effect in the Bible. An English writer recently said that he believed that the fruit was the grape, and that man sinned in making wine! This, too, is silly in the light of the fact that there could not have been fermentation before the fall brought death into the world, for fermentation has in it the principle of decay. Many writers — especially a group of Roman Catholic theologians, centuries ago — have expressed the thought that the fruit was sex, and have sought to make the union of Adam and Eve the matter of original sin. This suggestion was put forth by many of the protagonists of monasticism who conceived the idea that the married state had in it something which was essentially sinful. How pitiful such an explanation is in the light of God's command that they should be fruitful and multiply and replenish the earth! There is, of course, no sin whatsoever in the marital relationship which God declares to have been created as an illustration of the oneness and union of the Church with the Lord Jesus Christ in an eternal fellowship (Ephesians 5:32).

It may be asked, then, if it is possible to say with certainty what the fruit was which was forbidden to the first pair. We answer without hesitation. The fruit was the tangible symbol which God placed in the garden as the sign of man's creaturehood. It was something to impose a restraint upon him, something to remind him of his dependence upon God. What kind of fruit makes no difference at all. Why not accept it simply as a fruit which grew upon a tree? Its nature is secondary.

We may be sure that any questioning of the Word of God is Satanic in its origin. Whether the doubt comes from a group of atheists, from secular educators, or from theologians, its source is always the same. Satan can never win any victory, even a Pyrrhic one, over the Christian who holds to the Word of God. "The name of the Lord is a strong tower; the righteous runneth into it and is safe" (Proverbs 18:10), and the Word of the Lord is a citadel even stronger than the name of God, for it is declared that the Lord has magnified His Word above His name (Psalm 138:2). Is it not strange, in the light of these declarations, that men who would shrink from blaspheming the name of God will, nevertheless, commit the much more heinous sin of doubting the Word of God? Some who consider themselves Christians, even ministers, even conservative ministers, who would never damn an enemy with the name of God, will teach the young that the Word of God contains myth, folk-lore and legend. One may hear on every side today the repetition of Satan's question, "Yea hath God said . . . ?" (Genesis 3:1), but it is always Satan's question, even though it be spoken across a pulpit, or taught in the Sunday school literature of a denomination.

That Satan is at work against the Word of God is also brought out by our Lord in His parable of the sower. He announces that He, Himself, is the sower, and that the seed is the Word of God. As soon as it is sown, the enemy comes along and seeks to snatch away the seed which has been scattered. It is the garden of Eden over again, and in this phase of the battle Satan has partially succeeded. Beginning with Eve, he has gained the point to the extent that multitudes of people have been detached from the only source of spiritual life, the Word of God. Thus, with their defense destroyed, they are open to all attacks and are sure to be defeated.

The second point in Satan's attack was to get man to doubt the goodness of God. After having inserted in the mind of the woman doubt as to the finality and absoluteness of the Word of God, the devil went one step further and said, "For God doth know that in the day ye eat thereof, then your eyes shall be opened, and ye shall be as gods, knowing good and evil" (Genesis 3:5). The inward nature of this lie of Satan has been somewhat obscured by our English translation of the Hebrew word *Elohim,* the most-used name for God in the Old Testament. It should read "You shall be as God . . ." Lucifer was making the blunt suggestion that man had rights and should declare his independence; that he should take the place of God which was rightfully his in view of the fact that he was such a noble creature, above all the animal life in his dominion. There was also included in the phrase the insinuation that God was arbitrarily holding back something good from man, and that man would be far better off if he would only turn away from God's command and transgress in the single point where restraint had been laid upon him.

10 : *Man, a Casualty*
(CONTINUED)

THE difference between the nature of the man and the woman is seen in the way in which they met the temptation. It was quite consistent with the character of Satan that he should have approached the weaker of the two first, and when her husband was not with her to furnish advice and counsel. It should be noted that the legalists who warred against the doctrine of grace, as taught by Paul, were able to stir up trouble for him by beginning with "the devout and honourable women" (Acts 13:50). It was to the highest and best in her nature that the shining one appealed, and it was here that Eve succumbed. The New Testament tells us that the woman took the fruit and ate it, truly believing that she was going to better her husband's condition by her act. This revelation comes to us through Paul's epistle to Timothy, where we read: "For Adam was first formed, then Eve. And Adam was not deceived, but the woman being deceived, was in the transgression" (I Timothy 2:13, 14).

EVE DECEIVED

Satan came to Eve on the good side of her woman's nature. The temptation was similar to that which might come to a woman today if she were told that a certain course of action would result in such advancement for her husband that he would be able to buy the home they had wanted, and that their children would receive a college education. Eve transgressed with the thought that she was doing something good for her husband and their eventual posterity. Thus in the second phase of the battle of the garden, Satan seemed to have won a complete victory. He had detached the woman from the Word of God, and he had detached her, by deception, from the belief in the goodness of God.

SATAN'S SEEMING VICTORY

Likewise, in the third phase of the battle, Satan would seem to be complete victor. When the sinning woman goes to her husband, he joins her in what he knows to be a rebellion against God. The fall

89

of man would not have been complete if Adam had transgressed first. Then Eve could rightly have said to the Lord that she had merely followed that which was inherent in the nature of her creation, namely, to be one with her husband and follow his example. But when Eve transgressed first, in the absolute ignorance of deception, and when Adam followed her, eyes wide open, without any self-deception at all, he was deliberately rebelling against God; and his rebellion was as distinct and specific as was Satan's original rebellion.

This is the reason the Bible never places the blame for the fall upon the woman. The humorous papers and some literature may speak of the difficulties our mother Eve got us all into by eating the apple, but there is never a word of blame or responsibility put upon Eve in the Word of God. Rather do we read: "By one man sin entered into the world, and death by sin; and so death passed upon all men, for that all have sinned . . . By one man's offence death reigned by one . . . By the offence of one judgment came upon all men unto condemnation . . . by one man's disobedience many were made [constituted] sinners . . ." (Romans 5:12, 17-19). And again, in Corinthians, "By man came death . . . As in Adam all die . . ." (I Corinthians 15:21, 22).

Here is plainly the background of the injunction of God that women are to keep silence in the churches (I Corinthians 14:34), and women are not to be suffered to teach (I Timothy 2:12). It should be recognized, of course, that the church has no reference to what we call a church building. There were none such for centuries after Christ. The church was the Sunday morning assembly of the believers around the communion table, generally gathered in someone's house for the purpose of remembering the death of the Lord and to profit by the Spirit's instruction in the Word. Here was a place where God would not speak through a woman.

WOMEN'S HERESY AND MEN'S

By way of digression, it is enlightening to note the familiar pattern of difference which runs through those false religions which have come from women teachers as opposed to those which come from men. The religion put out by an Annie Besant, a Mrs. White, a Mrs. Eddy or their imitators, is much more subtle than what might be called a masculine heresy. For Theosophy, Seventh-day Adventism, Christian Science, New Thought, Unity and other religions which have come from women, stress the love of God, without His hatred for sin, and with fair words deceive. They offer a "key" to the Bible which says that the Book is true, and then denies its truth. Men are different in their heresies. Boldly they affirm that the Word of God is not true. Modernism strikes at the first chapters of Genesis as folklore and legend, and declares the birth of our Lord to be a biological impossibility. He was mistaken, they say, when He declared Moses to be the author of the Pentateuch, and so on throughout the account. There is a brazen characteristic in most of the heresies put forth by men which is not found in the women's heresies, and there was this same difference in the sin of the garden as seen in Eve and in Adam.

The spectator of the universal drama can dispel the cloudy confusion that hangs over much of the Bible and much of life for so many people if he understands the following important truth. In the sin of Adam, where Satan *seemed* to win a decisive victory there was, as a matter of Scriptural fact, a profound defeat for Satan which is the key to much of the rest of human history.

Let us state it in a series of facts about the fall. Satan succeeded in detaching man from obedience to the Word of God. True. Satan also succeeded in detaching man from a belief in the goodness of God. True. Thereby Satan won man away from confidence in God and dependence upon God. True. But though Satan won all of these victories, *he lost the whole battle in the fact that he did not succeed in attaching man to himself.*

HIS OWN WAY

In the beginning there had been one will, the will of God, the Creator. After the rebellion of Lucifer there had been two wills, that of God and the rebel. But *now there are billions of wills*. A significant verse in this connection is: "All we like sheep have gone astray, we have turned every one to ——" We have turned every one to what? In the fact that we have gone astray, we read that we have all left the will of God. But in the turning away from God, did we all turn to Satan? Was it a mere change of allegiance? Was it like Italy, fighting with Germany in the Spring of 1943 and with the Allies in the Autumn? Far from it. "All we like sheep have gone astray, we have turned every one to *his own way*" (Isaiah 53:6). This is the revealing statement. There are no longer two wills in the universe; there are more than two billion wills in this world alone.

The sin of Adam was, in the final analysis, the echo of Satan's own declaration of independence. Satan had had a glimpse of the glory of God and wanted it for himself. "I will be like the Most High . . ." he cried. When Adam sinned, there was the same rebellion: "I, too, will be like the Most High."

The cry of Adam against God has been remarkably expressed by an English poet, William Ernest Henley, in his *Invictus:*

Out of the night that covers me,
  Black as the pit from pole to pole,
I thank whatever gods may be,
  For my unconquerable soul.

In the fell clutch of circumstance
  I have not winced nor cried aloud,
Under the bludgeonings of chance
  My head is bloody, but unbowed.

Beyond this place of wrath and tears
  Looms but the Horror of the shade,
And yet the menace of the years
  Finds and shall find me unafraid.

It matters not how strait the gate,
  How charged with punishments the scroll;
I am the master of my fate,
  I am the captain of my soul.

The poetic fool! Even as Adam was a rebellious fool. For all of this cry against God was inherent in the sin of Adam. It is the beginning of that which wishes to put self in the place of deity. The fool has said in his heart, "There is no God" (Psalm 14:1), and he has said it in order that he might take the throne which he thinks he has emptied.

But let us come back to Satan's place in all this. How does this revelation of the nature of the fall of Adam affect Satan in the invisible war? The Bible and man's history give the answer. We can best sum it up in a parallel.

We have seen that back in the beginning God put a curse upon the earth when Lucifer rebelled and it became a ruin, waste and desolate, and darkness covered the face of the deep. Then God withdrew into the majestic silence of His infinite heaven and left Satan to brood over the chaotic mass of earth. All the angelic hosts were spectators of that horrible scene. What would Satan do with his ruined planet? Little by little, it was seen that he could do nothing. He was utterly powerless before the chaos which had come from a simple word of judgment from the Almighty God. Then there came a stab of light from this same creative Word of God. The devastation was revealed in all its chaos, and for the first time there may have echoed from star to star that laughter of God which shall one day rock the world, "He that sitteth in the heavens shall laugh: the Lord shall have them in derision" (Psalm 2:4).

A PREVIEW OF HISTORY

All of this seems strangely like a preview of the pageant which was to follow in the history of man. For once more there was a rebellion, and from the lofty heights for which God had created man, the creature fell to ignominious depths. Two separate battles are now being waged: Satan against God in the invisible warfare, of which history records the first phases and in the latter phases of which we ourselves live. Will Satan be able to organize mankind into a kingdom for himself? That is the one question which motivates all of his frantic efforts. Will man be able to organize himself, humanity, civilization, so that he can bring a semblance at least of peace and order into his realm? That is the question at which men toil and with which they wrestle.

Before we are through, we shall see that the living mass of humanity is more incapable of organization by man or the devil than was the ruined earth in its primeval darkness. For the earth was but matter, with no will of its own. If Satan had brought all of his angels to attempt to heap its waters into one place that land might appear, they would have had but an engineer's task. An able enough engineer might have accomplished something. Water will stay in its place if it is properly damned. Land can be graded and leveled. Rock will be held to earth by the force of universal attraction which we call gravitation. But man has a rebel will. It is active in rebellion against God, and, in many instances, it is in rebellion both against Satan and against authority when one human will is lifted above another. Land and sea are without desires, lusts, appetites, which are without limit. There is no satisfying the restless craving of the man without God. Augustine expressed it perfectly in his famous words: "Oh, God, Thou hast formed us for Thyself; and our souls can know no rest until they rest in Thee." There are those in the midst of humanity who have come to rest in God, through the Lord Jesus Christ. Yet rather they have come by no effort of their own, but through the creative work of God, paralleling His work of the six days. "For God, who commanded the light to shine out of darkness, hath shined in our hearts, to give the light of the knowledge of the glory of God in the face of Jesus Christ" (II Corinthians 4:6).

How far did man fall by his disobedience? How far did man go astray when he took the path of his own will? Is it possible for him to climb back by himself to the heights which Adam knew before the rebellion? Can man find his way back to God through the fields of desire in which he has been wandering? When properly understood these questions, really one question, reflect the things which divide men in their religious thinking today. How far did Adam fall? Humanism says man did not fall, that he is on his way up. Sacerdotalism affirms that man slipped over the edge, but that he may be pushed back again by the sacraments: that baptism takes away original sin; that the death of a piece of bread turned into Christ takes away man's continuing sins; that extreme unction removes more sins at the moment of death, and that in purgatory man can purge more of his sins. This leaves little for God to do!

Some branches of Protestantism hold that though man fell down it was only to a shelf, and that he has the will to choose to go back up if he wishes to exercise it. Others believe, and we are of that number, that man fell all the way, fell into a pit described in the Scriptures as "death." Man is in a threefold incapacity. His will, his mind, his heart are all estranged. He cannot know, he cannot please, he cannot understand God. "The natural man receiveth not the things of the Spirit of God: for they are foolishness unto him: neither can he know them, because they are spiritually discerned" (I Corinthians 2:14). "Because the carnal mind is enmity against God: for it is not subject to the law of God, neither indeed can be. So then they that are in the flesh cannot please God" (Romans 8:7). "There is none righteous, no, not one. There is none that understandeth, there is none that seeketh after God. They are all gone out of the way . . ." (Romans 3:10-12). "The heart is deceitful above all things, and incurably sick" (Jeremiah 17:9, Hebrew).

These quotations somewhat anticipate our thought, but it must be seen early in the invisible war that Satan can do nothing for fallen man, and that fallen man can do nothing for himself. God Almighty must do everything for man that is to be done to bring him back to his unfallen position, and even to a place above that from which he fell.

God, man or the devil: these are the three possible sources of hope. The strategy of the invisible warfare has been planned by God in order that these questions shall be answered, once and for all, in the presence of all created beings whether human, celestial or infernal. Human history is the record of the attempts of man and Satan to do something for man. When asked why an omnipotent God permits the holocaust of human history, the answer from the Word of God must be that He permits it in order to demonstrate to the universe that neither Satan nor man can do anything for themselves or for each other. If it were otherwise, these forces, which are at enmity with each other and both against God as their common enemy, could say either separately or together: "We have done it. We have succeeded in organizing ourselves and are no longer dependent upon God. We have demonstrated our capacity and ability. We have established a kingdom, and we do not need the plans of God for His kingdom of heaven over the earth . . ."

Mr. H. G. Wells has said that, faced with what we see around us in the world, we are forced to conclude either that God has the power and does not care, or that God cares but does not have the power. The logic is incomplete. There is a third possibility which is most certainly the expression of Biblical thought. It is that God both cares and has the power, but that He is planning something which demands the coming chaos of man's world in order to demonstrate to all that help is to be found in Himself alone. God knows that the world is in a terrible condition. God has the power to alter it, but will not do so today because of His greater purpose. God cares tremendously. This is evident in Calvary. But He knows that His care can be manifest today only to the select company of individuals who have accepted the principles that rise from His eternal decrees. These admit the principle of their own spiritual bankruptcy and have turned utterly to the Lord Jesus Christ as God's one and only answer to the problem.

There is a sense, therefore, in which God does not exercise any care over the rebels who people this world. Something of this is seen in the prayer of the Lord Jesus Christ: "I pray not for the world, but for them which thou hast given me; for they are thine" (John 17:9). This is what Mr. Wells saw without the spiritual insight to understand. This is why the worldlings, seeing the disasters of human suffering, draw the conclusion that God is not caring for His creation. They do not understand God; they do not understand the meaning of care, and they do not understand the difference between the creatures who refuse the Lordship of God and those who have bowed to it in Christ and have thus become the children of God.

In short, they do not recognize that there is a war on, and that God neither will nor can yield. There must be the unconditional surrender to Him of His universe. He is Lord of all strategy, and, when in His judgment certain lessons have been made obvious to the dullness of the fallen creation, He will move to end the present phase of the struggle and bring in the righteousness which shall, most certainly, come to the creation in the moment God has chosen for it. Meanwhile the war goes on, and it is fought entirely under a set of rules which have been drawn up by God and which He is able to enforce, even now, upon the reluctant enemies in the armies of Satan and in the camp of humanity.

11 : *The Articles of War*

THE invisible war is waged by men and Satan against each other and against God. The Lord, high over all, is not in the lists as an opponent, a combatant. He is the eternal One, working out His eternal decrees. Man and Satan are opposed to each other, the two in their positions each subordinate to God, forming a triangle with Him who is above all. We shall see that there is hatred from Satan toward God, hatred from man toward God, and hatred from God toward the sin that is in Satan and the sin that is in man. We shall also see that God Himself created the force of hatred that was to exist between man and Satan and between Satan and man. It is this latter that is one of the major factors in Satan's frustration, since it is the existence of this enmity which makes it forever impossible for the two to cooperate in the organization of mankind against God.

AN IDEOLOGICAL TRIANGLE

An analogy from World War II may clarify this. Many people thought that some of the nations were on the wrong side of the conflict in the late war. Fascist-minded Roman Catholics, for example, thought that the United States should have been allied with Germany and Italy from the beginning in order to fight against Russian Communism. As a matter of fact, America and Great Britain were allied with their potential enemy to fight Nazism and Fascism in line with the policy of meeting the nearest menace first, even at the cost of strengthening our greater enemy with goods and supplies that might later be used against us.

There was an ideological triangle: Russia against Germany, Russia against capitalism; Britain and America against Germany, Britain and America against Communism; Germany against capitalism, Germany against Communism. The lines were drawn in such fluid fashion that before the conclusion of hostilities some nations fought on opposite

96

sides. Italy, for instance, began as a back-stabber for the sake of greed, and ended as a recognized ally of Britain and America for the sake of her own stability. Russia began with a treaty of benevolent neutrality with Germany, and then felt the might of German attack.

SPIRITUAL WARFARE

In the same way, the great spiritual warfare is a triangular warfare. Lucifer became Satan, and declared war upon God. God, by nature hating rebellion, sin, unrighteousness and imperfection, immediately manifested His righteousness by judgment and the conflict was on. For God, of course, it could not have been a mere contest between Lucifer and the Most High. The Almighty does not condescend to enter the lists as the opponent of one of His creatures. There was to be a conclusive test before all the witnesses of the universe in order to demonstrate that no created being could succeed apart from the divine will, or bring order either to the chaos of judged creation or to that of judged mankind. There is only one will in the universe that can provide peace and order and righteousness, and that is the will of God.

When man sinned he was detached from God, but he did not become attached to Satan. On the contrary, man turned to *"his own way"* (Isaiah 53:6), a way that brought forth hatred from the human heart toward God and demanded hatred from the holy heart of God against man's rebellion and willfulness. "The carnal mind is enmity against God; for it is not subject to the law of God, neither indeed can be. So then they that are in the flesh cannot please God" (Romans 8:7, 8). Thus we see the God of the universe at the top of a triangle with lines emanating from Him toward Satan and toward man. There is a two-way hatred along each of these lines: hatred from Satan against God and from man against God, and oppositely from the holy God against the rebellion and sin in His creatures.

TWO-WAY HATRED

But it is equally important that we should realize the existence of a two-way hatred along the base line of this triangle, hatred between Satan and man and between man and Satan. As soon as man sinned, God announced that the rules under which the rebellion should be fought would be made by Him. God would establish the rules under which sin should be sinned. We can well imagine that Satan would have desired man as his ally, if not as his subject, but God would not allow it that way. In His first pronouncements after sin entered the heart of man God decreed that there would be hatred in both directions between Satan and man, and that He, God Himself, would put that hatred there.

Having broken the one restraint imposed by God upon them, Adam and Eve fled when they heard His voice. The effects of the fall were already visible, even to man. Because he had thrown off his dependence upon God, man must seek to rely upon himself. But the creature, looking around at the perfection of his God-given environment, was overawed by the discrepancies, already discernible to his high intellect, between what he had been and what he now saw himself to be. At that moment fear was born in the heart of man. It was inevitable that it should be so. God had created the rules of the warfare, and He had, in His great love, created this fright to haunt the mind of man, lest man should sit down in self-satisfaction and remain in a fool's paradise of self-deception until the day of his necessary doom. The first of the laws establishing the conditions under which sin should be sinned had come into being: man would run from God, but he would be pursued by his own fears. All his lifetime, fear would clutch at him, and though he might seek to create fictions which would give him a working basis of life without fear, he would never wholly escape it.

No Freedom From Fear

Modern psychiatry, which has done so much to bring out the evidence that bodily ills are often caused by emotional and mental disturbances, seeks to effect the cure by isolating the fear and bringing it out into the open where the patient, supposedly, can see it and, therefore, be no longer afraid of it. The psychiatrists may succeed with some types of fright, but the unsaved world will always be subject to fears that the true Christian need never know. We "sorrow not as others who have no hope" (I Thessalonians 4:13), and we have been delivered from the "fear of death" which is bondage throughout the whole lifetime to those who know not the Lord of the resurrection (Hebrews 2:15).

The Bible recognizes two distinct types of fear of the Lord. Unfortunately our word "fear" has been used in a pejorative sense for so long that one of its noblest meanings is often obscured. When Adam says, "I was afraid," he was not possessed of that fear of the Lord which is the beginning of wisdom. He had the fright of the Lord. A young bride, cooking her first meal at home, proceeded with extreme care that all might be exactly perfect for her young husband. Telling about it afterward, she said, "I was so afraid I would burn the roast." When someone said, "Afraid? Why? Would John beat you?" her answer was a mere look of disdain that such a meaning had been put on the word she had used. She did not mean that she was frightened of her husband, but that she loved him so much that she wished with all her heart that everything should be according to his pleasure. The "fear" of her husband was the beginning of good cooking. The term "fear" of the Lord was never meant to express any fright of the Lord.

ADAM'S FEAR

What now took hold of Adam was a fright of the Lord that was terror. He ran away. Just as a child, unaware of the law of gravity, might step out of a window and thus step into the law of gravity, so Adam stepped out of the will of God and stepped into the laws governing war against God. He was now doomed to be possessed by his fears.

When the Lord overtook the fleeing, hiding man and asked him the reason for his flight, a second result of the fall was immediately seen: man had become a coward and a liar. He attempted to shift the blame from himself to the woman and, in reality, back to God. "The woman whom *thou* gavest to be with me, she gave me of the tree, and I did eat" (Genesis 3:12). To blame the woman was bad enough, but to blame God by inference was much worse. God had given the woman to man as a help fit for his need, but Adam was saying to the Lord, "If You had not given me this woman, I would not now be in this predicament." Thus he sought to deny his own individual responsibility, and to shift the blame directly to the woman and indirectly to God.

The Lord turned to the woman and said: "What is this that thou hast done?" In the woman's answer, the same psychological sins appear. She had become a coward and deceitful. And she too sought to put the blame elsewhere, upon the enemy, Satan. "The serpent beguiled me, and I did eat."

MAN'S REST DISTURBED

Man had chosen to lie down in sin, but the Lord had planted the nettles that were to grow in his bed. Fear, cowardice, and deceit are to disturb man's rest.

The Lord did not discuss the matter further with the woman. But He turned to the serpent and said: "Because thou hast done this, thou art cursed above all cattle, and above every beast of the field; upon thy belly shalt thou go, and dust shalt thou eat all the days of thy life . . ." (Genesis 3:14). The serpent, however, was merely the mouthpiece of Satan, and the curse that turned the serpent into the loathsome, crawling reptile that we know is relatively unimportant, especially if compared with the curse that is pronounced *through* the serpent upon Satan. After the pronouncement upon the serpent, the Lord continued to speak, and addressing now the rebel, Satan, saying, "And I will put enmity between thee and the woman, and between thy seed and her seed; it

[He] shall bruise thy head, and thou shalt bruise his heel" (Genesis 3: 15).

In this passage is the first announcement of the creation of hatred by God, a hatred that is to flow along the base line of the triangle between man and Satan, and which completes the enmities, holy and unholy, that move around the triangle of God, man and the devil. It is against the black background of these hatreds that the doctrine of the love of God will shine all the more resplendently. The hatred that was created by God between man and Satan, Satan and man, was to be especially marked in its outgoing from Satan against the Son of Man, the Lord Jesus Christ, who is here announced for the first time.

Someone may question our statement that God created this hatred. But here is the explanation of one of the frequently misinterpreted and misapplied verses of the Bible. In Isaiah's prophecy we read: "I am the Lord, and there is none else. I form the light, and create darkness; I make peace and create evil. I the Lord do all these things" (Isaiah 45:6, 7). There have been those who have attempted to protect God from implications which they draw from this verse and which are not really there at all. Even Dr. Scofield in the annotated reference Bible, making one of his rare mistakes, commented on the word "evil" in this verse. He writes: "Heb. *ra,* translated 'sorrow,' 'wretchedness,' 'adversity,' 'affliction,' 'calamities,' but never translated *sin.* God created evil only in the sense that He made sorrow, wretchedness, etc., to be the sure fruits of sin." This note is misleading, for it is based upon the technicality that the word *ra* is never translated by the English word "sin." Though it is true that the word is rendered a total of thirteen times by the English words synonymous with sorrow and adversity, it is also true that it is translated by the word "evil" and "wickedness" several hundred times, including such usages as that in the great indictment of mankind at the time of the flood: "And God saw that the wickedness of man was great in the earth, and that every imagination of the thoughts of his heart was only evil *ra* continually" (Genesis 6:5). Dr. Scofield's note would have been correct if he had written, "Heb. *ra,* the common word for moral evil, but sometimes used as the antithesis of peace, as well as the general antithesis of good. God did create the wretchedness and the sorrow and the calamity which always follow sin."

Without violating what we know of the holy nature of God, and without contravening any of the great teachings of the Word of God, the passage can be understood in another way that not only explains the meaning of the verse but casts light upon our general theme. Sin originated in the heart of Lucifer, as we have seen at length in discussing Ezekiel's prophecy. It arose there by a process that we might liken to spiritual spontaneous combustion. It was followed by a declaration of independence of God, an action that announced that the rebel would no longer take his authority and power from the Creator but would seek his authority in himself. Apparently Lucifer, drunk with his own beauty, had decided that he was as worthy of worship as was the Creator, and that he would turn the divine worship unto himself. This was the origin of sin. In the passage in Isaiah, there is the announcement that God creates evil. It is not a denial of Ezekiel. It is rather a statement of the articles of the divine warfare: God creates all the rules under which Lucifer's rebellion shall be carried on. Lucifer declares war; but God announces that He is the Lord of strategy and will keep the combat within the bounds appointed, and that He will not permit the enemy to pass over the limits set by the divine wisdom.

It is difficult, perhaps, to find an illustration that, without oversimplifying the matter, will cover such a point as this. But suppose that the single manifestation of dependence upon God, instead of being a prohibition against eating a certain fruit, should have been a prohibition against stepping on a certain cornice stone of a high building. Man is in total ignorance of any of the consequences of stepping on the stone. He does not know that the stone will rotate beneath him and precipitate him into a void beneath. He is ignorant of all that will succeed in definite order. He knows nothing of the law of gravity, of the law of increasing momentum, of the law of physical impact, of the law of the tensile weakness of human bones and of all the other laws involved in such a step. He finally decides that he is not going to be restricted by an order which tells him that he may walk freely over the whole edifice but that he may not step upon the cornice stone. He is impatient at what he regards as an infringement of his rights of personality, and he steps firmly upon the stone of disobedience. The force of gravity immediately draws his body toward the earth, the crushing impact breaks his bones in many places, and the man is instantly killed.

When Lucifer stepped out of the will of God and when Adam stepped out of the will of God, they stepped into a set of moral and spiritual laws created by God which instantly and inevitably operated. Some of those laws included even the nature of evil. Although no illustration can fully reveal a truth, let us change the figure of speech in order to develop the idea and bring it into further light. Some of the highways of Georgia go for many miles through vast marshes and cypress swamps. A car may be driven at high speed along these splendid highways, but at almost every foot of the way it is possible to run off into the swamp. As highway is to swamp, so every type of righteousness has a corresponding type of unrighteousness. If a man stays on the highway of honor, he is in peace. If he goes off the highway of God, all ramifications of dishonor are set in motion, and in these he is entrapped. If a man stays on the highway of truth, he is in righteousness and peace. If he goes off the highway, he falls into the inevitable consequences. God has created the *nature* of lying; and, since one lie cannot stand alone, it requires two lies to cover up one, four to cover up two, eight to cover up four, and so on through the tangle of falsehood in which the liar becomes inextricably enmeshed.

Several years ago two couples sat in our study while we tried to salvage the two homes from the wreckage caused by the adultery of the man from one home and the woman from the other. In the course of the conversation, the guilty woman burst out with this cry: "But tell me how it is possible for something that seemed so beautiful, so noble, so real at the beginning to have degenerated into something that is so degrading and hateful?" We explained that this was the nature of the rules that God had made for sinning. We read the passage in II Samuel where Amnon committed his great crime against Tamar. At the point in the story where the sin had been committed, there is a profoundly significant verse: "Then Amnon hated her exceedingly; so that the hatred wherewith he hated her was greater than the love wherewith he had loved her" (II Samuel 13:15).

The divine principle of the disintegrating effect of all sin is clearly expressed in the Bible. "But every man is tempted, when he is drawn away of his own lust, and enticed. Then when lust hath conceived, it bringeth forth sin: and sin, when it is finished, bringeth forth death" (James 1:14, 15). You may continue applying this principle to every manifestation of human will against divine will which is possible in the choices of the heart of fallen man, and you will find that it is always in operation. God has made the rules under which sin shall be sinned. He has created the terrain of deviation from His highways of righteousness. The slightest tangent of departure brings us into the territory of evil, and under the operation of all its laws.

When we understand this principle, we can understand the state of mankind, the reasons for the perversions of the vicious, and the hypocrisies of what men call their human virtues. God made all things perfect: His was perfect wisdom, perfect justice, perfect righteousness. But a second will — not God's and therefore not perfect — was flaunted against His, and then multitudes of human wills. In order that it might be demonstrated forever that there is no good apart from His will, God in His love and grace created the nature of the whole horrible pattern of consequences which must follow the choice of any other will than His. If this truth could become established as a definite part of our thinking and be held constantly before our minds, perhaps we would not depart from the will of God so often. If man would say to himself that it is *impossible* to win, he might not try so often. Any thought of victory over God is an illusion. Satan continues to act like the croupier in a dishonest game where the dice are loaded against the victim, who is allowed to win little amounts so that he will risk his all at the moment when it has been determined that he shall not win.

The existence of this divinely created hatred between Satan and man is the explanation of much of human history. When God said, "I will put enmity between thee and the woman, between thy seed and her seed," He also added, "It shall bruise thy head" (Genesis 3:15). God announced not only the creation of a hatred from Satan toward men, but also that the final doom of Satan shall take place through the Seed of the woman. Since Satan knew that he was to be defeated and destroyed by means of a child that should be born of the human race, it is readily understandable that he should, from that moment, attempt to guard against the eventuality, and that he should seek to destroy the line of the promise in order to destroy the possibility of fulfillment.

Satan's enmity against mankind is, in reality, an enmity against God because God has been pleased in His sovereign grace to plan salvation through the Word made flesh; and Satan's primal hatred is, therefore, Christ. His hatred of mankind was, first, a racial hatred, blindly attempting to destroy all men that he might blot out the line of the promise. Then, when Satan discovered that there were some men who had been chosen by God for an eternal purpose, his chief hatred was turned against them. This is seen in the hatred of the children of this world, the seed of Satan, for the children of God because they are attached to Christ. "If ye were of the world," the Lord tells His disciples, "the world would love his own: but because ye are not of the world, but I have chosen you out of the world, therefore the world hateth you" (John 15:19). The more closely we walk with Him, the more we shall feel the hatred of the enemy.

12 : *The Articles of War*
(CONTINUED)

THERE is a sense in which Satan's enmity is not only an enmity against God but is definite hatred of man himself. Satan had ground for hating mankind because he knew not which baby born might become the Seed which would bruise his power. He had further ground for a jealous hatred because of the subsequent announcements through the Word of God that the Lord purposed to take all of the glories and functions with which He had originally invested Satan and place them on some of the sons of fallen Adam. These He would lift higher than the angels, higher than Satan himself, to the very throne to which Satan had aspired. He would give them the place and title of sons, and would ultimately call out one group, the Church, to be the successor of Satan as prophet, priest and king.

CAIN AND ABEL

History does not move very far from the garden of Eden before we see the working of Satan in the two sons of Adam. If Satan can destroy them, he will have obliterated the seed of the woman and frustrated the accomplishment of God's designs. Cain was so given over to Satan that the Word later says that he was "of that wicked one" (I John 3:12), and therefore slew his brother. Thus death has eliminated Abel, and sin has eliminated Cain, for God will not work through sin. But God gave the first couple other children, established the line of one of these sons, Seth, and the war goes on.

THE RACE CORRUPTED

By the sixth chapter of Genesis, we see that Satan was making a determined effort to corrupt the whole of the race. There can be little doubt of the fact that the language of the first verses of this chapter speaks of a stupendous attempt by Satan to infect the whole of mankind by demon possession. Some of the angels who followed Satan in his original rebellion left their first estate and sinned in a yet further disobedience of God's commands. While the Bible everywhere teaches that Satan has hosts of fallen angels that do his bidding, there is also a statement that certain angels have already been confined in the place of their eternal punishment. It is further stated that this occurred at the time of the flood. "God spared not the angels that sinned, but cast them down to Tartarus and delivered them into chains of darkness, to be reserved unto judgment; and spared not the old world, but saved Noah" (II Peter 2:4, 5, Greek).

It would appear that the angels that are still free are aware of this and seek to avoid what their companions have already experienced. The legion of demons in the maniacs of Gadara cried out against Jesus, asking if He had come to torment them "before the time" (Matthew 8:29), and requested that He command them not to go into the bottomless pit (Luke 8:31, Greek *abyss*, same as Revelation 20:1). The entire human family, with the exception of Noah and his household, was evidently corrupted by this irruption of demon forces into the earth. How senseless the complaints of those who accuse God of cruelty for destroying the world when it is understood that He wiped out the most blatant attempt to destroy the human race that is on record. The flood was an act of the marvelous loving-kindness of God in preserving the race intact so that the Redeemer, the Lord Jesus Christ, might be born of the Virgin; for certainly He could not have become incarnate in the womb of a demon-possessed woman.

SATAN'S HATRED OF THE JEWS

As defeat followed defeat in the war that was now becoming very visible to man, the hatred of Satan increased. When the nations were divided at Babel and Abraham was chosen as the head of God's people, he was told that through him and his seed all the families of the earth and all the nations of the earth — two distinct and entirely different promises — should be blessed (Genesis 12:3; 18:18). Anti-Semitism is born of this hatred of Satan for the people through whom God is going to demonstrate ultimately the triumphs of His righteous government. This phase of the battle is summarized in the Apocalypse: "And there appeared a great wonder in heaven; a woman [Israel] clothed with the sun, and the moon under her feet, and upon her head a crown of twelve stars; and she being with child cried, travailing in birth, and pained to be delivered. And there appeared another wonder in heaven; and behold a great red dragon, having seven heads and ten horns, and seven crowns upon his heads . . . and the dragon stood before the woman which was ready to be delivered, for to devour her child as soon as it was born" (Revelation 12:1-4). This is a vision summing up all of the struggle of Israel through the centuries. Of course, it ends in triumph as the Lord provides miraculous power to defeat the enemy. It cannot be otherwise when the plan of God is involved, and in this, as in all else, the devil once more knew the taste of dust.

THE FALLEN ANGELS KNOW THEIR END

Thus we may follow the hatred of Satan for the family of Israel. Nor should we be astonished at this. God tells us that the angels of heaven are careful students of the Bible. There are a score of words in the Greek that are translated by our word "look." The word that is used of the angels looking at the Scriptures (I Peter 1:12), means "to stoop to a thing in order to look at it; to look at with head bowed forward; to look into with the body bent; to stoop and look into; to look carefully, to inspect curiously, as of one who would become acquainted with something."

Should we then be surprised that the angels of Satan should be less careful students of the strategy of the one whose enemy they have become? We have just seen that demons knew that their "time" was coming. They can know this only from the Bible or from the direct announcement of God. Thus they must know that their present power over this fallen earth is one day to be wrested from them and put into the hands of the Jews who are to administer it for the Lord Jesus Christ, whom they (Israel) will then know and serve. There will be no peace established on this earth by any league, conference, alliance or union of nations until God sends the Lion of the tribe of Judah to reign through the instruments He has chosen for the administration of this earth.

Anti-Semitism is one of the most comprehensible things in human history when seen against the background of the invisible war. It is the most inevitable thing in Satan's dealings, just as Satan's frustration and defeat are the most inevitable in the plan of God.

SATAN WORKS AGAINST ISRAEL

In line with this same strategy, we see that Satan moved David to number the people of Israel against the command of God, and thus brought wrath upon the nation. Satan led the people to follow false gods, thus bringing the curse and the dispersion which enabled Satan to work on the remnants in isolated and alien circumstances. Today, Satan works against the regathering of Israel in the land which God has sworn to them. The Arabs block them physically from possession of the land while theologically, every device is used to bury the truth in obscurity. Some hold that the Anglo-Saxon nations are the supposed lost tribes and that therefore there are no promises to the Jews. The amillenarians take all the promises that belong to the Jews and apply them to the Church, leaving the curses, as Satan likes to do, for the Jews. The cults of Jehovah's Witnesses, the Seventh-day Adventists and others hold various theories that deprive Israel of her kingdom glories. But just as the Lord has always fulfilled His promises and kept Satan short of his goal, so He will continue faithful to the end. He will one day rule this earth through a redeemed Jewry.

SATAN'S HATRED OF THE MESSIAH

When the Lord Jesus Christ was born Satan's hatred came to white heat. We can see the hatred of Satan at every point in the earthly story of the life of our Lord. Joseph was moved to cast off Mary because he knew that she had not been his wife as yet and drew the natural conclusion that there was sin on her part. But the Lord manifested Himself and Joseph accepted Mary because of this divine revelation. The child of promise, the seed of the woman, the branch of David, was born, the Eternal Word was made flesh. Satan moved Herod to kill all of the babies from two years old and under according to the time which he had diligently inquired of the wise men. But God had arranged escape in advance, and had brought gifts of gold to the family of the young child so that a flight into Egypt was made possible. At twelve years of age He was left behind in Jerusalem among the followers of Satan and the enemies of God. The child was growing up before His Father as a tender plant and the heavenly care was about Him.

As soon as our Lord was publicly manifested, Satan immediately confronted Him and sought in the three temptations to turn Him aside from the path laid down for Him in the counsels with the Father. When he had been routed with the sword of the Word, Satan left the Lord, but returned again and again, both personally and through the religious leaders who had become veritable children of the devil, to destroy the Lord before He could come to the hour of the cross. It was Satan who stirred up the people of Nazareth to take Christ to the brow of the hill and thrust Him to His death on the occasion of His first public sermon. He had announced the doctrine of salvation by grace apart from works on the basis of the sovereign will of God (Luke 4), and the heart of man rebelled against it and turned easily to the enemy who would exalt the flesh. "But he, passing through the midst of them, went his way." Again and again Satan played the old plot with different scenes and characters. Sometimes they picked up stones to stone Him; they sent officers to arrest Him; their leaders attempted to incite the people against Him. Always the nerve of their action was paralyzed. Their desire was that of the carnal mind which is enmity against God. Now, for the first time in history, God was visibly before them as the object of their hatred. They were the sons of those who had killed the prophets, but they themselves would have killed their God. He described them fully in the parable of the tenants who killed the messengers and when the owner, last of all, sent His Son, cried, "This is the heir; come, let us kill him, and let us seize on his inheritance" (Matthew 21:38). Always He escaped unhurt. He was master of every situation. He said, "No man taketh it [my life] from me; but I lay it down of myself" (John 10:18).

When human allies failed, Satan moved directly to kill the Son of God. On one occasion the Lord's disciples were with Him in a boat on the sea of Galilee. They were lifelong fishermen who were in their home waters. They had thought that there was not a wave that could be unfamiliar to them. But suddenly a storm of such fury broke out that even these hardened mariners were chilled with fright. They rushed to the Lord as He lay asleep in the boat and roused Him with their cry of anguish, as they deemed themselves on the point of death, "Master, save us; we perish!" The gospel narrative states that the Lord arose at the call of the frightened disciples and "rebuked the wind." Let the deniers of Scripture realize that if Satan were not behind the power of that storm, then the action of Christ must be compared with that of a child who, hurt by stumbling against a chair, begins to kick at the chair, crying out with petulance against it. But if we understand that Satan had raised that storm to kill the Lord Jesus, so that He might not live to go to the cross to become the Saviour, we see the whole pattern of these attacks, and understand the force of the words addressed to the storm, "Peace, be still" (Mark 4:35-41). The verb in Greek means "to muzzle," and in ancient domestic life was sometimes addressed to a dog to silence him.

Finally, the prophecies were fulfilled and Satan bruised the heel of the Lord Jesus Christ and had his own head crushed in the bruising. We shall study the battle of the cross in some detail in its connection with the overcoming of the enemy, but we would note here that the redemptive work of Christ did not change the nature of the rebel. The key to the history of the last two thousand years is the same as the key to the history of the times before Christ. We shall never understand our own age if we do not comprehend the principle of interpretation in which we see Satan attacking the people of God. He seeks to build up his own kingdom, and he attacks the underground of God who remain faithful to the absent Sovereign of the universe.

In the first centuries of the Christian era the full force of Satan was unleashed to destroy the infant Church. Ten great persecutions, wave upon wave, threatened to sweep the believers from the earth. So terrible was the carnage that was wrought among the faithful that the Greek word for witness, *martyr,* has become accepted in our language as one which describes a man who dies for his faith. The fury of the Roman secular power was the fury of Satan. Violence having failed, the enemy shifted his attack to guile. After the centuries of persecution, there came the sustained effort of Satan to marry the Church to the world, which was finally accomplished by the "conversion" of Constantine and the enthronement of the church in the palace of the Caesars. This move from the catacombs to the palace was almost fatal, but God, through the spiritual darkness of the Middle Ages, had His own hidden ones who were faithful to Him. Though the church organization waxed exceedingly corrupt, God still preserved the elect seed and, in the course of His own time, He brought forth the Reformation to re-establish the great truths of grace which had been well nigh lost. Satan answered with the Inquisition and the religious wars. The order of the Jesuits was founded, and every attempt was made to crush the truth and all who held it.

Satan's age-long strategy remained the same. In the first recorded sentence which he had ever addressed to man, "Yea, hath God said?" Satan had attacked the Word of God. Every arm of infidelity was unsheathed against the divine revelation. The English deism of the eighteenth century was matched by the French atheism of the encyclopedists. In the infant republic that had sprung up on American shores, Tom Paine sowed his puerile rationalism against the Book that was the foundation of the spiritual life that had been planted in this wilderness, and which had given the first liberties in centuries to the Jews who were to be sheltered here until God's time for their return to the land. If Satan could destroy confidence in the Word of God, he would have some hope of achieving a victory over some of God's creatures. If he could not destroy faith in the Word of God, he would be defeated. Luther knew this when he wrote in the battle hymn of the Reformation: "One little word will fell him." In the battle against the Word of God which has been carried on even more vigorously since the invention of printing made the Book available to the millions, Satan has manned every approach and used every artifice at his disposal. The Bible was burned and banned, scorned and ridiculed. It was given lip service by those who denied the power of its truth. It was in the name of science built on false hypotheses that the great attack on the Bible and the Church came in the nineteenth century, and in our day psychology and psychiatry claim to duplicate the efficacy of the blood of Christ to break the power of sin in the life.

False cults by the score have sprung up outside the churches that are still creedally faithful, the heart of all of which is the denial of the person and the work of the Lord Jesus Christ. Within the bounds of the fellowship of those who confess the finality of the Word, living and written, there are divisions and sects which are based primarily on something that man is to do for God rather than on that which the Lord God has done for His people through the work of His Son, Jesus Christ. Also, within the churches whose creeds are still impeccable, various delusions of error find their place. There, to the accompaniment of organ music and suave preaching, multitudes of baptized persons are in the snares of sacerdotalism, legalism and, above all, of a form of godliness which denies the power thereof (II Timothy 3:5).

But, in spite of all of Satan's strategems, his doom is sure: for it is written, "The God of peace shall bruise Satan under your feet shortly" (Romans 16:20). This is possible because at the cross our God has already bruised Satan under the feet of the Lord Jesus Christ.

13 : *God Announces Victory*

THERE is only one Being in the universe who knows the end from the beginning, and that is our God in the three Persons of His being, Father, Son and Holy Spirit. From what we have seen thus far, it has been demonstrated that both Satan and man, by the very nature of their rebellion, had that short-sightedness which characterizes the creature and which is one of the proofs that our ways are not God's ways and that our thoughts are not His thoughts (Isaiah 55:9).

TIME SHALL BE NO MORE

The announcement to Satan in the garden of Eden not only set in motion the laws of history, chiefly characterized by Satan's hatred of the people of God — Israel and the Church — and by his hatred of the Word of God, but also pronounced the absolute doom of Satan and the impenitent children of Adam and proclaimed the final triumph of our God. Alongside the eternity of the single will of God had come the beginning of time and the introduction of a second will. This brief moment of time, God has assured us from the beginning, will come to an end. The kingdoms of this earth will become the kingdoms of our Lord and of His Christ, and His government will merge into eternity and the single will of God. The claims of other wills will have been demonstrated to be baseless and there will be but one will again in all the universe and forever. The rebel wills which may still smolder with their eternal hatred against the righteousness and justice of God will be restrained forever in an outer darkness, and will be unknown and unremembered to the universe of beings who are with God. This is the consummation we now await. The power of Satan is to be absolutely crushed and put away forever, while God's Deliverer, the Lord Jesus Christ, shall be exalted, and we who believe in Him shall share that exaltation.

111

A Moral Problem

The moment that we say that some members of the race of fallen Adam are going to be in heaven with a holy God, participating with Him in the rule and government of the universe, we raise a great moral problem and express a delimma that must be resolved. How can a holy God take any sinful creatures to Himself? How can any member of the race of Adam get to heaven? The thoughtlessness of the human mind is perhaps nowhere more clearly illustrated than in that easy nonchalance of the average person toward the idea of heaven.

The mass of fallen humanity looks upon some pleasant life after death as a part of the human birthright. The primitive mind of the American Indian looked upon life after death as a happy hunting ground. The unsaved of the past generation read and circulated a novel with the title, *All This and Heaven Too,* which evidently includes the idea that the earth is a beautful place, that life is wonderful, and that when we have drunk all the joys of this earth, we shall go on to the joys of heaven. While this is true for a regenerated person who has believed that God Himself has satisfied all the righteous demands of His holiness by Christ's death in our behalf, it most certainly is not true for the mass of unregenerate people who fill the earth and even many churches. Heaven is as far above the earth spiritually as it is physically. While it is true for the Christian that "all the hell we have is here on earth," it is just as true for the non-Christian that all the heaven he shall have is here on earth. The Negroes are more realistic and certainly theologically more accurate when they sing in the chorus to their spiritual:

"Heaven . . . heaven . . .
Everybody talkin' 'bout heaven ain't goin' thar . . ."

Surely Satan who before the fall had been the covering cherub occupied with the holiness of God, knew that this dilemma would arise out of God's holy hatred for sin and the consequent necessity of judgment upon any creature who departed from the single will of God. It would seem that the thought, or one thought at least, which was in the back of his mind in the seduction of the human race was that he had turned the tables on God and put the Lord in an impossible situation. For had not God wrecked Lucifer's earth, making it without form and void, a wreck and a ruin, and Lucifer could do nothing about it? Now, if Satan could get man to sin, he would have succeeded in making God's new creation a wreck and a ruin; and God's holiness would not permit Him to do anything about it.

SATAN'S REASONING

The thought of God's answer in the incarnation through which the redemption of an elect company would be wrought had never entered into the mind of the enemy. He saw merely in the straight lines of simple creature logic. His reasoning might be set forth as follows: This God is absolute in His holiness, and He is absolute in His justice. His blessings drop down like a waterfall, and man stands there in the place of blessing because there is no sin in him. But if I could only get him to step out of the place of blessing into the place of sin, God would have to pour upon him the acid-fall of His divine wrath. For the one thing that a God of holiness and justice could never, never do would be to condone sin in any way.

That Satan must have thought thus we conclude from his speaking actions which said: "God has created this puny creature, man, and has given him dominion over the province that was mine, yes, that is yet mine. I shall get man to sin and God will be frustrated, and He shall know the mouthful of this dust that has become my meat."

There is a great illustration of this idea in the story of Balaam. The children of Israel, after their victory over the Amorites, camped near the country of Moab. The king of the Moabites, Balak, was frightened at the fate of his neighbors, and his first reaction was to get Balaam, the hireling prophet, to come to his aid. The true God intervened and warned the prophet that he was to bless His people, for they were chosen of God. Balak sent more honorable messengers, with offers of richer rewards, but the Lord revealed to Balaam that, though he went under the permissive will of God to the king of Moab, he would have to speak the words which the Lord gave him to speak. Balaam followed the counsel of his greed and acted against the directive will of God. We are familiar with the story of the ass in whose mouth the Lord put the words to curb the selfish prophet. Then Balaam went to Balak and thrice over he prophesied great blessing for the children of Israel.

BALAK'S PLAN

What Balak had not been able to obtain by giving wages to a hireling prophet, he now obtained by a method of seduction. The women of Moab came round about the camp of Israel and the men of Israel took the women of Moab. There has always been a very closely drawn psychological line between the sex instinct and that of religion, and it was not long before the men of Israel began to attend the sacrifices of the gods of the Moabites, partook of their feasts, and bowed down to the idols. Then we read: "And Israel joined himself unto Baal-peor; and the anger of the Lord was kindled against Israel" (Numbers 25:3). This was just what Balak, king of Moab, had desired — that the anger of the Lord should be kindled against Israel; and, when he could not get a curse against the people from the lips of Balaam, he got a curse from the anger of the Lord against this people because of the spiritual departure from the Lord.

SATAN'S STRATEGY

This was exactly the strategy that Satan was employing in the garden of Eden. Man was in the place of blessing, and God, therefore, could not be filled with wrath against him. No word of curse could be pronounced against man by any being within the camp of the enemy, for man was not yet at enmity against God. But get the man to depart from the place of blessing, and God Himself would be forced, by the very nature of His being, to curse man and seemingly play Satan's game. Satan thought that this would have to be of necessity an eternal, universal curse, and that he would thereby have outplayed God and given God a taste of the frustration which was gritting in his own mouth. He did not know the depths of the heart of God or the nature of God's dealings with sin by the death of a substitute.

Is it any wonder that Paul, the great spiritual logician, should find himself crying out in an ejaculation of supernatural joy: "O the depth of the riches both of the wisdom and knowledge of God! how unsearchable are his judgments, and his ways past finding out!" (Romans 11: 33). Satan had understood the way of God's holiness and the way of God's justice, for he had felt the fullness of these ways in the separation which had been invoked against him and in the stroke of judgment which had come upon him. But he had no point of reference to gauge the loving-kindness of the divine heart. He had no knowledge of the doctrine of grace.

BEYOND MAN'S COMPREHENSION

Our finite minds cannot understand all of the divine plan. Somewhere along the line, we are going to find a question which causes us to admit that we do not know all the answers and that we must abandon ourselves to the full tide of faith, trusting God that understanding shall be ours in some future day. We may not be able to understand, fully, the positive statements of God as to His absolute sovereignty and the equally positive statements as to the place of man's will. We may not be able to comprehend the seeming overlapping of the total depravity of mankind and the total responsibility of each individual for his own position and condition. But that which best satisfies the mind of this writer, when we think of the reasons why God permitted a fall which He undoubtedly had the power to avert, is that without that fall there could never have been any knowledge of His loving-kindness, His tender mercy, His longsuffering, His free sovereign grace — doctrines of which Satan was seemingly in total ignorance.

In order to proceed with the study of God's method of working in the redemption of man and the defeat of Satan, it is necessary for us to go back for a moment and pick up one thread of truth which we have mentioned before. We again ask the question: When Adam sinned, how far did the human race fall? On the answer to that question depends all the rest of the development of doctrinal knowledge. We do not need to consider the humanistic doctrine that man did not fall, but that he is on his way upward to bigger and better things; nor will we spend time on the Roman Catholic doctrine that man slipped over the edge and that he is restored by the sacrament administered at the hands of a priesthood. Those who come to the Bible as to the supreme court will reject these two positions without hesitation since they are manifestly so far from the truth. On the other hand, the vast majority of people who believe that the Bible is the Word of God hold to one of two doctrines: namely, either that man fell a long way, but that he still has in himself the power of climbing out of the pit of sin, and that he is somehow the maker of his own destiny; or, the opposite doctrine, that he fell so great a distance that he does not have the power in himself to lift himself out of his lost condition. We hold, unquestioningly, that the Scripture teaches the latter of these two positions, although we shall at the same time demonstrate that man is fully responsible for his condition.

Now, when we show that the Bible teaches the doctrine of total depravity, we are not claiming that there is no good in man, but that there is no good in man *that can satisfy God.* We have already pointed out from Scripture that "the natural man receiveth not the things of the Spirit of God; for they are foolishness unto him; neither can he know them, because they are spiritually discerned" (I Corinthians 2: 14); and, "the carnal mind is enmity against God; for it is not subject to the law of God, neither indeed can be. So then they that are in the flesh cannot please God" (Romans 8:7); and, "There is none that understandeth, there is none that seeketh after God . . . there is none that doeth good, no, not one" (Romans 3:11, 12). These texts are indicative of a whole line of divine revelation which may be summed up in the Old Testament phrases: "The heart is deceitful above all things, and incurably sick" (Jeremiah 17:9, Hebrew); and "all our righteousnesses are as filthy rags" (Isaiah 64:6).

We repeat, these statements do not teach that there is no good in man, from man's point of view, but that there is no good in man from God's point of view, for God can require no less than perfection.

The story is told of a well-known New York playwright who had been born on the lower East side in the city. It was a rags to riches tale of a man of poor immigrant Jewish background who had nevertheless made good in his profession. One day, after he had made some of his fortune, he took his old Jewish mother out for a ride on his yacht which he kept anchored in the Hudson River. To impress her, the playwright came dressed in a naval uniform. "Look, Mom," he said, "I'm a captain." The old woman shook her head. "Izzy," she said, "by you, you are a captain. And by me, you can be a captain also. But by captains, Izzy; ah! by captains, you ain't no captain."

In the same way, man may think of himself as good. He may go to great lengths to convince his fellow men that he is good. He may dress up in all the uniforms of goodness. But in the sight of God, the Author of all good, man certainly is not good. He is a sinner, utterly destitute of any and all that can genuinely be called good by God's standards.

It was Chalmers of Scotland who said: "The righteousness of God is that righteousness which His righteousness requires Him to require." The righteousness which is required by man of men is an imperfect thing which cannot even be classified as a small part of the divine righteousness, but which is of an entirely different essence. God Himself thus differentiates the two. Speaking of erring Israel, He says: "For they being ignorant of God's righteousness, and going about to establish their own righteousness, have not submitted themselves unto the righteousness of God" (Romans 10:3).

Many unregenerate people are finer people than many Christians. It must be confessed that we would much sooner trust certain unsaved people in matters of morals, finance and similar manifestations of character than we would some saved people. Measured by man's standards, there are many human beings who are quite eligible for places of public honor and trust, for places of personal esteem but who are not eligible for heaven. The qualities which make a young man eligible to be a son-in-law in one's family do not make him eligible to be a son in the family of God. Scrip money may pay the grocery bill during a depression, but it will not be acceptable at a post office for stamps or at the Bureau of Internal Revenue for payment of income tax. There one will need good, Federal money. Character is scrip money that will pay the way in any of the circles of earth, but it will not be acceptable for the entrance price at the gate of heaven.

How, then, is man to be saved? Has Satan won the war by getting man detached from God and into a place where the laws of God's wrath must operate against sin? If we look at the problem closely, we are forced to admit that if God had immediately destroyed Adam and Eve He would have been perfectly just in doing so. They deserved destruction. If He had permitted the human race to increase and multiply and had then swept the whole of the race into the lake of fire, He would have been perfectly just in doing so. Man's departure from righteousness deserved the curse of God. We can never come to any growth in the knowledge of God until we are ready to admit that we personally deserve the wrath of God. It would be a very salutary experience for each of us if we would stop right here and taking the nearest paper and pencil write down so that we could see it in our own handwriting: "I, John Smith (put your name in here) truly deserve the wrath of God, and under the laws of perfect justice I should spend eternity in the lake of fire." We do not believe that any human being is truly saved until he has seen that truth in all its stark and naked reality.

How, then, is any man to be saved? God answered this dilemma by the doctrine of election based on the vicarious, substitutionary atonement as provided in the death of the Lord Jesus Christ. The great hatred which exists in some quarters against the doctrine of election is readily understandable in the light of the fact that Satan was ignorant of it, and that its introduction, as a sort of secret weapon, insured his own eternal defeat and provided for the salvation of the great company of believers who shall, under the graciously given title and position of sons of God, rule the universe for God throughout all eternity.

Christ announced the world's hatred of the doctrine of election in plain terms: "If the world hate you, ye know that it hated me before it hated you. If ye were of the world, the world would love his own: but because ye are not of the world, but I have chosen [elected] you out of the world, therefore [– *therefore* –] the world hateth you" (John 15:18, 19). The first epistle of John amplifies this in a beautiful way. It is, of course, a general New Testament truth that the expressions "sons of God," "the elect," "the saints," "the believers" and similar names and titles are synonymous. John specifically states that he is writing to those who have believed on the name of the Son of God, and who, therefore, are possessors of eternal life (I John 5:13). In an earlier chapter of this same epistle he says: "Behold, what manner of love [what special kind of love] the Father hath bestowed upon us [the born again ones], that we [the elect] should be called the sons of God [as distinct from the unsaved masses who are only creatures but not sons]: therefore [– *therefore* –] the world knoweth us not, because it knew him not. Beloved [in spite of all that anyone, saved or unsaved, may say about it], now *are* we the sons of God [and that is something the unsaved are not], and it doth not yet appear what we shall be . . ." (I John 3:1, 2).

When you find Christians who show antagonism toward the doctrine of election, you may be sure that it is a carry-over from their old carnal mind which is enmity against God. They are forced to delete great sections from the Word of God in order to eliminate the doctrine, and, what is more, they are forced to deny the doctrine, which is found throughout all the Bible, that man fell all the way, not part way, and that he is dead, totally dead, in trespasses and sins. But we must not be astonished, for it is merely an illustration of the great desire of fallen man to be exalted and to take some of the credit for salvation to himself.

14 : *God Announces Victory*
(CONTINUED)

We have long since adopted the old-fashioned method of the seesaw to test all doctrines. When children are riding two ends of a plank on a seesaw, we know that if one end is down the other is up, and if the first is up the second is down. So it is in the matter of all doctrines. There is an entire set of doctrinal interpretations which exalts man and abases God, and there is another set that exalts God and abases man. We may be absolutely sure that the path of truth, in every case, exalts God. How far did man fall? Only part way, say some, so that he still has the power within his lovable self to lift himself back to God. Man is up in that interpretation, and God is down. But did man fall all the way, so that not one man could ever have been saved unless God had moved to do it all? That abases man to the place where God has said he is, but it exalts God, and that is the true interpretation of the Word of God. The same rule of interpretation may be applied to all the doctrines in theology.

Thus we understand why, in the same verse which announced that there would be hatred placed between Satan and mankind, God declared that Satan would be destroyed by One who would be the offspring of the woman, and, that the Saviour would be bruised in His crushing of the enemy. Here is the announcement of the method whereby God could save a sinner, without any violation of His own holiness and justice. For God to send the whole of the human race to the lake of fire would not have involved any injustice; for God to take even one sinner into heaven would pollute heaven if no way were found for changing the sinner back into the likeness of a holy God.

TWO FACTORS

In the strategy of God, then, there are two factors: the election of some, not all, of the descendants of Adam to a place beside Himself in heaven, and the proclamation of the just and righteous basis for this procedure. At the same time, there is the proclamation of the ab-

119

solute responsibility of the individual. Some may think that there is a contradiction between these two statements, but we shall resolve any dilemma that may appear on the surface to exist between the two sides of this great question.

That God elects only some is evident in the world round about us as well as in the Word of God. We do not even pause to give attention to the claims of those, like the Seventh-day Adventists and Jehovah's Witnesses, who deny eternal punishment, while admitting the practical fact that only part of the human race will be saved.

Two Questions

For those who have given their faith over to the Word of God and who are not quite sure of what it teaches and therefore of what they do believe, we have two questions, the considered answers to which will clarify any Christian's thought in this matter. The first question is this: Ten million years from now, when you are in heaven, assuming that time is long past, the judgments of God are completed and eternity has long begun, will there be any child of Adam there who was not chosen in Christ before the foundation of the world (Ephesians 1:4)? The answer must be in the negative. The second question is equally pertinent: Will any one who was thus chosen in Christ fail to be there at that time? Again the answer must be in the negative. The logical conclusion must then be drawn: there will be in heaven the elect of God, chosen in Christ. If God had not moved thus, Satan would have won the invisible war.

I put these two questions to a woman missionary who was in despair because she, her husband and their fellow workers saw almost no fruit of their labors among the followers of Mohammed. Other missionaries, a few miles away among the pagan tribes of Africa were able to count their believers by the thousands. I pointed out that if God had sent the various missionaries, each to the other field, the numbers of the saved would have been just the same. The missionaries who saw a thousand saved in central Nigeria would have seen three saved in Islamic Kano, while the missionaries who have seen three saved in Kano would have won a thousand in the other field. The Church of Jesus Christ in the last century and a half has spent a hundred million dollars on Mohammedan missions and has seen only a few converts. The reason is that God, in His inscrutable providence, has not chosen many Mohammedans. If we are going to commit the folly of believing otherwise, we are forced to the conclusion that the salvation of individuals is based on the zeal of the missionary and that the Church has sent poor missionaries to Mohammedan lands and good ones elsewhere. The fact is that some of God's most devoted servants have spent their lives in being a savor of death unto death (II Corinthians 2:16) to the world of Islam, and to fulfill the plan of God.

THE BASIS OF SELECTION

What, then, is the basis on which God selects those that shall be with Him in heaven? The answer is found clearly in the Bible, especially in the epistle to the Romans.

In order to understand this declaration, let us stop a moment and set forth a brief résumé of the teachings of this greatest of all the epistles. Chapter one shows that all the Gentiles are under the wrath of God. Chapter two presents the same truth as it affects the Jews. Chapter three begins by lumping all mankind together and showing all to be lost, then clearly presenting the cross of Jesus Christ as the basis for the pardon granted by God. Chapter four illuminates the doctrine of salvation by grace apart from any righteousness in the individual by drawing illustrations from the lives of Abraham and David. Chapter five shows the results of the implanting of new life in the one to whom God imputes righteousness in Christ, and begins the story of the struggle between the old life of Adam and the new life of Christ; this teaching carries us through the sixth and seventh chapters. In the eighth chapter the great conclusions are drawn: the man who is justified is freed from all condemnation as he is looked upon as being in Christ, and nothing can be laid to his charge or separate him from the love of God.

WHAT OF THE JEWS?

Immediately there arises a question. If this be so — if the gifts of God are on the ground of His sovereign grace, totally apart from anything in man, why has God cast off Israel? The answer is that He has not; Israel is merely set aside for a time awaiting the day when God shall restore His ancient people to a place of usefulness in the midst of His plan. This question is answered in the next three chapters — nine to eleven — which contain our greatest passage on election. The remaining chapters from the twelfth to the end are occupied with the principles of living that grow out of our high and holy position as the chosen of God, and the practical application of these principles to the daily life of the believer.

In answering the question about the assured position of those who are called of God, the Word declares that the work which God does in any heart chosen by Him is done forever, "for the gifts and calling of God are without repentance" (Romans 11:29). The principle on which He has chosen the elect is locked in the sovereignty of His own being. He has done that which He pleased to do, and He has not been pleased to give us any reason for His choice. "When Rebecca also had conceived by one, even by our father Isaac; (For the children being not yet born, neither having done any good or evil, that the purpose of God according to election might stand, not of works, but of him that calleth;) it was said unto her, The elder shall serve the younger. As it is written, Jacob have I loved, but Esau have I hated" (Romans 9:10-13).

God's Love for Jacob

There is an old anecdote about this passage which puts it in its proper perspective. The story goes that a skeptic approached a Christian with a sneer that the Bible could not be true because of this passage. " 'Esau have I hated!' " said the skeptic. "Imagine that in the Bible, spoken about a God who is said to be love!" The Christian replied that there was, indeed, a great difficulty in the verse, and the skeptic complimented him on his willingness to admit it. "But," replied the Christian, "there is no difficulty at all in the phrase you have quoted. Esau was a hateful sinner, and we couldn't have much respect for a God who would love him in his unchanged and unchangeable condition. God in His justice must find an Esau hateful. The great difficulty lies in the preceding phrase, 'Jacob have I loved,' for Jacob was a liar and a swindler, and the fact that God could manifest love toward him constitutes our real problem. This can be understood only in the light of the death of Jesus Christ."

There is truly a great problem! That God loved Jacob is a wonder surpassed only by the fact that God loved me! Sometimes we sing the chorus:

> Wonderful Saviour! Wonderful Friend!
> Wonderful life that never shall end!
> Wonderful place He has gone to prepare!

Up to this point we sing with faith, believing what we have sung; but when we come to the last line how many of us have really comprehended the depths of the truth there are to be found in this statement:

> Wonder of wonders! I shall be there!

There is no human logic in the doctrine of heaven; the only logic is to be found in the punishment of sin by a holy God and the separation of the sinner from His holy Self. That He was able, in the depths of His being to find a way whereby sin could be put on a substitute and the sinner go free, is one of the greatest glories of His nature which He has been pleased to reveal to us. Again and again we must cry out: "O the depth of the riches, both of the wisdom and the knowledge of

God; how unsearchable are his judgments and his ways past finding out!"

Our purpose in this work is not to give an explanation of Christian doctrines, but an outline of the great invisible war which rages in the universe of time and sense and space. But it might not be invidious at this point to add a paragraph illuminating the doctrine of election. A group of young people asked us to create an analogy which would shed light on this most controversial of all doctrines and that would answer the false charge that election nullifies the need for evangelism.

After a year or two of thought on the matter, which remained in the back of the mind as one of many problems demanding elucidation, the following analogy came full-grown, one evening while we were walking through Times Square in New York. The largest electric sign in the world stood above us and we had recently read a magazine article about it telling how many thousands and thousands of light globes made up the sign. Suddenly, we saw the analogy of a much larger board on which were untold millions of dead globes, all of them unscrewed in their sockets and all of them with broken filaments. None of them, need it be said, was giving forth any light for, on two counts, it was impossible for the current to reach the point of illumination. This represents the human race. Every man is dead in trespasses and sins (Ephesians 2:1) — the filament is broken — and every man is alienated from the life of God (Colossians 1:21) — the bulbs are unscrewed.

How is life to come to any man? How is light to come to any bulb? We go to a man and proclaim the Gospel to him. It is as though we screwed the bulb in place. The man is by that act evangelized. We have fulfilled the function of the herald of the Gospel. No man can call on the Lord if he has not believed and he cannot believe if he has not heard and he cannot hear without a preacher (Romans 10:14). In other words, it is the proclamation of the words of the divine revelation concerning man's lost condition and God's saving work in Christ which brings the man in contact with the source of light and power. But as we twist all the bulbs we can lay our hands on, preaching the Gospel to every creature by every means, suddenly there are some that light up, and there are also some that remain in darkness. We know that at the moment that some shine forth it is because a miracle has been performed in them. They have been the objects of the new creation (II Corinthians 5:17), and they have been made partakers of the divine nature (II Peter 1:4). This new creation is not of blood, nor of the will of the flesh nor of man, but of God (John 1:13). Of His own will begat He us with the Word of truth (James 1:18). This is why neither the one who turns the light bulb a little way into the socket nor he who turns it in a little more is anything, but God who creates the filament. This is the significance of this same truth in another analogy where we read, "Neither is he that planteth anything, nor he that watereth, but God who giveth the increase" (I Corinthians 3:7).

If someone should object that God has said that He is no respecter of persons, we would answer that the true meaning of this is not that there is to be universal salvation, but rather that in choosing those whom He has willed to choose He would not look at any human differences. He takes a pauper as readily as a prince, and a depraved man as readily as one who is righteous in the sight of men. In fact, "Not many wise men after the flesh, not many mighty, not many noble are called: but God hath chosen [elected] the foolish things of the world to confound the wise; and God hath chosen the weak things of the world to confound the things which are mighty; and base things of the world, and things which are despised, hath God chosen, yea, and things that are not, to bring to naught the things that are; that no flesh should glory in his presence" (I Corinthians 1:26-29).

These studies were originally given as lectures in several different cities. One evening, in Washington, D.C., we told how the study of the Word had led us to abandon many of the methods of evangelism that are known only in America and where Americans have gone; the sing-two-more-verses-while-four-more-sinners-come-to-Jesus type of evangelism, and that we had long since come to the place where we threw ourselves on the grace and power of God, realizing our own nothingness, and depending entirely on Him. We preached the Word, and He would quicken whom He willed. We were content to be a savor of life unto life to those in whom He created the new filament of life, and of death unto death to those who remained in their dead and lost condition. At the close of the meeting, a major in the United States Army said: "You turned my bulb the night God created the filament in me in Boston eleven years ago." His father, a preacher, stood by, and we were happy to say that the father had planted and we had watered, but God had given the increase.

If someone again objects, quoting some of the "whosoever will" passages, we reply that these, when fitted into all of the Scriptures, and not taken by themselves to the exclusion of great bodies of truth, are the litmus papers which show the baseness of the human heart outside of Christ. For though we preach "whosoever will" on every possible occasion, we know the answer to that very important question: Who will will? We seek to preach to every man in the world, and we proclaim, as we must, "whosoever will may come. . . ." Yet we know that only those will come who are quickened — made alive — from their state of darkness and death by a definite act of God in the sovereignty of His eternal purpose in grace.

Before any man believes there are three works which must have taken place on his behalf, one from God the Father, one from God the Son and one from God the Spirit. The believer has, first, been chosen by God the Father before the foundation of the world (Ephesians 1:4); he has, secondly, been redeemed by God the Son (I Peter 1:18, 19); and he has, thirdly, been quickened by the Holy Spirit (John 3:3-8): only then, fourth in the sequence, he believes.

Now let us turn the medal and look at the effigy on the reverse side. We do not hold for a moment that man is an automaton and that he may be compared to a puppet on a string. There are some that believe thus, and they have been well described and refuted by many theologians. We quote the following from A. W. Pink and make it our own position: "Those who belong to this school of theology insist that it would be just as sensible to visit our cemeteries and call upon the occupants of their graves to come forth as to exhort those who are dead in trespasses and sins to throw down the weapons of their warfare and be reconciled to God. But such reasoning is puerile, for there is a vast and vital difference between a spiritually dead soul and a lifeless body. The soul of Adam became the subject of penal and spiritual death, nevertheless, it retained all of its natural powers. Adam did not lose all knowledge, or become incapable of volition, nor did the operations of conscience cease within him. He was still a rational being, a moral agent, a responsible creature: though he could no longer think or will, love or hate, in conformity to the Law of Righteousness.

"Far otherwise is it with physical dissolution. When the body dies it becomes as inactive, unintelligent and unfeeling as a piece of unorganized matter. A lifeless body has no responsibility, but a spiritually dead soul is accountable to God. A corpse in the cemetery will not 'despise and reject' Christ (Isaiah 53:3), will not 'resist the Spirit' (Acts 7:51), will not disobey the Gospel (II Thessalonians 1:8); but the sinner can and *does* do these very things, and is justly condemned for the same. Are we, then, suggesting that fallen man is *not* 'dead in trespasses and sins'? No indeed. But we do insist that these solemn words be rightly interpreted and that no false conclusions be drawn from them. Because the soul has been thus deranged by sin, because all its operations are unholy, it is rightly said to be in a state of spiritual death, for it no more fulfills the purpose of its being than does a dead body.

"The fall of man, with its resultant spiritual death, did not dissolve our relation to God as the Creator, nor did it exempt us from His authority; but it forfeited His favor and suspended that communion with

Him by which alone could be preserved that moral excellency with which the soul was originally endowed. Instead of attempting to draw analogies between spiritual and physical death and deriving inferences therefrom, we must stick very closely to the Scriptures and regulate all our thoughts thereby. God's Word says, 'You hath He quickened who were dead in trespasses and sins, *wherein* in times past ye *walked*" (Ephesians 2:1, 2). Thus the spiritual death of the sinner is a state of *active* opposition against God — a state for which he is responsible, the guilt and enormity of which the preacher should ever press upon him. If it be asked, Why speak of a state of active opposition against God as a being *dead* in sins? the answer is, because in Scripture 'death' does not mean cessation of being, but a condition of separation and alienation from God (Ephesians 4:18)."

The Word of God clearly teaches, then, the total depravity of man, his total impotence and his total responsibility.

If there should come into the heart of an individual any concern as to whether he were included in the divine plan, we may say to him that the general course of Scripture teaching authorizes us to believe that no such concern would ever arise in the heart of anyone who has not been chosen of God. God never plows a field He does not intend to plant. "The preaching of the cross is to them that perish foolishness" (I Corinthians 1:18). If you who read these lines contemplate the cross of Christ as God's eternal answer to the problems raised by the invisible war, and if you see that He proclaims that He is satisfied with the death of His Son instead of your death as the deserving sinner, and if you cast yourself utterly upon that redemption provided in the Saviour, you can know, beyond all doubt, that the preaching of the cross is to you "the power of God." To those who thus accept God's declaration of satisfaction with Christ as covering their every need we may declare, as God has given to every child of God to proclaim to those who are following in the same path of belief: Your sins are no longer retained; your sins are remitted. Be assured of your divinely given position and enter in, to possess the blessings that go with your inheritance.

15 : *Satan's Organization*

THERE are certain phases of the invisible war that can be understood only if we first have a knowledge of some of the opposing forces and the nature of their organization. The Word of God is the revelation of truth, and it contains the revelation of truth concerning the vast host of adversaries in this war that are invisible to our eyes, but which play a definite part in our history and in our lives. These beings, some of whom are faithful to God and some of whom are in rebellion, are commonly known as angelic beings.

MESSENGERS

We have pointed out earlier that the basic meaning of the original word for angel is "messenger." The Oxford English Dictionary has several definitions of the word "angel," two of which may be set down for our guidance: "A ministering spirit or divine messenger; one of an order of spiritual beings superior to man in power and intelligence, who . . . are the attendants and messengers of the Deity . . .

"From the literal sense of the Greek *angelos:*

"Any messenger of God, as a prophet, or preacher. A Hellenism of the Bible and theological writers; sometimes an affected literalism of translation."

This literalism of translation has given us the word in English, for the word "angel" is not really a translation but a transliteration. If the word had always been rendered by its true English equivalent, it would be found in our Bibles as the word "messenger." When we understand this it makes no difference that the Lord Jesus is identified as "the angel of the LORD," or that the pastors of the seven churches of Asia are called "angels."

We will have a more complete idea of the word if we take the second dictionary definition and change it to make it read: "Any messenger of God, as a prophet, or preacher, *or even Jesus Christ as well*

127

as the spiritual beings mentioned under the first definitions." With this
idea in mind we can proceed to study the orders of spiritual beings superior to man in power and intelligence, and differing from each other
in the same way.

<h2 style="text-align:center">HIERARCHIES</h2>

Earlier we likened these varied ranks to the gradations of an army.
Perhaps it would be even better to describe the comparison in the religious world. In the Roman Catholic system the various ranks include
deacons, archdeacons, bishops, archbishops, cardinals, and the Pope. It
is common today to speak of such a gradation of ecclesiastical dignities as
a hierarchy, but this is a young word, as words go, not having been used
for such a purpose until the seventeenth century. Three hundred years
earlier we find Wyclif using the word to describe "the three hierarchies"
of the angels. This is an allusion to the fourth century work attributed to
Dionysius the Areopagite, who divided the heavenly beings into three
hierarchies, each of which was supposed to contain three choirs or
orders. The highest of these hierarchies was composed of the cherubim,
the seraphim, and the thrones; the second included dominions, virtues,
and powers; the third contained the others mentioned in Scripture, principalities, archangels and angels.

There is certainly some part of imagination in Dionysius' division,
although there can be no doubt that all of the words are to be found
in the Bible. A good concordance will lead easily to all of the expressions except "virtues," and this is the old English word which translates
the Greek of a passage that speaks of "the mighty angels" (II Thessalonians 1:7).

<h2 style="text-align:center">A GRADATION OF POWER</h2>

We are not too closely concerned with the writings of the mystics
of the early centuries. The Scriptures, themselves, give us definite warrant, however, for the teaching that there is a gradation of power and
intelligence, and that some beings of every rank have remained faithful to God and that some of every rank have followed Satan in his
rebellion.

Perhaps the simplest way of setting forth the truth is to give a
sketch of the great picture and then to fill in some of the details. For
His own reasons God has not been pleased to give us an etched portrait
with every line finely drawn. But there are enough details that the picture need not be dull and hazy to the spiritual mind.

If we revert to the military illustration, it would appear that angels
of every rank in both camps are constantly at war with each other in
the invisible realm, and that, since there is no question of putting one

of these spirit beings to death, the victory or the defeat is gained by the application of power and the withdrawal of the inferior force. The importance of all this to believers in our day is that it can be demonstrated from the Word of God that the warfare in the invisible realm principally concerns individuals in the human realm.

In the book of the prophecy of Daniel, there is a revelation of truth to the prophet that includes, not merely the truth which he wrote down, but the method by which the truth was communicated to him through an angelic messenger. We are not here concerned with the prophecy, but we are concerned with the incidental teaching concerning the power and might of the messenger when compared to Daniel, the messenger's weakness when compared with another spirit being, and his ultimate triumph by the aid of the intervention of a still mightier spiritual being.

We will take the story out of the mold of the King James Version, for the stately prose of that translation is so familiar to our ears that we sometimes lose some of the shades of meaning because of that familiarity and the archaic speech.

THE ANSWER TO DANIEL'S PRAYER

In the tenth chapter of his prophecy, Daniel tells of the appearance of a messenger of God who came in answer to his prayer. Daniel had been reading the prophecy of Jeremiah, and there was something in it that he did not understand. He prayed for enlightenment and three weeks passed without any sign of an answer to his prayer. Suddenly, on the twenty-first day there appeared a being described in the following terms: "Behold a certain man clothed in linen, whose loins were girded with fine gold of Uphaz. His body also was like the beryl, and his face as the appearance of lightning, and his eyes as lamps of fire, and his arms and his feet like in colour to polished brass, and the voice of his words like the voice of a multitude" (Daniel 10:5, 6).

This appearance, of course, was for the sake of Daniel's eyes. There is no evidence in Scripture that this is the permanent appearance of the angelic being. On the contrary, we can deduce from several passages the fact that angels do not have bodies in the human sense of the word. The last verse in the first chapter of Hebrews tells us that they are all ministering spirits, sent forth to minister to those who shall be heirs of salvation. The Lord in His Resurrection, showed His hands and His side to the disciples, saying, "Handle me, and see; for a spirit hath not flesh and bones, as ye see me to have" (Luke 24:39). It would seem clear, therefore, that the angels are bodiless, though nonetheless real personalities.

DANIEL'S REACTION

The effect of this appearance on Daniel and his companions was very marked. Daniel alone saw the vision, but the men that were with him, though they did not see the angel, were possessed of great quaking, so that they fled to hide themselves. Daniel says, "Therefore I was left alone, and saw this great vision, and there remained no strength in me: for my comeliness was turned in me into corruption and I retained no strength" (verse 8).

Yet we shall see that this angelic visitant was an angel of low rank. We might say that he was a lieutenant in the forces of God. As soon as he was opposed by a major angel of the forces of Satan, he was stopped at once and could not go on with his mighty ministry in behalf of Daniel until there was an intervention by God Himself, who sent a still higher angel of the faithful ones to relieve the lieutenant from his struggle with superior adverse powers, thus permitting him to complete his mission to Daniel.

The appearance of the angel had caused Daniel to fall into a deep sleep, with his face to the ground. The angel touched the prophet and set him upon his hands and knees and then spoke to him, saying, "O Daniel, a man greatly beloved, understand the words that I speak unto thee, and stand upright: for unto thee am I now sent" (verse 11).

Daniel then stood trembling before him and heard the amazing story. The angel recounted that as soon as Daniel had prayed, twenty-one days before, his prayer had been heard in heaven immediately and he, the lieutenant angel had been sent with the answer. On the way he had to pass through territory guarded by angels that were faithful to Satan. These angels were evidently of the order of the principalities, for they are named the Prince of Persia and the Prince of Greece. It was the first of these two, the angel revealed to Daniel, who had resisted him for twenty-one days, accounting for the delay in the answer to his prayer.

Suddenly one of the mightiest of God's faithful angels appeared on the scene. This was none other than Michael, who is called, in Jude, the "archangel." As soon as this great power joined the combat, the angel of the revelation was permitted to leave to bring the message through to Daniel. The story continues, with the content of the revelation and the impression made on Daniel by the angel, and then tells us that the angel told Daniel his own immediate plans. He was about to return to the scene of the conflict where he had been fighting with the Prince of Persia until Michael had intervened. He was going to take up the conflict there, and another of Satan's angels would enter into the conflict, whether with the angel or with Daniel is not quite clear. This angel was called the Prince of Greece (verse 20).

The introduction of Michael into the story leads us to a further illustration of the principle of domination by imposing the power of higher rank. Michael is described by the angel of revelation as being interested in the special prophecies concerning the Jewish people. The words are: "But I will show thee that which is noted in the scripture of truth: and there is none that holdeth with me in these things, but Michael your prince" (verse 21). Calling Michael "your prince" would be obscure were it not for the fact that later in the same book we find it written that "At that time shall Michael stand up, the great prince which standeth for the children of thy people . . ." (Daniel 12:1). This would lead us to believe that Michael is God's angel in charge of Jewish affairs upon the earth, and that since the Jews are chosen by God for special purposes Michael's position is a very high one. In fact, he is the angel who is called the "archangel." Dionysius speaks of the choir of the archangels, but the Bible gives no warrant for believing that there is more than one archangel.

In the epistle of Jude we read, "Likewise also these filthy dreamers defile the flesh, despise dominion, and speak evil of dignities. Yet Michael, the archangel, when contending with the devil he disputed about the body of Moses, durst not bring against him a railing accusation, but said, The Lord rebuke thee" (Jude 8, 9). Michael is occupied with the task of burying the body of Moses. The book of Deuteronomy tells us of Moses' death and the fact that he was buried by God Himself (Deuteronomy 34:5, 6). Jude tells us that Michael was the messenger of God in this work and that Satan came to interfere with him. The reasons for the conflict are obscure, but we may suppose that they centered in the fact that there was to be something special in the manner of the disposition of the body of Moses since God had planned to raise him from the dead in the time of the Great Tribulation as one of the two witnesses (Revelation 11:3-6). The Pharisees had thus understood the prophecies and questioned both John the Baptist and Jesus to find out if either of them claimed to be Moses.

At all events, Satan interfered with Michael's work, and as Michael was of lower rank than the former chief-of-staff of the host of the Lord, there was nothing that Michael could do to Satan directly. He did not even bring against him a railing accusation because of the great dignity of his position as the anointed cherub. He did have available, however, the power to call upon the Lord directly. This he did and Satan's rebuke came from the Lord Himself (Jude 9).

The display of the forces of Satan, as recorded by Daniel, leads us to believe that the entire globe is organized under principalities, corresponding to earthly governments. If there is a Prince of Persia and a Prince of Greece, we may not be astonished if there is a Prince of Russia or a Prince of India, a Prince of Britain and a Prince of the United States. This is not a mere conjecture for it is bluntly stated that earth government is in the hands of Satan. Paul tells the Ephesian believers that it is necessary for them to be clad in the whole armor of God, "for we wrestle not against flesh and blood, but against principalities, against powers, against the rulers of the darkness of this world, against spiritual wickedness in high places" (Ephesians 6:12). Satan may even have corporals in charge of municipal affairs.

We must not think that the number of spirit beings who followed Satan in his rebellion is any small one. At Gadara the Lord confronted the poor man who was possessed by the powers of Satan. He called upon the evil force to declare itself by name and the evil spirit answered, "My name is Legion: for we are many" (Mark 5:9). If we may put any stress on the meaning of the name it is highly significant to note that in the time of Augustus a Roman legion counted 6,100 foot soldiers and 726 horsemen.

But though Satan is powerful, God is all powerful. The Lord Jesus pointed out that He could pray to the Father who would immediately give Him more than twelve legions of angels (Matthew 26:53). And if He so desired He would not have to confine Himself to angels who had been long in His service. Our God is the Creator, and He who could of stones raise up children to Abraham (Matthew 3:9) could with a single word call into being fresh multitudes of yet uncreated hosts.

16 : *Satan's Organization*
(CONTINUED)

WE may be sure of the fact that the Lord's forces have never been outnumbered at any moment unless the all-wise Creator had a definite purpose in permitting Satan to gain a temporary advantage in order better to teach him and the watching universe the utter impotence of any will outside the divine will. Satan may do his very best with the forces he has under his control, but we can be sure that the end result is discomfiture, frustration, defeat and rout. He will never have his diet of dust mingled with any sweetness.

Those who think the devil is gaining victory are like the servant of Elisha. In one of the leading magazines, there was an article on limerick poetry which included the following example:

> God's plan made a hopeful beginning,
> But man spoiled his chances by sinning.
> We trust that the story
> Will end in God's glory,
> But, at present, the other side's winning.

For some people this may raise a wry smile at the supposed humor of the man who wrote it, but his ignorance of the spiritual truth like the ignorance of Elisha's servant, causes real pity from those who know. Ignorance of the plan of God leads to ignorance of the omniscience and the omnipotence of God.

BEN-HADAD AND ELISHA

One of the most striking stories in the Word of God is that of the attempt of Ben-Hadad, king of Syria, to defeat the plan of God by destroying His prophet Elisha. The king's enmity had been stirred against Elisha because Elisha was able to know all of the plans which were spoken in the secret bed chamber of the king by the leaders of his army. When the king became aware that he was being consistently outwitted in the field, he angrily asked his counselors which one of them was a traitor. They told him the truth, that their secret conversations were

133

communicated to Elisha (probably by angels), and Elisha, in turn, communicated them to the king of Israel, enabling him to escape from the greatly superior forces of the enemy. When Ben-Hadad learned this, he decided to send an expedition against Elisha, to take him prisoner. It is worthwhile to notice, in passing, that a single man of God, yielded to God, can become so important in the invisible warfare that the earthly enemy king finds it worthwhile to send an army against him, and that, in the spiritual realm, a great number of fallen angels will be deployed by the prince of this world, in order to frustrate the plan of God.

The army of Ben-Hadad reach the little valley of Dothan in the middle of the night, having learned that the prophet of God was living there at the moment. The troops were thrown about the village, leaving no loophole for human escape. At the dawn, when the servant of Elisha went out to begin his daily tasks, he saw the indications of the enemy force, round about on all sides and rushed back into the presence of his master with words of warning and inquiries of consternation and doubt. "Alas, my master! how shall we do?" (II Kings 6:15) is the phrase which God has recorded to reveal the state of his mind.

Elisha's Answer

The answer of Elisha is a verse of very great importance to us in our study. "Fear not," said Elisha, "for they that be with us are more than they that be with them" (verse 16). "They," "us," "they," and "them," are the four words which line up all of the forces, earthly and supernatural, and calculate the extent of the powers that oppose each other on the field of battle. The human alignment can be counted. The "us" refers to Elisha and his servant, just two people. The "them" is indicated for us in the narrative with the statement that Ben-Hadad, on hearing that Elisha was in Dothan, "sent thither horses, and chariots, and a great host: and they came by night and compassed the city about."

Ordinarily the human eye cannot see the spiritual forces that are arrayed in the invisible realm. The eye of faith can look into the Word of God and know the truth of the power of the Lord we serve, and can be sure that nothing can ever touch us unless it has passed through the will of God. We can be sure that though there may be wisdom on the other side, omniscience is on our side alone. We may be sure that though we find an enemy to be potent, we can find that our God alone is omnipotent. We deal with the only Being in the universe who has never made a mistake, who has never been astonished, who has never been caught at a disadvantage, who has never been surprised at a superior force or strategem. This is the thought that is in the mind of the worshiper when he sings, "The Lord is high above all nations, and his glory above the heavens. Who is like unto the Lord our God, who dwelleth on high" (Psalm 113:4, 5).

THE HOSTS OF HEAVEN VISIBLE

Elisha knew that the forces of God were greater than the Satanic forces that watched over Ben-Hadad. Satan could not muster enough to make his group of angelic powers more than "they" that were with Elisha. The prophet prayed and asked the Lord to open the eyes of his servant. It would spoil the grandeur of the vision to tell it in any other words than those which have been given us by God Himself. The simplicity of the phrase, thrown up against the glory of the fact, gives us to see something more than a picture of the imagination. For "the Lord opened the eyes of the young man; and he saw: and, behold, the mountain was full of horses and chariots of fire round about Elisha" (II Kings 6:17).

The writer once passed by Dothan. It lies in a little valley to the east of the road that runs south from Galilee through Samaria. We stopped there and walked over the brown fields toward the mound that possibly was the site of the ancient town. The hills round about were bare and dry in the summer sun, and there was no movement save the shimmering air that rose from the parched earth. We sat in the shade under a scrawny tree that furnished a little shelter from the hot sun and read portions of the story of Elisha, including the one we have just told. We could well imagine the startled servant coming out in the morning and, walking toward the well to draw some water, seeing the glint of fresh morning light on the shields of the Syrian soldiers. But we closed our eyes to see the mountain full of horses and chariots of fire, and, since we live in an age when God has ordered our standard to be faith and not sight, we saw more than the angelic hosts that do God's bidding on our behalf. Certainly, it is true, there are guardian angels that protect us from the onslaughts of the enemy. Certainly, it is true, that the faithful angels are the servants of us, who are the heirs of salvation. Certainly, it is true, that they that are with us are more than they that are with any foe or combination of foes. But that day, as we thought of these things we were reminded of an even greater verse that has the same alignment of pronouns covering the earthly warfare and the heavenly.

THE HOLY SPIRIT IN US

We on this side of the cross have something far greater than Elisha ever had. There is that which transcends sighted vision of invisible things. The Lord told His own disciples that the Holy Spirit dwelt with them, but that the day would come when He would dwell in them (John

14:17). Having a member of the Godhead come to take up His abode within us puts us on a spiritual plane above that which was known to men of the Old Testament. The Lord Jesus Christ said that John the Baptist was no whit behind Moses, Elijah, Elisha, or any of the other mighty men upon whom the Spirit had come; of all that had preceded him there was not a greater than John the Baptist (Matthew 11:11). And we have the word of our Lord that the least and lowliest from the time of the coming of the Holy Spirit to dwell within, would be considered in God's sight, greater than John the Baptist because of the presence of the Holy Spirit within.

It is in the light of this great fact that the New Testament writer lines up the invisible forces to show us the fullness of the supply that is available to us. "Ye are of God, little children," the believers are told, "and have overcome them: because greater is he that is in you, than he that is in the world" (I John 4:4). Let us remember this when we face difficulty or feel that the forces that are against us are more than we can meet. "He," "you," "he," "the world," are the four words which draw the line of demarcation, ranging all of the forces, earthly and spiritual, and calculating the extent of the powers that oppose each other on the field of battle. Even more, for not only are there horses and chariots of fire round about Elisha of old and the Elishas of this age, but there are the angelic hosts for even the humble servants of Elisha. Still more it is our privilege to fly the flag of joy in our lives every day, as the flag is displayed in a kingdom on whatever castle or palace the king is using at the moment, for we have not merely angels with us but the King of kings, Himself, is in residence.

Then what do we care though Satan's organization is close-knit and widespread? Only the mind of unbelief can think, even for a moment, that at present Satan's side is winning. "We know that an idol is nothing in the world, and that there is none other God but one. For though there be that are called gods, whether in heaven or in earth (as there be gods many, and lords many,) but to us there is but one God, the Father, of whom are all things, and we in him; and one Lord Jesus Christ, by whom are all things, and we by him" (I Corinthians 8:4-6).

17 : *The Battle of the Soul*

NOT even modern wars are fought with great intensity at every moment. World War II had preliminary months that were called "the phony war." The interval between World War II and the inevitable World War III has been called "the cold war." From the human point of view, it may appear that there are similar phases of relaxation of intensity in the invisible war. But in this realm as in the realm of character, "Man looketh upon the outward appearance." There is no truce in the invisible war. There is no armistice in the invisible war. What may appear to be only a skirmish may in reality be a major engagement. The importance of a spiritual battle is not to be measured by the number of troops engaged but by the principles involved and, above all, by the exhibition of another phase of the impotence of any will that is not the will of God.

There are hundreds of millions of battles being fought every day in the invisible war. The field of each battle is the heart of man. In order to comprehend the true nature of the warfare, we must dissipate one or two false ideas that have become almost a part of the framework of human thinking, and which have been planted and fostered by Satan. In our western civilization, which includes the majority of those who are believers in the Lord Jesus Christ, false ideas have been spread through the great secular literature which has grown up about the theme of this conflict. From the point of view of the Bible, these are not only erroneous in their doctrinal teaching but are factually misleading, conducive to low standards of living. How many wrong concepts have been introduced into popular thought through Dante's *Inferno,* Milton's *Paradise Lost,* and Goethe's *Faust!* The principal error is that Satan and God are struggling for man's soul, and that man has the deciding voice in his destiny. Anyone who has been born again knows, if he is honest with his own experience, that the primary decision to believe God's Word about man's own condition and about God's satisfaction

137

with the death of the Lord Jesus Christ came when God entered the Adamic nature of the sinner, making him alive in Christ with a life that was capable of believing. It is a great error to think that faith precedes life; the clear teaching of the Bible is that life precedes faith. Man does not like to believe this because it takes the credit away from man and gives all the glory to God, who has said, "I am Jehovah: that is my name: and my glory will I not give to another . . ." (Isaiah 42:8).

The idea that life follows faith comes partly from a misunderstanding of the passage in John's gospel: "Verily, verily, I say unto you, He that heareth my word, and believeth on him that sent me, hath everlasting life, and shall not come into condemnation: but is passed from death into life" (John 5:24). Most readers take this to mean that the life is a consequence of the belief, as though the passage could be paraphrased: "If you hear My Word and believe on Him that sent Me, you will obtain everlasting life." Many sentences in English are capable of almost opposite interpretations, and this is one such sentence. A good example of double interpretation is taken from one of the national picture magazines. The story concerned the daughter of a former President of the United States who, the article stated, had been exploited by an ambitious music teacher and a business manager with few scruples. The concert tour had turned out badly. The girl had a nice parlor voice but not one of concert caliber. The article ended: "It could not have happened to a nicer girl." In common American speech that means that the girl was very, very nice, and that it was unfortunate that she was the victim of such exploitation. This was the sense in which the magazine meant the line. In good English the sentence also could mean that if the girl had been nicer, such a thing would not have happened to her.

Let us parallel the sentence in John to bring out its real meaning. Imagine a battlefield over which troops are advancing under heavy fire. They flatten themselves to the ground and hold their prone position until the enemy artillery is silenced. For the sake of our example, we will imagine that all of the soldiers are either dead, or alive and unwounded. When the command to advance is given, he that gets up and walks has life. Does that mean that life is given to the soldiers who get up and walk, or that the soldiers who possess life manifest it by getting up and walking? It is obvious that there can be only the latter meaning. This is the exact meaning of the passage in the fourth gospel. "He that hears my word and believes on him that sent me, does so because he has eternal life planted within him." The hearing and believing are the marks of the existence of the new life of God implanted within the individual.

When this is understood, we can realize that there is no struggle between God and Satan for the possession of man's soul. God is irresistible, and everything that He has planned will come to pass. Satan can never, under any circumstance, frustrate the grace of God. What God has promised He will perform. God promised Christ before the foundation of the world that He would give to Christ the whole body of those who had been thus chosen in eternity, and Christ Himself declared: "All that the Father giveth me shall come to me, and him that cometh to me I will in no wise cast out" (John 6:37).

In *Faust* Satan has Goethe advance the idea that a man can sell his soul to the devil. I like to counterbalance that story with one written by a far greater German, Martin Luther. Luther once had a servant who left him in anger at the time a dinner was being served. Years later when the servant was dying, Luther went to see her. She was weeping and said, "Oh, Doctor, I sold my soul to the devil the day I walked out of your house in a temper." Luther answered her, "Suppose you had signed a bill of sale while you were working for me, agreeing to sell one of my children as a slave. Would that agreement have any value?" The poor woman answered, "Of course not. I would have no right to sell one of your children." Luther then pointed out that she had become a child of God years before and that she was not her own but had been bought with the price of the blood of Jesus Christ. She had no right whatsoever in the eternal disposition of her soul. By her choices, after she had been regenerated, she could set the course of her daily life but not the course of her eternal life. By her choices she could establish her rewards in heaven but not her entrance into heaven.

The battle between the Lord and Satan in the soul of man cannot be over the possession of the soul. The battle is within the soul of the redeemed one as to whether he will honor and glorify God or whether he will live to his own ends. There are two stories in the Bible which indicate that sometimes God Himself chooses the field of battle, as with Job, and that sometimes Satan ventures to select the scene of the struggle as with Peter.

We are going to retell part of the story of Job, taking it in the same order in which it is set forth in the Bible. It may appear without outline, but life is sometimes disjointed, and episodes occur that seem to have no connection with what precedes and what follows. As we tell this story there will be one thread through it all: The revelation of truths which give us understanding of the spiritual forces engaged in the invisible war and which explain to us much that would otherwise be incomprehensible in our daily living. Some years ago, when I was a university student in France, one of the professors of history, knowing my Christian position, said: "Ah, Monsieur, if only a scholar had had the choice of materials for your Bible! What a different book it would be! All those endless genealogies of Jewish scoundrels, and forty chapters given to an unfortunate farmer who had a bad case of boils! If only we had that number of pages on the methods used by the Pharaohs to collect their taxes — that would be something of value!"

There is little use in argument with a mind that holds such a perspective; though I gave him the correct answer, there was seemingly no impression made upon the learned man. The genealogies of the Old Testament are of paramount importance in human history because they cover the ancestry of the Lord Jesus Christ in His humanity and concern the people which God has chosen to be the ultimate administrators of the world. Job's boils are of importance because they were raised by Satan in the midst of a direct conflict with the Lord of all the universe. They were the result of Satan's attempt to prove to the watching angelic host that God was unable to satisfy a human soul with spiritual things when the material things were taken away.

We will not spend any time discussing the so-called "problem of the book of Job." We do not believe it is a parable or an allegory. We believe that it is as literally history as is the story of the battle of Guadalcanal. The battle for that island in the midst of the war against Japan is not without its parallelism with the battle of Job. Japan, by her attack on Pearl Harbor, had declared war on America. The Japanese thought that they were secure behind the vast reaches of the ocean and the many thousands of pin-point islands upon which they had put a skeleton force for defense. They thought that we would have to advance in a frontal attack, island by island, on their terms. But our General Staff, surveying the situation, said in effect, that they did not choose to fight the war on the terms of Japanese strategy, but that they would make their own plans as to where and when the attacks would fall.

The Japanese waited, on the defensive, not knowing where the attack would fall. Suddenly, the men on the island of Guadalcanal heard the thunder of artillery and the drone of airplanes. Shells and bombs began to explode in their positions and the battle of Guadalcanal was on. Of all the millions of people in America, only a few had ever heard of the name of the island before the newspapers announced the attack. Maps had to be published with arrows pointing to the spot in order that people might get a general idea of where it lay. To some, even to some who had boys fighting in the occupation, it was just some place that was a very long distance away, and they had no point of reference for location or comparison. They even took the pronunciation of the name from the radio announcers. The island got its fame from the fact that our General Staff made the sovereign choice to do battle there.

It is on precisely the same grounds that the name of Job has its place in history. There are thousands of islands larger and better known than Guadalcanal. There were thousands of human beings with more claim to fame than Job. He was not a monarch upon a throne. He was not a Pharaoh or a Nebuchadnezzar. He was a farmer with a stock inventory that may have been large for the time and the section, but which would be considered a second-rate operation by the great farmers of the plains and the pampas of the world today. The man had seven sons and three daughters. His stock consisted of seven thousand sheep, three thousand camels, five hundred yoke of oxen, and five hundred she asses. There were a number of servants to take care of the animals and the household. How does the personal story of a man who never commanded an army, who, to our knowledge, never wrote a word, who never left a mark in art or architecture, who never made a law or a statute, who never achieved greatness as measured by human standards – how does his story occupy such a large place in Biblical history? The answer is that the Lord God Almighty, surveying all the members of the human race, as the General Staff surveyed the islands of the ocean, said, "Job shall be the next battlefield in the invisible war. All of the forces of the enemy will be permitted to hurl themselves against this man. I will provide him with strength and sustain him in sorrow and disaster. It shall be seen by men, angels, and demons that spiritual life from the throne of heaven is sufficient to attract a soul. In a world where prosperity and luxury are the aims of most effort, where personal health and happiness is the object of most prayers, where the companionship of loved ones is the highest fellowship, I will permit the enemy to take away the flocks and the herds; I will allow his sons and daughters to die; I will suffer his body to be smitten by plague and wracked with pain; I will let his wife turn from him and take the side of the enemy; I will send his friends to give him the counsel of despair. He will be brought to the nadir of human desolation. Yet he will sit, intransigent, uncompromising, unhesitating, with his eyes filled with eternal things and his mind aware of realities that are beyond the scope of human vision. He will understand that there is no will that can compete with the will of God. And, as a result of this battle, not only will he be vindicated in his steadfast resolution, but also there shall be comfort for thousands of thousands of souls throughout the coming centuries, and Satan will have a large mouthful of dust for his pains."

"And so it came to pass." Men read those words, and they may have no more than a literary effect upon their minds. But they mean that, suddenly, in the midst of a calm, ordered, and peaceful life, all the forces of Satan broke loose. War, banditry, death, disease, contentiousness, strife and debate came flooding into the life of a man who was admittedly upright and who had done nothing specific that would deserve such strokes if they came as punishment or chastisement.

The sufferings of Job began not only by the permission of God but by the direction of God. In the opening verses of the Book of Job, the court of heaven is revealed to us with all of the angelic hosts present, even the fallen ones, for Satan was there among them. The Lord called Satan to account for his movements. "Whence comest thou?" was the question to which the fallen prince answered: "From going to and fro in the earth, and walking up and down in it" (Job 1:7). This would seem to be an honest enough answer, even suggesting that Satan was telling God how industrious and active he was, perhaps even suggesting that he was active in God's behalf. There has been a disagreement between two Bible commentators, Pember and Jennings, as to the nature of the original work of Satan. Pember wrote that Lucifer had been occupied before the fall with the government of the universe for God. Jennings, asserting that this was wrong, taught that Lucifer had been occupied with setting forth the righteousness of God, being the anointed cherub that covered the throne of God. Jennings holds that Satan's words in the first chapter of Job indicate that this malignant being was still pretending before God to be actively interested in the glory of the Creator and that his deepest wish was to protect that glory from the evil in Job's heart. Perhaps the difficulty between these two writers is simply that neither saw the whole picture, neither realized that both were right indeed and that Satan was even more than either of them had seen. Lucifer, as we have shown in an earlier chapter, was in a threefold office for God. He was prophet, priest and king. God no longer spoke through Satan — he had forever lost the office of prophet. He knew, however, that he still possessed the office of government, Prince of this world, and he could well have pretended at this moment that he was busily occupied with the office of priest, and that in this capacity he was revealing to God that the latter had been deceived with Job. It can well be imagined that the father of lies would still seek to deceive God if he could. If he could make the lie stick he would be freed from a difficult position into which he had been maneuvered by the integrity of Job and the failure of all the attacks on that righteous man.

At all events, Satan, going to and fro in the earth, had received the reports of all his minions through the various orders of his hierarchy.

His subordinates had evidently brought to his attention the existence of this man, Job, who could not be turned aside by any of their seductive arts. Here was a man whose soul they had been unable to move by the attractive incentives of worldly power, whose body they had been unable to lure by the ravishing enticements of the flesh, and whose spirit they had been unable to flatter to a pride that would have dethroned God from the worship rightfully His due. Job had indeed been a very good man, and he was able to point to his goodness in his later discussions with the comforters who came to advise him in his distress. He was able to say of public opinion with respect to himself: "The young men saw me, and hid themselves: and the aged arose, and stood up. The princes refrained talking, and laid their hand on their mouth. The nobles held their peace, and their tongue cleaved to the roof of their mouth. When the ear heard me, then it blessed me; and when the eye saw me, it gave witness to me: because I delivered the poor that cried, and the fatherless, and him that had none to help him. The blessing of him that was ready to perish came upon me: and I caused the widow's heart to sing for joy. . . . I was eyes to the blind, and feet was I to the lame. I was a father to the poor: and the cause which I knew not I searched out. And I brake the jaws of the wicked, and plucked the spoil out of his teeth" (Job 29:8-17).

It is no wonder that Satan was aggrieved that such a righteous man should live and move in the midst of his principality. His hatred against Job must have mounted at every good deed that Job accomplished and at every wicked deed that Job blocked. Thus, when the Lord asked Satan if he had considered Job, whom He ennobled with the title "My Servant," Satan knew only too well the nature of the humiliation that was now before him. It may even be possible that this sentence hides a great irony. If Satan had been attacking Job and if Job had been remaining steadfast, all heaven, which rejoices over the conversion of one sinner, must have rejoiced at the uprightness of this steadfast soul who stood unmoved in the midst of the opposing forces that would have struck him down could they have reached him.

When God mentioned the name of Job, Satan lashed out with an answer which contains one of the most glorious truths of the Bible: God's hedge about the believer. When the father of lies is forced to admit a truth that is going to bring sublime comfort and strength to weary souls who, for a little while, have become tired with the struggle for life, we may be sure not only that it tore him but also that such an admission of defeat will contain truth that is pertinent to our victory and our strengthening. "Does Job fear God for naught?" he cried. "Hast not thou made a hedge about him, and about his house, and about all that he hath on every side?"

This answer shows the extent of Satan's onslaught. It reveals that Satan had been attacking Job personally, that he had been attacking him through his family, that he had been attacking him through his possessions and that this attack had been from every possible angle and with every possible device known to Satan. But the answer reveals much more than this. In admitting that there was a hedge about Job, Satan admits that he has tried to reach Job and has failed repeatedly. He reveals that he hates upright men and that he would strike through to the believer if he could, but that he cannot because of the protective love of God that overshadows all of those who have put their trust in His saving grace. If Satan could only pass the hedge! But he admits that he cannot. There was a barrier of cloud between the children of Israel and the armies of Pharaoh. That which was light to the people of God was darkness to the enemy. That which is a defense to us is an obstacle to Satan. He would strike at us if he could. His arm is long enough but God intervenes. He would pierce us with his fiery darts, but God is our shield and our buckler, our strong defense and our high tower. In the Psalms, God tells us these truths in song. In the history of Job, Satan confesses them. How safe we are! It is because of this principle that "we know that all things work together for good to them that love God, to them that are the called according to His purpose" (Romans 8:28).

Satan continued to answer God with a subtle and evil attack against Job. Satan sought to put Job in the wrong and to show that he himself was the protagonist of the righteousness of God. It might be paraphrased: "Here you have a creature that seemingly is going about doing good, and everyone thinks he is the last word in goodness. But I know him down underneath and in reality he is an arrant *hypocrite*. He is good simply because he is healthy and wealthy. If you would just prick him with calamity, all of that insipid righteousness would ooze out, and You would see him for what he really is. He would curse You to Your face if he were deflated and the real core of his being allowed to become evident."

Having already experienced defeat at the hands of Job, Satan was now to know the full bitterness of complete rout. He should have realized that the God of the hedge, the God who had been taking care of Job, would continue that loving care. He was evidently driven on by that hatred which always motivates Satan both against those who refuse to yield him allegiance in his attempt to organize and rule the earth and against those who turn from the visible and tangible prizes of this earth to gaze upon the invisible though no less real delights that belong to those who prefer the unseen because it pertains to the only true God.

Carried on by his vindictive hostility, Satan overreached himself. A boxer who has been struck by a blow that excites his anger and who seeks to retaliate with a destructive thrust that will finish his opponent, sometimes succeeds only in throwing himself off balance and in opening up his defenses for his own defeat. Thus Satan, forced on by his arrogant pride and his envious malice, challenged God to take away Job's possessions by claiming that the result would be a curse from the creature upon the Creator.

The Lord answered with pointed brevity. He would take the hedge down, but with a definite limitation. Satan had permission to do what he pleased with the family and possessions of Job. But he was rigorously forbidden to touch Job himself.

18 : *The Battle of the Soul*
(CONTINUED)

W HAT comfort there is for the believer when the attacks rise against him in his life, his family, his business, and his other associations, to know that God sees the end from the beginning and is allowing it for His own glory and the believer's good! Satan can do what he pleases with those who are not of the family of God, but God's own may not be touched without permission. Those who are outside the faith are taken captive by the devil at his will (II Timothy 2:26). Even more than this, we have in the story of the Gadarene maniac the evidence that the demons could not even touch the swine which were feeding at the top of the hill until the Lord had given permission (Luke 8:32, 33). The scene indicates the panting desire of the demons who were about to be cast out of the maniac to possess some sort of body, even if it were only the body of a pig. But even the animal creation is safe from Satan, and in the instance cited, only the specific permission of the Lord allowed them to enter the swine which then ran headlong down the steep place into the sea.

SATAN'S POWER LIMITED

In the light of these truths how the words of the Lord to Satan concerning the limitations of the attack against the believer take on renewed force. There has gone forth from the throne of God a decree which forbids our enemy to move against us in any way that is outside the plan of the Father. How safe we are! No weapon that is formed against us shall prosper (Isaiah 54:17).

Now the full force of Satan's spite flares forth against Job. Soldiers pillage. Servants are murdered. Goods are stolen. Winds blow. Lightning strikes. Houses fall. Children die. These are the acts of Satan. Today men call such things "acts of God," and insurance companies use these very words in writing policies designed to protect us from the losses involved in such calamities which they, not knowing the truth,

146

attribute to an inscrutable Creator. He, who suggested to Eve in the garden of Eden that God was unkind and would keep from them the joys and privileges that would come from eating the forbidden fruit, has sold to many of the human race the idea that calamities and disasters are all from God. God is the Creator of the universe, and every force of nature within the universe has been created by God and is subject to His complete control. But there can be no doubt that Satan is able to use some of these forces and that he does use them to his ends. He uses them against the unregenerate at his own whim, and he uses them against the children of God whenever the Lord takes down the hedge and permits him to hurl their force against the believer. In this sense they are acts of God for a believer but they are always acts of the devil for the unsaved.

SORROWFUL YET REJOICING

Job stood fast. Satan's thrust was parried. The blow fell, but faith knew how to ward off its worst effects. The attack reached the emotions, as Job mourned for his children; but the blow did not wound his spirit, for that was fortified in the Lord; and Job lay in his mourning, sorrowful for his loss yet rejoicing in the Lord (cf. II Corinthians 6:10). "Job arose, and rent his mantle, and shaved his head, and fell down upon the ground, and worshipped. And said, Naked came I out of my mother's womb, and naked shall I return thither; the Lord gave, and the Lord hath taken away; blessed be the name of the Lord" (Job 1:20, 21).

There is something almost majestic in the calm deliberation of this aggrieved saint, who proceeds methodically with the physical preparation of the outward signs of mourning. There was no wild outcry of wailing. There certainly was no cursing of God. If we can read between the lines, we can almost hear him say to the servant: "Bring me some water and soap, and bring my razor, that I may shave my head." As the three remaining servants stood by in wonderment, his hand did not tremble as he brought the sharp instrument to his head. Satan's children may use the razor to cut their throats when they have been bereft of loved ones and despoiled of property, because this has been their life and they now have nothing left to live for. But Job continues his task; the locks fall from his head, and the tears fall within his heart and are all gathered in God's bottle (Psalm 56:8). The Scripture adds that in all this trouble Job sinned not, nor did he charge God with injustice.

Here is faith triumphant. Job had no thought of any personal proprietary rights either in children or in possessions. He recognized that everything possessed in life was a trust from God. The Lord who had given to him had a right to take from him if He so desired.

God is the only being in the universe who knows the end from the beginning, and His perspective is that of perfection. Job believed this and so he was able to worship God.

SATAN'S REPORT

As the roar of guns on Guadalcanal caused an echo all over the world, and a nation went about its work with one eye on the headlines and one ear on the news reports, and a prayer in the heart for sons and brothers fighting in a far island, so heaven was interested in the conflict that was raging within and about Job. Once more God convened heaven's court, and the angel hosts were present. Again Satan was singled out and required to bring in a report on his doings. This time his statement that he had been going to and fro in the earth and walking up and down in it seems evasive and face-saving. He had been in Job's backyard, and all heaven knew it. He had had some dust on earth, but he was to eat more in the sight of all heaven.

Once more the direct question is asked about Job. This time the answer is a snarl and a lie. The first time he had spoken some truth. This time he dares to lie directly to God. This is, in itself, an indication of Satan's character. Most lies are told when there is a possible chance that the one to whom the lie is told may be deceived. There is a momentary advantage to be gained for the liar by his deception. But here is a lie to God, who is light and in whom dwelleth no darkness at all. "Skin for skin, yea, all that a man hath will he give for his life. But put forth thine hand now, and touch his bone and his flesh, and he will curse thee to thy face" (2:4, 5).

The annals of man are filled with stories of men who have given life away cheaply, flippantly, pointlessly. There is no coin of stupidity and shallowness that has not been accepted by man in exchange for life. Though it may seem preposterous and irrational, men have given life for the smile of a worthless woman who cared nothing for them. Though it may seem foolish and absurd, men have given life for the bravado of a dare. There were no tabloids at the time of Job to record the prattle about such deeds of oddity, yet they must have been known since we find a record of Lamech, who boasts, "I have slain a young man who did no more than wound me. I have killed a fellow who did nothing but hurt me. If God thinks that he has to go around protecting Cain by a mark on him to keep someone from hurting him, he doesn't have to worry about me. If he would avenge Cain sevenfold, I will avenge myself seventy and sevenfold" (Genesis 4:23, 24). Such men take or give life without a thought. The lie, then, has in it more of effrontery than deceit.

SATAN'S FOLLY REVEALED

The plan of God is to lead this foe to reveal his own folly. Satan is mighty from our point of view but insignificant from that of heaven. He is allowed to make declarations before the court of heaven that reveal the hollowness of his pretension and to commit actions before men that show the evil of his purpose. Furthermore, he who had pretended to an ability to rule the universe without God is to display his intrinsic weakness when faced by a being even lower than the lowliest angel. It is to be demonstrated that a frail child of Adam, availing himself of the spiritual power provided by a loving God, is mightier than the highest of all created beings.

Again the Lord answers with brevity: "Behold, he is in thine hand; but save his life" (2:6). Now Satan has permission to touch Job, but not to the point of death. Here, again, we see some of the power possessed by Satan. He has the power to bring disease and suffering upon man, and in some cases, to end his life on earth. What light this throws on some of the tales of wonder that are published from time to time by the false religions of earth! Satan has the power to put his hand on an unsaved individual and to make him ill; he then has the power to take his hand from that individual, thus effecting a cure, to the glory, perhaps, of either a Mary Baker Eddy of New England or of a Mary of Lourdes. We should never forget that all religion in the world that does not accept fully the person and work of the Lord Jesus is Satanic religion. The New Testament significantly sets forth the fact that spirits controlled by Satan are behind the shrines of the earth religions, and that all prayer that is made at these shrines is prayer to Satan and that all worship offered there is garnered by him (I Corinthians 10: 19, 20).

Once more the full force of Satan's spite flares forth against Job. "Satan smote Job with sore boils from the sole of his foot unto his crown." But again Job stood fast, parrying the thrust of Satan. The blow fell, but faith knew how to ward off its worst effects. It did not wound Job's spirit, for that was resting quietly in the Lord. "He took him a potsherd to scrape himself withal; and he sat down among the ashes." There may be a time when physical pain comes almost as a release from the greater sufferings of the mind and heart. Certainly Satan misplayed his strategy, for a mind that had suffered the loss of ten children in a day's calamity would find a good case of boils somewhat in the nature of an opiate.

At this point, Satan attacked with something much worse than boils — Job's wife turned against him. Totally failing to comprehend what was happening to him, like Elisha's servant who saw the soldiers but did not see the angels, this companion of his life and mother of his children said to her husband, "Dost thou still retain thine integrity? curse God, and die." How can we account for this defection? According to all the teaching of Scriptures, we must credit it either to the separate origination of this evil within Job's wife as a child of Adam or to the prompting of Satan and her willing compliance therewith. In either case it is of Satan.

This woman falls far short of the task that was given to her by God in her position as a wife. Woman was originally given to man as a help fit for his use. Failure to give him comfort and strength in the time of his great spiritual need, which was now compounded by a physical need, was treason since this was her one reason for existence upon the earth. A woman should be like a warm hearth fire by which a man, when he has labored in the cold world, may come in and warm himself before going out once again to his labor. For her to have been passive in the time of his need would have been for the fire to die down to ashes. For her to speak positively against him was for the fire to flare up and burn him. She was a tool of Satan. Job had the courage to speak to her from the depths of his misery: "Thou speakest as one of the foolish women speaketh." The term is one that is used for insanity. He continued with a rebuke that was at the same time a magnificent expression of faith. He asked, "What? Shall we receive good at the hand of God, and shall we not receive evil?"

Here was a declaration of Job's faith in God's sovereign right to do with His creature as it pleases Him. It was the expression of faith in the fact that the Father has never made a mistake. The Lord knows what He is doing. Since He is omniscient and omnipotent, and since His name is love, it must follow in any kind of logic that whatever He does is the best that could possibly be done in any set of circumstances. Job knew this, and so he was just as ready to accept disaster at the hand of the Lord as he was ready to accept the rich blessings which he had known for so many years. In all this Job did not sin with his lips.

The next phase of the battle, which is the longest in the record of the fight, may be treated briefly. Job was visited by friends who attempted to meet his need with worldly logic. Their idea was that there must be a spiritual cause back of every adversity and that Job's condition was *prima facie* evidence that he must have offended God. This idea dominated the Middle Ages and it is still current in much of the thinking of the spiritually untaught today. There was some excuse for Job's comforters in that they lived before the major part of the Bible was written. There is no excuse for those that have lived since. The Lord Jesus answered the disciples when they asked whether the calamity of the man born blind was caused by his own sin or that of his parents by a categorical, "Neither hath this man sinned, nor his parents; but that the works of God should be made manifest in him" (John 9:3). Here was a New Testament Job, chosen to suffer blindness from birth, that he might be a field of battle in the invisible war. The glory of God would be manifest in Him, and Satan's impotence would be further displayed.

When the last of Job's comforters had spoken, the Lord appeared to Job in order to end the battle that had been raging about him and within him. The opening words of His message were words that repudiated their thesis: "Who is this that darkeneth counsel by words without knowledge?" (Job 38:2). Never perhaps was so much said in a phrase, and it could well be written on the title page of most of human philosophy. The Christian must disclaim it because God has already done so. It is an illustration of the declaration, "For it is written, I will destroy the wisdom of the wise, and will bring to nothing the understanding of the prudent. Where is the wise? where is the scribe? where is the disputer of this world? hath not God made foolish the wisdom of this world? For after that in the wisdom of God the world by wisdom knew not God, it pleased God by the foolishness of preaching to save them that believe" (I Corinthians 1:19-21).

Job had been right in maintaining his integrity before the comforters. He knew God well enough to know that salvation came from God and not from man. We have no historical statement in the Bible that links Job with any of the prophets to show a contact with the stream of truth that came through the revelation of God about the Saviour, the Lamb, but most certainly Job had such knowledge. He had cried out to his adversaries: "For I know that my redeemer liveth, and that he shall stand at the latter day upon the earth; and though after my skin worms destroy this body, yet in my flesh shall I see God" (19:25, 26). He further knew that God had a definite plan for all His redeemed, and that it was best to be in that plan. He said, speaking from his ulcered condition on the ash heap, "For he performeth the thing that is appointed for me: and many such things are with him" (23:14).

When God revealed Himself to Job, however, there was a great change in his attitude. He who had withstood the philosophers for more than thirty chapters listened in silence when God spoke. Then he answered in one of the great climaxes of human faith: "I have heard of thee by the hearing of the ear: but now mine eye seeth thee. Wherefore I abhor myself, and repent in dust and ashes" (42:5, 6).

Then the Lord showed His wrath against the philosophers and ordered them to bring a blood sacrifice. Finally, a most moving incident is recorded. Job prayed for these men who, in the midst of his suffering, had caused him so much misery. It was a revelation of the forgiving character of his heart, of the love of God that dwelt within him. The Lord canceled Satan's permit to touch Job, put back the hedge for his protection, and restored him the outward marks of divine favor. We read, "And the Lord turned the captivity of Job, when he prayed for his friends; also the Lord gave Job twice as much as he had before" (42:10).

There have been many thousands of Christians who have passed through fires as fierce as Job's and who have come out unscorched. Some have ended this life without seeing their vindication and triumph before their earthly enemies. That must wait until the day when all such wrongs shall be made manifest before all heaven and earth. Though we may suffer without seeing the double restoration of lost goods, there is one detail in the mathematics of God's love that should bring great comfort, courage, and hope to the Lord's people when they are put in the furnace of adversity. They can never lose their children. They may go to the cemetery and see the casket containing their remains lowered into the ground, but the loved ones who have gone are still the children of their parents.

The opening lines of Job's epic had given an inventory of his possessions. He had seven sons, three daughters, seven thousand sheep, three thousand camels, five hundred yoke of oxen, and five hundred she asses. In the last paragraph of the narrative, after the statement that the Lord gave Job twice as much as he had before, there is the new inventory of his possessions. There are fourteen thousand sheep, six thousand camels, a thousand yoke of oxen, and a thousand she asses. The order of the inventory is inverted to teach us, more sharply, the great lesson of comfort. In the beginning the number of children was placed first, and just as the reader, having checked the items one by one, discovers that there are, indeed twice as many animals as Job possessed in the beginning, the number of the children is given, and it is, once more, seven sons and three daughters. It takes a moment to realize that what God is saying by this is that sheep and camels and oxen and asses must be double in number because they have no eternal existence, but that in giving Job seven more sons and three more daughters Job now had fourteen sons and six daughters. Half of them were living at home with him and the other half had moved to the heavenly Father's house where Job would meet them in the morning. That is true for every Christian parent who has lost a child. Our loved ones are safe in His keeping. If you have four children and one dies, never say that you now have three children. Say that you have four, and that one of them has gone to heaven.

Such battles as that which was waged in the soul and body of Job are being fought in every part of the world every day. In homes for incurables, in the lives of many of the blind, of the deformed, yes, in the lives of outwardly robust men and women who have the iron of conflict in the soul, the battles rage. Sometimes, as in the case of Job, God Himself indicates the Christian in whom He is prepared to give battle to the enemy. At times Satan comes with a sneer telling God that He is unwilling to fight in some believer who appears to be weak.

We may close this chapter with an illustration of such a conflict. It is not actually recorded in the Bible, but we know that it happened because it is possible to reconstruct the story from a later incident which implies that which is not written. We shall tell the story and then substantiate it with collateral proof from the words of our Lord Himself. One day Satan came to the Lord Jesus Christ and sneered at the motley company that followed Him as disciples. Were these to be compared with the noble creatures who graced the courts of Rome or the learned halls of Athens? What did the Lord think He would be able to do in the invisible war by such tatterdemalion disciples? Above all, this fellow Simon! If Satan had a chance to blow on him, pouff! Simon would be blown away like a bit of straw. The idea in the challenge seems to be that Satan is suggesting to the Lord that the only thing that keeps weak followers in line is the hedge of the Lord. Men will not stand and avail themselves by faith of the power that has been provided but will crumple before the first blast of Satan's onslaught.

This incident took place, even though there is no primary record of it in Scripture. We reconstruct it from the fact that the Lord Jesus came to Peter and said, "Simon, Simon, behold, Satan hath desired to have you, that he may sift you as wheat" (Luke 22:31). Satan made the request; the Lord says so. But is there any indication of Simon's failure in the fact that the Lord does not call him by his new name of Peter, nor does He address him as Simon Peter? Instead he repeats the human name, "Simon, Simon," which perhaps is derived from a Greek word suggesting characteristics of vascillation and weakness. There was certainly nothing in Simon that could resist the winds of Satan, but Satan was permitted to blow his fury against the weak disciple. What happened? The chaff was winnowed and the wheat remained. When it was all over, there was less of Simon and more of Peter, which means "rock." He had long since been made a partaker of the divine nature, but he had to become aware of the nothingness of his own self-inheritance in which he had so long boasted. The secret of the victory lay in the intercession of Christ: "But I have prayed for thee, that thy faith fail not: and when thou art converted, strengthen thy brethren" (verse 32). The term "converted" has no reference to regeneration, which had taken place long before in the life of Simon who had become Peter. This is made sure by the fact that the Lord refused to wash Peter's head and hands in the Upper Room, but told him definitely that he was already clean through the word that had been spoken unto him (John 13:10; 15:3). The "conversion" was a spiritual turning within the Christian, and such may take place many times in the course of life though the implanting of new life can take place but once.

At all events, Satan blew his winds against Peter; the chaff was taken out; the wheat remained; the disciple became one of the most stalwart, the instrument of God's power and might; men took knowledge of him that he had been with Jesus; and the day came when he laid down his life as a martyr for the name of his Lord.

Let us be watchful that when such battles come to those near us that we may be quick to comprehend what is happening in the lives of our loved ones, lest we be like Job's wife, and when the battle swirls within our own being, let us remember that our Lord will never permit that we be tested above that we are able but will with the testing make a way of escape that we may be able to bear it (I Corinthians 10:13).

19 : *The Devices of Satan*

ALTHOUGH he is the wisest of all the creatures that ever came from the creative word of God, Satan is strictly limited in wisdom. It does not appear that Satan has originated any new ideas, plans, or methods since the time the Scripture unveiled his portrait and showed all his lineaments. It was Tertullian who wrote, about the end of the second century, *Diabolus est Dei simia* — the devil is God's monkey. Certainly all that Satan can do is to imitate and copy or ape the things which he has seen God do or which he finds in the Bible as a part of the plan of God.

TRICKS AND STRATAGEMS

To the Corinthians Paul wrote that we are not ignorant of Satan's devices (II Corinthians 2:11). The word is a very interesting one. The dictionary definition is "something devised or contrived for bringing about some end or result; an arrangement, plan, scheme, project, contrivance; an ingenious or clever expedient; often one of underhand, or evil character; a plot, stratagem, trick." In the days of the King James translation, Shakespeare was writing in *Twelfth Night,* "Excellent, I smell a device." The original word in the New Testament was one used from the time of Homer for the source of thought, intelligence, and thus for intentions, projects and plans, generally in an evil sense. It is the word used for the *minds* that are blinded or corrupted by Satan (II Corinthians 3:14; 4:4; 11:3), and the *mind* which shall be kept by the peace of God (Philippians 4:7). It is the *thought* that is to be brought into captivity unto the obedience of Christ (II Corinthians 10:5).

We may paraphrase the line, then, to read that we are not ignorant of the schemes, the plans, the stratagems, the tricks of Satan. We know how his mind works. This is a very important truth. Every general staff seeks to know the psychology of the enemy leaders in order that they may anticipate their movements in warfare. God has given us such a portrait of the mind of Satan that all of his devices are known, and we need never be caught off-guard.

How Satan's Mind Works

In another phrase, Paul told the Christians that they were to put on the whole armor of God in order that they might be able to stand against the *wiles* of the devil. The English word is practically synonymous with *devices* in the other verse, but the original word is just a slight twist away from that which has been transliterated as our word for *methods*. Its deepest meaning would be the pursuit of an end by devious ways, and thus it means fraud and artifice. Putting the ideas expressed by the two words *devices* and *wiles* into one common meaning, we find that the Scripture tells us that the workings of Satan's mind, in fraud, trick, stratagem and artifice need not be unknown to us. The reason that Paul was able to say that we are not ignorant of these things is, of course, because we have the clear revelation of the teaching of the Word of God concerning them. Surely one of Satan's greatest stratagems has been the attempt to keep men in ignorance of the real nature of his being and the fraudulent dimensions of his pretensions.

We shall consider in this chapter the devices and wiles of Satan concerning himself, his existence, his nature, his appearance, his past, present, and future place of abode, his power and his knowledge.

His Incognito

It was Baudelaire who said: "The devil's cleverest ruse is to make men believe that he does not exist." For multitudes of people, generally among the more highly educated, the idea of a devil is something to be received with an amused tolerance. Denis de Rougemont, at the outset of his book *La Part du Diable* writes: "Recognize immediately that this stratagem of spreading the idea of his own non-existence has never been more successful than at the present time. Even those who 'still' believe in God believe so little in the devil that I shall certainly be accused of obscurantism, or simply of a lack of seriousness, if I persist in my project of writing a whole book on the subject. The first trick of the devil is his *incognito*. God says, '*I am He who is.*' But the devil, who is possessed with the desire to imitate truth in twisting it, says to us, like Ulysses to the Cyclops, '*I am nobody.*' What are you afraid of? Are you going to tremble before the non-existent?" This Swiss author then goes on to state that the Bible proclaims the existence of the devil on almost every page, but unfortunately he does not have a sufficiently large knowledge of the Bible to enable him to use his very great talents in presenting the devil from the standpoint of the Word of God. He, himself, falls into some of the traps set by the devil, and, while he sets forth many shrewd observations on the nature of temptation, and while he makes the flat statement that anyone believing in the truth of the Bible must certainly believe in the objective reality of Satan, he does not comprehend the real nature and purpose of Satan in the invisible war.

No Enemy, No Need for Defense

To deny the existence of Satan leads to the denial of the existence of God as He presents Himself in the Word. To deny the existence of the true God is to deny the existence of pardon and to leave the sinner in the midst of his sin. It can readily be seen, therefore, why the enemy does not want men to think he exists. If there is no enemy, there is no preparation for defense. If there is no preparation for defense, the enemy can attack wherever he will. Conversely, of course, the denial of the existence of God carries with it a denial of the existence of Satan. The result is the same by whichever avenue the question is approached.

Sometimes the same result is achieved by the denial of another world. Of course, if there is no other world, there is no personal God and no Satan, and we are back at the same objective. If there is no heaven, there is no hell. If there is no eternal Judge, there is no sin and no author of sin. If there is no truth, there is no lie and no father of lies. De Rougemont writes: "The Fallen Angel says, 'I am thy heaven, there is no other hope.' The Prince of this world says, 'There is no other world.' The Tempter says, 'There is no judge.' The Accuser of the brethren says, 'There is no pardon.' The Liar sums it all up by offering us a world without obligations or sanctions, closed upon itself but recreated unceasingly in the image of our complaisances, 'There is no reality.' Finally, Legion speaks the ultimate blasphemy, 'There is nobody.' The modern world (and each of us in it) in the measure in which it dreams of deifying man by his knowledge, or in which it denies transcendence, or in which it gives itself to the empire of power or of passion, or in which it drowns the individual in the irresponsible anonymity of the masses — the modern world (and each of us in it) surrenders to the law of Satan. By the same stroke it becomes incapable of knowing whom it is really serving. . . . Thus Satan's own action serves to hide him from the eyes of the one he dominates. Satan disappears in his successes and his triumph is his incognito. The proof that the devil exists, acts and succeeds lies in the fact that the intelligent world does not believe in him anymore."

HORNS, HOOFS AND TAIL

For those who see that the devil must exist, he has set forth another ruse to argue his non-existence by circulating false ideas as to his being. He seeks to argue his non-existence by presenting nothing more than horns, hoofs and tail. In the Middle Ages, when the vast majority of men were illiterate, the Church presented miracle plays that told religious stories from a stage. Virtue was besieged by vice, with Satan prompting, and nobility came to the aid of virtue which always triumphed in the end. How was the devil to be portrayed on the stage so that the lowest serf could recognize him at once? A figure dressed in red, with horny protuberances upon the head, with cloven hoofs, and with a tail was evolved to represent the devil. Furthermore, this one was portrayed as the master of hell and the one who was in charge of tormenting souls in hell. From whence arose the idea of a physical caricature of the being whom we have already seen was the most beautiful, the most wonderful creature ever to come from the creative word of God?

The evolution of this idea seems to have come about in the following way: In Isaiah's prophecy against Babylon, it is said that the site of the ancient city should be desert and that certain wild animals would dwell there. In the King James Version these are presented as "wild beasts of the islands" (Isaiah 13:21, 22). These words represent a series of Hebrew words of which the meaning, in some cases, is obscure. When we stop to think that the average human being cannot distinguish between a hare and a rabbit, either by sight or by definition, or between a coyote, a wolf and a jackal, the difficulty in identifying wild animals as described by rare words in a dead language may become more apparent. The most important French translation of the Old Testament renders the five words quoted above as "animals of the desert," "owls," "ostriches," "goats" and "jackals."

SATYR

We are concerned with only one of these words, that which is rendered "goat" in the French and "satyr" in English. In the Hebrew the word is *sair,* and we can well understand how men who were translating the Bible, and who came to involved lists of wild animals totally unknown in Renaissance England, took the word *satyr* that sounded somewhat like *sair,* and inserted it for the translation. But there is a vast difference. The word "satyr" is used both in Latin and Greek for the woodland gods or demons, in form partly human and partly bestial, supposed to be the companions of Bacchus. In Greek art of the pre-Roman period, the satyr was represented with the ears and tail of a horse. Roman sculptors assimilated it in some degree to the faun of their native mythology, giving to it the ears, tail, and legs of a goat, and budding horns.

The Hebrew word should have been simply translated by some term such as "wild goat," which the English Revised Version uses. Instead the word *satyr* was used (perhaps also because Luther had translated the word *Feldgeister* — field-spirits — following perhaps the Septuagint *demons*), and the career of Satan as a monster, already launched in the pagan world, seemed to have the stamp of the Scriptures. The comic figure of the miracle plays, degenerated into the swinish figure portrayed by Dürer; and, although Michelangelo depicted him as the massive personification of the forces of evil, he has become, in modern times, the sleek, suave character, the slim gentleman-devil of Gounod's *Faust,* or the light-hearted statuettes (for there is a Mrs. Devil in France) which stand in the foyer of one of the leading salons of Parisian fashion.

So there are those who, fascinated by the traditional image of the devil which is so evidently puerile, have no thought that perhaps the real devil is at work in quite another form, perhaps even their own. How illogical is the unpardonable sophistry of these doubters who argue: "The devil is a smart little fellow in red, with horns and tail; I could never believe in a smart little fellow in red, with horns and tail; *therefore* I do not believe in the devil." That is all that he wants.

There is still another subterfuge in which Satan has hidden himself in order better to deceive some. He has his followers who deny his existence by thinking of him, not as a personal devil, but as the mythological figure of evil. We can see how subtle the devil really is when he is able to concoct a notion of his hiding in sin itself. De Rougemont points out that this trick of Satan is very effective because men would be terrified at the sight of the real Satan, while sin awakens a feeling that is less fright than desire. He writes, "If we were able to see the devil himself in the midst of every sin, we would be much more prudent, for sin attracts but the devil frightens. The artistry of the devil, therefore, is to make himself invisible in our temptations. He is a master at showing white paws, like the bad wolf in Little Red Riding Hood. In truth, the devil is not dangerous when he is so visible that he frightens us, but only when he is where we are not able to see him." A retired minister, given a television set by his people, was shocked at some of the things he saw. He attached a card to the edge of the screen, reading, "Be careful! The devil is in this box!"

What might have been the result if the so-called Lord's prayer had been correctly translated, "Lead us not into temptation but deliver us from the evil one"? — for the Greek word that is translated *evil* in the

Prayer Book and common versions is the word used for the *evil one* or the *wicked one* in many New Testament passages (Matthew 13:19, 38; John 17:15; I John 2:13, 14; 3:12; 5:18, 19).

De Rougemont has one more apt phrase in connection with the devil hiding himself in sin. "As soon as you think you see him because he has acted in some manner that is extreme, as soon as you attempt to unmask him within sins, he slips out of your grasp by having men of science teach you that sin does not exist: what really is the matter is some trouble with the endocrine glands, or some fantasy of the sub-conscious mind, or some mental malady, or an improper social adjustment. . . . We are not responsible for anything. We are not bad; we are merely sick. . . ." In view of the currency gained by false psychological concepts, it is important to realize that these ideas are Satanic in every part and that Satan is hiding within these modern phrases just as he hid in the satyrs and the red comedy figure.

In addition to these devices and wiles of Satan in connection with his existence or non-existence, and his attempts to hide himself in various forms or fictions, the father of lies is especially concerned with spreading false ideas about his origin, his past history, his present abode and his future destiny. We have touched on certain phases of this at previous points in this study, but at the risk of repeating we feel it necessary to set forth in one place the whole of the Bible truth concerning Satan's abode. We have pointed out that sin did not begin in heaven; it began on earth. Satan's great movement was toward heaven, and God has permitted the occupation of a portion of His domain by Satan ever since the first arrogant cry, "I will ascend into heaven" (Isaiah 14:13). We will wrestle against the spiritual hosts of wickedness in the heavenly places (Ephesians 6:12). Many have been deceived by the use of the prophetic past in our Lord's statement, "I beheld Satan as lightning falling from heaven" (Luke 10:18). De Rougemont begins one of the chapters of his work on the devil with the quotation of this text and the opening sentence: "The Bible teaches us that Lucifer is an angel fallen from heaven." The Bible does not teach us anything of the kind.

One of the common lies which the devil has made to pass among men as a good coin is the idea that Satan is now in hell, that he is the ruler of hell, and that he has the power to punish men in hell. The truth is that the devil has never yet been punished; that he does not know what hell is like except from the Word of God; that, when he ultimately reaches the place of his punishment, he will be there as the chief outlaw prisoner and not as ruler, governor, jailer or tormentor.

There is great *confusion* arising from this widespread *illusion* that Satan is at present in hell and that he is the ruler of that place.

The late C. S. Lewis has written the most famous book of the last generation on the subject of the devil. *The Screwtape Letters,* while containing a portion of whimsey, are nevertheless strongly loaded with excellent teaching concerning the methods which the devil uses in se-ducing men and women to his ends. We might even suggest a careful reading of the book as a postscript on this present chapter. C. S. Lewis frames his whole work as written from Screwtape in hell, which the demon calls "our Father's house," and has him speaking of Satan as "Our Father Below." This may be clever, but it is untrue. Satan is not yet "below." In Screwtape's nineteenth letter to Wormwood, we read, "When the creation of man was first mooted and when, even at that stage the Enemy (*i.e.,* God) freely confessed that he foresaw a certain episode about a cross, Our Father (*i.e.,* the devil) very naturally sought an interview and asked for an explanation. The Enemy gave no reply except to produce the cock-and-bull story about disinterested love which He has been circulating ever since. This Our Father na-turally could not accept. He implored the Enemy to lay His cards on the table and gave Him every opportunity. He admitted that he felt a real anxiety to know the secret; the Enemy replied, 'I wish with all my heart that you did.' It was, I imagine, at this stage in the interview that Our Father's disgust at such an unprovoked lack of confidence caused him to remove himself an infinite distance from the Presence with a suddenness which has given rise to the ridiculous enemy story that he was forcibly thrown out of heaven." Spiritually, of course, Satan is exiled, but physically he still has access to heaven and does not yet know hell.

De Rougemont gives Satan the title to hell in even more definite phrases. "And certainly he could have everything, since he is called the Prince of this world in the gospels, but he will never have anything other than this world. He will never reconquer heaven, which is really the soul of this world. He will have nothing more of our universe than the material carcass. And Satan will probably use the debris of this transformed and debased House for the fuel to heat his hell." Nothing could be further from the truth than to speak of Satan's hell. Satan has no hell. There is only one hell and that is God's hell. He prepared it, and He prepared it for the devil and his angels (Matthew 25:41). If men ultimately go there, it is because God enlarges it, so that its mouth may open without measure (Isaiah 5:14). The Lord Jesus taught very definitely that it is our God who has the power of eternal punishment and who exercises it. "Fear not them which kill the body,"

162   *THE INVISIBLE WAR*

He told the disciples, "and which are not able to kill the soul: but rather fear him [God] which is able to destroy both soul and body in hell" (Matthew 10:28).

In the tympanum, the triangular space over the entrance way of the doors of many Gothic cathedrals, there is a sculpture, sometimes in bas-relief, sometimes in haut-relief, that frequently portrays a great error. Under the point of the arch, there is the bearded head that represents the Father. Beneath this there is a dove with outstretched wings, representing the Holy Spirit. The center of the triangle is the enthroned figure of Christ, surrounded by the Virgin and angels or apostles. Beneath the feet of the Lord, the remaining oblong space is filled with a representation of the supposed last judgment. In the center, there is a set of balances on which the souls are weighed, while the recording angel checks the procedure from a scroll. To one side, angels attach wings to the souls of the blessed who rise open-mouthed with song toward the angels. On the other side, there are imps and demons who prod the souls of the howling, grimacing damned toward the flames of torment which were sometimes painted red to make the scene more terrifying. We can be assured from the Word of God that Satan was the author of that artistic idea, and that it is merely a part of his lies to hide his past, glorify his present and obscure his future.

The devil certainly knows all that the Bible has to say about him, and he understands it only too well. The unfallen angels of God eagerly plunge their gaze (the Greek verb is very strong) into the depths of Scripture to fathom the meaning (II Peter 1:12). The demons also believe and tremble (James 2:19). We may be sure that the chief of the rebels knows every line and word of the Scriptures. He quoted it to Christ (Matthew 4:6), and has himself been sorely wounded by its thrusts, not only when it was wielded by the Lord, but when used by believers, for we are told that "they overcame him by the blood of the Lamb, and by the word of their testimony" (Revelation 12:11), which is a testimony of alignment with the Word of God.

20 : *The Devices of Satan*
(CONTINUED)

THE devil knows, then, that his doom is sure. He knows that his power has always been limited by the lacks in his own being, and that his malignancy has never been allowed to spread beyond the limits of God's permissive will. He knows, as we shall see in detail, that at Calvary he was exposed to the gaze of all the angelic hosts, and that from the moment the judgment was given, it was merely a question of time until the verdict should be enforced against him. He knows that the sentence will be executed even as the Word spreads it forth on the record, so that he will one day go to the lake of fire that was prepared for him and his angels (Matthew 25:41). We can well understand, therefore, why the devil seeks to make people think that he has power which he never possessed, and that this power is somehow independent of God's power and not subject to it. If it could be maintained that he had any stake whatsoever in the government of hell, he would be seen, in some sense, as an eternal victor. But he is limited to lying about his prestige and position, thus exhibiting the ragged tatters on the lining of his pride.

If Satan thus sets forth lies concerning his origin, his abode, and his future, we need not be astonished that he should lie concerning his attributes. While he has great power, the devil is, nevertheless, not to be thought of for one moment as having all power, or even as having any power outside of the permissive will of God. Satan is a creature. If we understand the meaning of that word, the whole matter is said. Satan was bold enough to come to the Lord Jesus Himself and say, "Mine is the kingdom, and the power and the glory" (Luke 4:5, 6). But the Lord Jesus speedily taught His disciples to ascribe the kingdom, the power, and the glory to the one true God (Matthew 6:13). Christ said as He was about to return to heaven, "All power is given unto me in heaven and in earth" (Matthew 28:20). The Spirit taught

163

John to tell the Church, "Greater is he that is in you than he that is in the world" (I John 4:4).

SATAN NOT OMNIPRESENT

An error that is more common is the thought that Satan is omnipresent. There are those who think that Satan can be present at the same moment in America and in Africa, in China and in England, hurling his fiery darts personally at whomsoever he will. This simply is not true. It is doubtful that many who read these words have ever known the personal attention of the devil. If an old soldier in a convention of veterans began to spin a tale about a personal, hand-to-hand combat with Hitler or Mussolini, his comrades would laugh at him. The great leaders of the enemy power were not out in foxholes grappling with privates of the rear rank. Elisha was a foe of sufficient importance to engage a mighty force of Satan's hosts, but Satan himself is not mentioned as being present. Daniel only drew a captain or two of the principalities and powers to impede the transmission of the divine revelation. Paul, on one occasion at least, had no more than a messenger of Satan to buffet him (II Corinthians 12:7). The greatest of the angels who remained faithful to God did meet Satan face to face. Michael, the archangel, when carrying out an order of God concerning the body of Moses, was interrupted by Satan, personally, and Michael could deal with him only by committing him to the Lord for rebuke (Jude 14).

Among those human beings who met Satan personally, according to the Scripture, the following may be named: Eve (Genesis 3:1), Peter (Matthew 16:23; Luke 22:31), Ananias (Acts 5:3), and, perhaps, Paul on an occasion other than the one mentioned above (I Thessalonians 2:18). We say *perhaps* because there is a shade of difference between a temptation that is brought personally by the devil himself and one that is brought by one of his minions. There may not be much comfort in this for one who is buffeted by a messenger of Satan, but we believe that the distinction should be made in order to point out certain facts concerning Satan's limitations. The daughter of Abraham, who was bound by Satan for eighteen years (Luke 13:16), was undoubtedly held by a member of Satan's legions. We believe that a similar idea is expressed in such passages as those that speak of Satan tempting (I Corinthians 7:5) and getting an advantage over the believer (II Corinthians 2:11).

JUDAS

In mentioning the fact that seven characters in the Bible are set forth as having been the object of Satan's personal attack, we pur-

posely made no mention of Judas. The reason for this is the statement
by Christ that He had chosen the twelve, one of whom, Judas, as the
original text shows, is "the devil" (John 6:70). That the disciples did
not have the remotest idea that Judas was anything different from the
rest of them is proved by the fact that when the Lord later announced
at the Passover table that He would be betrayed by one of them, there
was no thought at all among them that Judas was the one, but each
began to say, "Lord, is it I?" This seems to be a case of utter and absolute Satanic possession of Judas by Satan, perhaps at intervals at
first, and then finally, when the Lord gave Judas the sop at the table
and Satan entered into him again to carry him through to the desperate
end. Judas was never at any time a believer; never at any time a child
of God. He became a child of the devil, and the devil carried him
through to the grave.

De Rougemont has an excellent passage on suicide which is worth
summarizing here. Speaking of the temptation of Eve, he points out
that it was not evil within her that tempted her but the imagination
of a good that was better than that which God had offered her. It was
a temptation to utopia, and every movement toward any utopia is always a Satanic temptation. First, it was imagination, then, the desire
for a good that was beyond reality and that the divine plan did not offer.
It is later, several generations of sinners in history beyond Eve, and
after continual yielding to sin within, that evil comes to dominate the
individual, to become second nature. He then quotes Baudelaire: "Man
and woman know from birth that voluptuousness is found in evil. The
unique and supreme voluptuousness lies in the certainty of doing evil."
Then De Rougemont concludes, "But at this point complicated mech-
anisms are set loose leading through perversion, self-chastisement, and
a torn conscience to the desire to destroy oneself. To destroy oneself
in order to become innocent! To escape in one's own way from the
consequences of the evil which one has done; to chastise oneself without recovery. This is the mystery of suicide and the logic of Judas,
the last temptation, the supreme utopia."

GOD KEEPS HIS OWN

While Satan undoubtedly receives reports from all his lieutenants,
he is not everywhere himself. Though he may attack a Christian, there
is always a term to his attack. Even as angels came and ministered unto
Christ when the devil left Him after the temptation (Matthew 4:11),
so we may be sure that our God wards off the attacks of the enemy
upon all His own after a predetermined limit and ministers to us Him-

self. God will never permit that we be tested beyond our ability to meet the test (I Corinthians 10:13).

CHILDREN OF WRATH

The old Adamic nature is sufficient in itself to hold many millions of lost souls in check. Note that we do not call them Satan's subjects, or even the children of Satan. We do not believe that everyone born of Adam is thereby a child of Satan. The Bible indicates that all are born children of wrath (Ephesians 2:3), but that one becomes a child of Satan as another becomes a child of God. We will bring this out more clearly in the chapter on Satan's motives and religion. Satan's forces are occupied only with his great effort to build his kingdom and to oppose those who are children of God through faith in Christ Jesus. The rest of the world rests supinely in his embrace, for the Greek word in I John 5:19 describes the world in the arms of Satan in a term that pictures a harlot in the arms of the one who has hired her: body given over, perhaps, but still with a mighty will of her own. We must never forget that man has a nature that in essence desires nothing but his own will. For an Adamic nature to desire the will of Satan there must be a perversion of the will and a conscious bending to Satan which might even be described as a Satanic regeneration. The verb *keitai* which is used to describe the world *lying* in the wicked one is the same as that in Homer's often repeated proverb concerning the issues that *lie* in the laps of the gods (*Iliad* 17:514; 20:435; etc.; *Odyssey* 1:267; etc.).

NO COMMON DWELLING GROUND

Even though Satan may travel with the speed of thought and even though he be overlord to a vast host of subordinates that report to him, he can never be on the throne of God nor can he ever come inside the body or being of one who has been born again and whose body has become the temple of the Holy Spirit (I Corinthians 6:19). We put forth this statement categorically in spite of the works of the English group known as the Overcomers, whose bible is frequently Mrs. Penn-Lewis' book, *War on the Saints*. We know of no more insalubrious idea than that which would turn Christians to introspection, looking for attacks of Satan within, or to a circumspection that would have Christians seeing defilements in shaking hands, or touching in any way a person who might be possessed by the devil. There is no fellowship between righteousness and unrighteousness. There is no communion between light and darkness. There is no concord between Christ and the devil. There is no common dwelling ground for faith and infidelity. There is no agreement between the temple of God and idols (II Corinthians 6:14-16). Before these definite assertions of the Word of God we must stand firm. There may be attacks upon the Christian by the enemy, but the Christian may not be possessed. The Bible shows attacks on the physical health of Job. It teaches that Christian leaders have the right of delivering erring Christians into the hands of Satan for such attacks (I Timothy 1:20), even to the point of physical death as a judgment so that the released soul might go immediately to heaven, yet with all works burned away, saved as by fire (I Corinthians 3:15). There are temptations from without upon the soul that come from Satan through the flesh (I Corinthians 7:5). There are temptations from without upon the soul through the world (I John 2:15-17). There are temptations upon the soul that come directly and personally from Satan, but even though there are possibilities of enemy action, there is no possibility that the devil can possess the soul or body of the the one who has been born again.

THE IGNORANCE OF SATAN

Yet another device of Satan is to make men believe in his wisdom beyond its real limits. Without question Lucifer was the wisest creature ever to come from the Word of God. Although Satan has retained the wisdom of Lucifer in a perverted sense, he most certainly is not omniscient. There are two things, at least, that Satan does not know. He may be psychologically shrewd and a good guesser, but he does not know what goes on within the mind and heart of man, and he does not know the future.

In one of the Psalms, David sings, "O Lord, Thou hast searched me and known me. Thou knowest my downsitting and my uprising; thou understandest my thought afar off. . . . No word ever reaches my tongue until long after thou hast known it" (Psalm 139:1-4). Such language, used of God, could never be used of Satan. He has the age-long experience of the evil seducer. He knows the gestures and the glances of the human race without exception. His skill to know the motives and the thoughts of men is far above that which mere man possesses. All of us, to a greater or less extent, read the minds of those round about us, but we cannot enter into their minds to know that we have read them correctly. Satan, to a much greater extent, can read the minds of men from without. The Bible will not countenance the opinion for a moment that the devil has the power, possessed only by God Himself, and which He uses by means of the Word which is the "discerner of the thoughts and intents of the heart" (Hebrews 4:12).

Perhaps in no field has Satan won the interest of more people than that which he has created by the circulation of the idea that he can know the future or that he can reveal the future to man. His first lie to Eve included a promise of knowing something that was hidden. The same search after the future is the underlying fact of the great event that took place on the plains of Shinar and which caused the Lord God to intervene in a judgment which confounded the tongues of men and instituted the curse of nationality. The tower of Babel was not a tower that men were attempting to build beyond the soaring heights of the surrounding hills, but as the original language shows, it was a ziggurat on whose top was a zodiac where the priests consulted the stars for their prognostications, and where centered a cult of the sun and the moon and the stars.

In the great judgment upon Babylon set forth in the prophecy of Isaiah, there is a résumé of the history of Israel with respect to their seeking knowledge of the future apart from God. We read: "Stand fast in your enchantments, and in your many sorceries, with which you have labored from your youth; perhaps you may be able to succeed, perhaps you may inspire terror. You are wearied with your many counsels: let now the astrologers, the star-gazers, the monthly prognosticators, stand up, and save you from the things that shall come upon you" (Isaiah 47:12, 13). The key phrase is that they had labored at their sorceries from their youth. It was against these practices that the Lord had warned Israel even before they had come into the land of promise. They had left the deviltries of Egypt, which were all bound up with the worship of the astrological gods, and were now going into Palestine, where they would have pagans round about them. But they were to take heed to themselves, the Lord told them through Moses, "lest you lift up your eyes unto heaven, and when you see the sun and the moon and the stars, even all the host of heaven, you be drawn away and worship them" (Deuteronomy 4:19).

As the centuries passed, the children of Israel became corrupted in precisely this thing. The Lord sent the Assyrians to conquer them because they had attempted to know the future through the Satanic means that had been set up in all of the pagan nations. We read of the Assyrian invasion, "And this was so because the children of Israel had sinned against Jehovah their God . . . and the children of Israel did secretly things that were not right against Jehovah their God: and they built them high places in all their cities (i.e., towers with zodiacs for astrological prophecies concerning the future as at Babel) from the tower of the watchman to the fortified city . . . and they worshipped all the host of heaven and served Baal" (II Kings 17). Throughout the latter years of the history of the children of Israel, the story is the same, told over and over. They built high places; they worshiped the host of heaven. The Lord sent judgment upon them.

The implications in any religious idea which seeks to gain knowledge of the future by means outside of the Word of God is that the divine revelation is not great enough for man. He deserves better of God than the narrow confines of such a limited book; therefore, man will seek out the knowledge of the future apart from God. The idea is an old one. Eat of this fruit, and ye shall be as gods, knowing the end from the beginning.

The history of man's efforts to find out the future and the methods he has used in the search would fill many shelves of books. The literature of divination is not small. All of the sibyls, the auguries, the prophecies, the omens, and the portents of the past can be matched by methods that are in use today. In the past, men studied the flight of birds, the passage of clouds, the entrails of freshly killed fowls in order to know the future. They consulted oracles and witches, soothsayers and seers, and all because they did not like to retain God in their knowledge (Romans 1:28). Today men decide their actions on the basis of the old deviltries as well as the new. There are still multitudes who read horoscopes and consult the stars. Others act on the toss of a coin, the cut of a pack of cards, the movement of a ouija board. Some of them do this without knowing that *ouija* is the combination of the word for *yes* in both French and German. The devil always says *yes, yes* to his followers. They do not like *No* for an answer; therefore, they shall have *Yes*. And all of this on the pretense of a being who has not the remotest inkling of what is going to take place tomorrow, other than what he can read in the prophecies of the Bible, or can foresee in the manner of a good political commentator or columnist.

The failure of Satan to know the future is a sure proof of his creaturehood. The Lord has set forth a definite challenge on this point which Satan could never meet. "Set forth your case, says Jehovah; bring your proofs, says the King of Jacob. Let them bring them forth, and declare unto us what shall happen; tell us the former things, what they are, that we may consider them, that we may know their outcome; or declare to us the things to come. Tell us what is to come hereafter, that we may know that you are gods. . . . Behold, you are nothing, and your work is nought; an abomination is he who chooses you" (Isaiah 41:21-24).

Though God has defied men to announce the future, it is certain that such power is claimed by spirit-mediums, although the events do not bear out the claim. Jennings, in his work on *Satan* has an excellent paragraph on this claim. "We must still remember that when men turn away from light, a double darkness is upon them, and that they thus put themselves in a peculiar way in the power of the evil one, so that the 'strong delusion' of which we read in I Thessalonians 2 has many a forerunner in minor, but still very striking, delusions even in the present day.

"In that day God shall permit him to deceive the whole world by the very evidences that made Israel say, 'Jehovah, He is God; Jehovah, He is God' (I Kings 18:39). Fire shall then appear to come from heaven. An image made of dead matter shall appear to have life since it apparently breathes freely (Revelation 13:15). Who will be able to withstand such 'proofs'? So today those who have commerce with those evil spirits often have the chains of deception riveted the more tightly upon them in somewhat the same way. They have to do with *superhuman* subtlety, *supernatural* skill and intelligence, and consequently it naturally transcends the powers of human skill to fathom the delusions. The more men give themselves up to this unclean traffic, the more the powers of evil are permitted to ensnare them. Future events are foretold, and while at times these prophecies are utterly at fault, yet at times it would appear as if God permitted their literal fulfillment, possibly even by the direct agency of the same spirit-powers that gave the prophecy. Marvelous memory and knowledge of the individuals' lives do these spirits show; marvelous skill, derived both from their powers by creation, and 6,000 years of dealing with mankind, in discerning motives do they possess; and equal skill in using what they know; yet is the highest Prince of all these spirits but a creature, and of limited powers; he cannot infallibly foretell as to the future."

We would not give the present spirit mediums as much credit as Jennings does. We believe that the portion of fraud in their dealings is much greater than many imagine. Today is not yet the day of the grand delusion, but the day approaches and the Christian must be ready at every moment to test all claims by the Word of God. Here in our hands is the one infallible means whereby we can detect that which is of the truth and that which is of the father of lies.

Finally, there is one device of Satan which is used most frequently and which is practically overlooked by the vast number of people who take even the slightest interest in religion. This ruse, one of the simplest and most easily detected, yet one of the hardest to point out to most people, is that Satan gets ordained and speaks from Christian pulpits. We are not at this point to be occupied with what he teaches when he gets there; that will form the subject of another chapter when we discuss the motives and religion of Satan. We present here the simple fact that Satan's ministers speak every Sunday from many thousands of pulpits.

Several years ago, in a Bible conference lecture, in speaking of the source of error in Christian theology, I said, "Do not forget that the Bible teaches us that we are to expect error from the pulpit. There is that verse in the Corinthian epistle which says, 'When you look for the devil do not forget to look in the pulpit.'" To my surprise, the audience burst out laughing. I said hastily, "Oh, I'll admit that that is my own translation of the Greek," and once more there was laughter. I pointed out that it was not a laughing matter; that I was most serious. The Revised Version runs thus: "For such men are false apostles, deceitful workers, fashioning themselves into apostles of Christ. And no marvel: for even Satan fashioneth himself into an angel of light. It is no great thing, therefore, if his ministers (often with a D.D. and other degrees) fashion themselves as ministers of righteousness, whose end shall be according to their works" (II Corinthians 11:13-15).

Truth comes from the Word of God. Error comes from the pulpit. If you think it over, you will realize that this must be the case. Spiritual and religious errors are for the most part disseminated from the pulpit. It is the false doctrine that is preached in thousands of sermons that gives currency to the false ideas that are held by the multitudes. The dividing line between truth and error is strictly on the question of the point of reference. There are those who appeal to something outside of the Word of God, and there are those of us who appeal entirely to the Word of God.

It goes without saying that we have dealt with only a few of the devices and wiles of the devil — those that concern his person, his appearance and his deficiencies. We have not spoken of his ways of seduction and enthrallment. Some of these will be seen more clearly, perhaps, in the chapters that follow. Many, of course, will become evident only in the midst of conflict as the individual learns to lean upon the power that has been provided in Christ and to measure all things by the Word of God. Even at this point, we must break off in the middle and say that those who overcame the attacks of Satan did so "by the blood of the Lamb and the Word of their testimony" (Revelation 12:11).

21 : The World, the Flesh and the Devil

"T HE author of confusion and lies," as Robert Burton called Satan in *The Anatomy of Melancholy,* has done one of his most effective bits of mystification in creating bewilderment even among many Christians, concerning his methods of attack. These are threefold. We do not know what student of the Word of God first coined the phrase, "the world, the flesh and the devil." The oldest usage of this triple division of the field of attack is to be found in *The Book of Common Prayer* in a prayer for an infant, "Grant that he may have power and strength to have victory, and to triumph, against the devil, the world and the flesh."

THREEFOLD ATTACK

In this chapter, we shall show that the enemy attacks us from these different angles because man is a threefold being. We will then show the nature of the difference between these three temptations, and finally, we will show the methods set forth by the Word of God through which the Christian may have victory in each of the three spheres.

When God created Adam, the act of creation is described as follows: "And the Lord God formed man of the dust of the ground, and breathed into his nostrils the breath of life; and man became a living soul" (Genesis 2:7). The verse reveals to us that the body was made of the dust of the ground, that the spirit came from the breath of God, and that the combination produced the soul. It would be correct, in the light of this verse, for a man to say, "I am a soul, I have a body and I have a spirit."

There have been many theologians who have denied the tripartite nature of man. They find no difference between the soul and the spirit. However, the Word of God definitely does make such a difference, and we shall see that the difference is an important one in the psychology back of the differences in temptations that come to a man. One of the most obvious verses which tells us how we are to distinguish between the soul and the spirit is in the epistle to the Hebrews: "The Word of God is living and powerful, sharper than any two-edged scalpel, piercing even to the division of soul and spirit, of joints and marrow, and is the critic of the thoughts and intentions of the heart" (Hebrews 4:12).

BODY, SOUL AND SPIRIT

We shall give only a brief summary of the use of the words *body, soul and spirit,* for it will not only be instructive for our purpose, but will also show the extent of the task.

The Hebrew word that is most frequently rendered "soul" is *nephesh.* It is found 754 times in the Hebrew text, and it is translated "soul" 472 times. In the other 282 places, it is rendered by no less than forty-four different English words or phrases. Apart from its use in translating the word *nephesh,* "soul" is found only two other times in the Old Testament (Job 30:15 and Isaiah 57:16). Twenty-two times the word is used of the lower animals without any possible connection with man, thus showing that the Bible teaches that animals have souls, though definitely they do not have spirits.

Man is a soul, and as a soul he conserves his own identity though he may have the same name as other men. John Smith on Third Avenue does not get himself confused with John Smith on Fourth Street. The Post Office department may send their mail to the wrong addresses, but if they are sober, they get to their right homes. So do the animals, for our Lord pointed out "the foxes have holes, and the birds of the air have nests" (Matthew 8:20), and we know from observation that each goes to his own home and it is never confused with any other. Evidently an animal or a bird has an individuality as distinct as that of man. The soul is self-consciousness.

The New Testament word *psuche* does not alter the meaning that we have gathered from the Old Testament word. It is found 105 times in the Greek Testament and is the only word that is translated "soul." It is thus used 58 times, and no other word is so rendered. It is also seen as "life" 40 times, "mind" three times, and once each as "us," "mind," "you," "heart," and "heartily." It is *psuche* which is the word used to translate the Old Testament *nephesh* when there is a quotation in the New Testament.

MAN'S SPIRIT

The soul, which is the self, the ego, the I, has a spirit. The words for this idea are as definite as the ones we have just looked at. In the Old Testament, we have *ruach* which is found 389 times in the text, and it is translated "spirit" 237 times. In the other 152 places, it is rendered by twenty-two different English words. Apart from its use in translating *ruach*, "spirit" is found only two other times in the Old Testament (Job 26:4 and Proverbs 20:27). While at times the word signifies wind or breath, its metaphorical meaning is used for the life of God and for the name of the third person of the Trinity, the Holy Spirit. This is what was breathed into Adam when he was created, and this is that which distinguishes man from animals.

No man, be he ever so low in the scale of human intelligences, ever failed sooner or later to recognize that there was something about him and superior to him. Aristotle said that "man is by nature a political animal"; Seneca said that "man is a social animal," and in another place, "man is a reasoning animal." Chrysostom said "man is a gentle animal," and Augustine called him "an earthly animal." There may be a measure of truth in all of these, but it would be far closer to the truth as revealed in the Scriptures which use the word "soul" and "spirit" to say that man is a religious animal. We substantiate the use of the word "animal" by the usage of the word "soul," and we substantiate the word "religious" by the usage of the word "spirit."

The New Testament word *pneuma* does not alter the meaning of the Old Testament word. It is found 379 times in the Greek Testament of the best critical editors. Used with the word *Holy*, it is translated "Holy Spirit" or "Holy Ghost" 93 times. It is rendered "Spirit" 130 times and "spirit" 150 times. The full count is completed by the use of the word as "ghost" twice, and once each as "spiritual," "spiritually," "life" and "wind."

SPIRITUAL PSYCHOLOGY

There is, indeed, a great need for a detailed study of spiritual psychology (note the union of our two words in that phrase), but this is sufficient to establish the fact that man is a soul and that he has a spirit. We do not need to expand the fact that he also has a body. It is, indeed, the body that is the foundation that holds the other two in place so that if the body be destroyed the soul and spirit depart.

Why, then, do some theologians claim that there is no difference between soul and spirit? For much of popular theology is founded on the dichotomy of man into body and soul, rather than on the Biblical trichotomy of body, soul and spirit. Perhaps an illustration will explain. When man was created, he was somewhat like a three-storied house. After the fall, he was more like those houses which had gone through bombing: the third story had fallen into the second; the walls of the second were gaping so that a passerby might see the debris of the two mixed up together, and the first story was lined with cracks though part of the house might still be fit for dwelling. When Adam sinned, the spirit of man fell down into his soul. The two are almost inseparable in the unregenerate.

There is no adjective in our language for the word *soul*. Previous students have seen the need for such a word, and the great dictionaries give us *soulish*, but mark it obsolete for more than a century. In the Greek of the New Testament there is such an adjective. The spiritual concepts of lost men are really soulish concepts. They rise from the natural (soulish) man that receiveth not the things of the spirit (I Corinthians 2:14). We do not need to press the obvious analogy that the body is like a cracked wall. In view of the confusion of soul and spirit in the unsaved man, is it not comprehensible that philosophers and theologians have thought that they were one and the same? It is the Word of God that divides the two asunder.

A NEW SPIRIT

When a man is born again, the work of the Holy Spirit plants within him a new spirit. It is a new third story that is held from above by the power of God. As the old man was three-stories held up by the body, and always bearing downward by what we might call a soulish, gravitational pull, so the new man is three stories with the center of his being in the new spirit and is always being pulled upward by a spiritual, magnetic attraction. The Christian life is the development of the forces of the new spirit so that their influences come to combine the whole soul and being of the Christian. "I" am crucified with Christ, means that the old soul has to be dealt with in the only way that will bring any change. "Nevertheless I live" means that the life from above is penetrating the fastnesses of the soul and that the sphere of victory is being enlarged constantly in the life of the believer.

Satan's entire strategy is, therefore, directed to continuing the confusion of soul and spirit and of using every artifice possible to increase the pull of the flesh which lusteth against the spirit. Because of the tripartite nature of man, the devil has arranged his attacks to assault each phase of man's being. Against the body, he brings the temptations of the flesh. Against the soul he brings the temptations of the world. Against the spirit, he comes himself, even though through one of his lesser agents, seeking to win the allegiance of the old spirit to a worship of himself. It is thus important that we distinguish sharply between the three types of temptations. Failure to do so is in itself a victory for the enemy.

The importance of delineating the lines of the conflict and recognizing the various avenues of attack from the flesh, the world, and the devil may be illustrated by a simple analogy of the visible war. Suppose that during the last war there had been a sudden explosion in one of the great hotels of Miami Beach that were being used in the training of thousands of airmen. Suppose the Federal Bureau of Investigation, charged with the maintenance of our guard against sabotage, hastily concluding the attacks to be from land, immediately began a search for the enemy spies who might have introduced the explosive by trunk or package to the destroyed area. Roads are blocked, cars examined, suspects questioned, and a general frenzy of search is continued, futile because there is no enemy on land.

In the meantime, the captain of a large enemy submarine sits quietly offshore, and with his high-powered glasses, examines the scene of the devastation which he has caused by hurling a huge mortar shell into the beach resort. When he is well satisfied with what he sees, he turns, with a sardonic smile, to give the order to submerge and continue unmolested. He is at peace because his enemy has been so stupid that they have confounded an attack from the sea with an attack from the land.

The analogy can be continued easily by the introduction of the third element, a high-flying aircraft. Let us suppose that the explosion was caused, not by a bomb planted by saboteurs, not by a shell fired from a submarine, but by a bomb dropped from thirty thousand feet. How foolish would be the defenders if they raced around in automobiles looking for someone who was not there, if they dashed over the waters in highspeed boats looking for someone that was not there, if all the time the enemy was far in the clouds above them! Each branch of warfare has its own defense and when the enemy strikes, he must be met by the defense that is suitable to his attack. Saboteurs are sought by the F.B.I., submarines are searched out by planes and destroyers to be finished off with depth charges, while aircraft must be located by radar and pursued by faster craft. To misjudge the source of any attack, or to attempt a defense against one thrust with means adapted to meet another is to risk harsh defeat.

The flesh, the world, and the devil are just as different in their modes of attack as are the varied branches of service in earthly warfare. The success of our defense will depend upon our understanding of the differences between the three and the use of the divinely appointed methods for their defeat.

Many years ago, an elderly woman came to a minister at the beginning of his ministry in a certain church and began to warn him against a woman in the congregation. He should not entrust her with any spiritual task because, according to the gossip, she was "worldly." The pastor had been apprised of the true situation in the church and came to the accused's defense. His informant persisted, saying that the woman in question danced, drank cocktails, smoked and used too much makeup. The pastor knew his Scripture and said, "On the contrary, you have not told me one item that would make me think she is worldly. She is what the Scripture calls 'carnal'; it is you who are the worldly one." The woman was aghast and protested that she did not do this, she did not do that; that she abstained from this and avoided that. The minister replied, "Nevertheless, you are the worldly one. All the things you mentioned against her are in the realm of the flesh. You are worldly because you are the one who wishes power and who loves display. You want to be the head of organizations. You delight in show and position. When the various circles were meeting in different homes, the other women finally returned to the church for the meetings because none of them could keep up with you. When the women had gone to your house, you had made an ostentatious show of your linen, your china, your crystal. As you have had no children, you have had more income to spend on other things. Your conversation concerned the cloth and napkins you had bought in the Azores, the ornament from Dresden, and the antique from a little shop in England. Your supposed coat-of-arms was framed in a prominent place on your wall, and every time anyone remarked on any of your heirlooms you explained from which ancestor it had come and described without understatement his particular honors in life."

We do not know the result of the incident. We use it merely to illustrate the fact that there is widespread confusion on the part of the average Christian as to what would constitute worldliness and what would constitute carnality.

The Bible is not a book of rules but contains a great set of principles that will enable every Christian to come to a right decision on every choice in life. Man's nature is so complex that an event that may come to one man as a testing in the field of the spirit may reach another in the field of the soul and still another in the field of the flesh. We must realize, also, that the word *flesh* in the Bible is sometimes used to cover the entire being of the man, including his fallen soul and his fallen spirit. In Galatians we have two verses that balance each other, the one giving a list of the works of the flesh and the other a list of qualities which comprise the fruit of the Spirit. "Now the works of the flesh are manifest, which are these; immorality, impurity, uncleanness, sensuality, idolatry, sorcery, hatred, quarreling, jealousy, bad temper, strife, dissensions, heresies, envyings, murders, drunkenness, carousing, and such like" (Galatians 5:19-21).

Over against these sins which proceed from man's fallen being there is the fruit which the Holy Spirit is cultivating in the life of the believer: "The fruit of the Spirit is love, joy, peace, patience, kindness, goodness, faithfulness, gentleness, self-control" (Galatians 5:22). As we examine the nature of individual temptations more closely, we shall see that the sins mentioned in the first list are all-inclusive. Some come to a man when he succumbs to temptations from the world. Jealousy and dissensions might be included in this group. On the other hand, idolatry and sorcery might come to a man directly from Satan or one of his agents. Still other temptations might fall at times in one field and at times in another, depending on the individual and the circumstances.

A similar list of the works of the flesh is to be found in the gospels, spoken by our Lord Himself, in connection with a rebuke administered to the Pharisees. He had been reproved by these blind leaders because His disciples did not conform to all of the ritual washings prescribed by the Talmud. The Lord replied that filthiness in a man did not come from without but from within. When He was alone with His disciples, they asked Him for a further explanation. He answered: "That which comes out of the man, that defiles the man. For from within, out of the heart of men, proceed evil thoughts, lust, fornications, murders, thefts, greed, wickedness, deceit, sensuality, envy, slander, pride, foolishness; all these evil things come from within, and defile the man" (Mark 7:20-23).

In other words, man is not to cast the blame for his nature or for his sin on outward circumstances, or on an alien personality. Man is to bear the brunt of the responsibility himself. It is his own fallen nature which is essentially at fault. Let no man say, "I couldn't help it. The devil tempted me." God never meant that the devil should be a comfort and an excuse for man. True, the devil is responsible in one sense for all temptations that come to man, whether directly from himself in the field of religion, or from the surrounding world in which man is placed, or from man's own base passions. This is true only because Satan caused the original seduction of man. But man is also responsible — totally responsible.

22 : *The World, the Flesh and the Devil*
(CONTINUED)

W<small>E</small> shall not tarry here on the demonstration that some of the sins of man result in the defeat of Satan's larger purposes, and that Satan is frustrated in his attempt to regiment the human race because man wishes to follow his own propensities for carnality or worldliness rather than accede to the desire of Satan to have a perfect kingdom which he can show to God as proof of his own ability to organize and govern. Let us rather present an analogy which will show the interlocking responsibilities of both Satan and man for the acts of man.

A hunter goes into the forest to get a deer and at last sees one on a hillside and wounds him. The deer turns and crashes out of sight into the woods. After some moments, the hunter reaches the spot where the deer had been when shot and begins to follow the bloody trail. He goes on and on, up and down the pathless forest, and ultimately comes to a stream where the prey has eluded him by going in the water for some distance and coming out at an unknown spot. The man searches in vain and finally gives up in defeat and goes home. Some weeks later a certain village is struck with an epidemic of enteric fever. An investigation reveals that a wounded deer, infected with the typhoid bacillus, has fallen into the water supply and, unable to rise, has died there. Who is responsible for the epidemic, the hunter or the deer? Of such differences are great theological arguments sometimes made. The hunter is Satan; the deer is man. Satan fired the fiery dart; man was wounded. Man has the nature that is susceptible to wounding, and out of his fall has come all the ills that infect the world today.

THE FLESH

Let us now consider in detail the flesh, the world and the devil. We are defining the "flesh" in its metaphorical meaning. We do not refer to the soft substance of the living body, which covers the bones and is penetrated with blood. God created that flesh and gave it to

179

man, and the proper use of its every function is normal, natural and moral. There is no sin involved in any thing in connection with the human body in itself. But there is a figurative meaning of the word *flesh* (especially when it is used in antithesis to the spirit), which has an ethical sense, and denotes mere human nature, the earthly nature of man apart from divine influence, and, therefore, prone to sin and opposed to God. It is this flesh which has frequently debased the body and turned some of its highest functions into the most ignoble. But we must be careful of the word *flesh* as having to do merely with the sins of the body. It is true, as we shall see, that fleshly sins tend to vice and depravity and worldly sins sometimes tend to nobility of character. But we follow Luther in his *Preface to the Epistle to the Romans,* where he writes, "Thou must not understand 'flesh,' therefore, as though that only were 'flesh' which is connected with unchastity, but St. Paul uses 'flesh' of the whole man, body and soul, reason and all his faculties included, because all that is in him longs and strives after the flesh."

There is a definite way for the Christian to deal with the flesh quite different from the way he must deal with temptations from the world or from the devil. After the whole man has been surrendered to God in that acknowledgment of His lordship as a general principle, and after we have given ourselves over to Him for what the Bible calls the crucifixion of self, there must be a definite flight from the temptations of the flesh. "Flee also youthful lusts" (II Timothy 2:22); "flee fornication" (I Corinthians 6:18); "abstain from fleshly lusts which war against the soul" (I Peter 2:11). The watchword against temptations of the flesh is: flight.

THE WORLD

The world, also, is not to be considered in its literal meaning but in its symbolic. We do not refer to the earth globe, or its inhabitants, and only secondarily to the ungodly multitude, the whole mass of men alienated from God, and therefore hostile to the cause of Christ. We use the definition which the Oxford English Dictionary gives: "worldly affairs; the aggregate of things earthly; the whole circle of earthly goods, endowments, riches, advantages, pleasures, etc., which, although hollow and frail and fleeting, stir desire, seduce from God, and are obstacles to the cause of Christ." It is of all this that Satan is the prince.

The world operates entirely by the senses. The Lord declared that the world could never receive the Holy Spirit because they could not see Him (John 14:17). He announced its antagonism when He told the disciples that they were not to expect treatment differing from that which He Himself had received, and which led to His death. "If ye were of the world, the world would love his own; but because ye are not of the world, but I have chosen you out of the world, therefore the world hateth you" (John 15:19). He told the Heavenly Father in the garden prayer that "the world hath hated them, because they are not of the world, even as I am not of the world" (John 17:14). It was into this environment that the resurrected Lord sent His disciples (John 17: 18), announcing that He had already overcome it (John 16:33).

The further teaching of the New Testament on this word is most enlightening. It is revealed to us that God has made the wisdom of this world foolish, and that no one can know God by means of it (I Corinthians 1:20). He has told us that the devil is in the world (I John 4:4), and that before we were saved we walked in its course, according to the prince of the power of the air, the spirit that now is at work among the unsaved, the children of disobedience (Ephesians 2:2).

ADORNING

Perhaps one of the most significant statements made about the world is hidden under the translation that has been given to the word in a passage in Peter. The subject under discussion is the fact that Christian wives should be in subjection to their husbands even if the latter were unsaved, and that such a man might be won by the behavior of his Christian wife who was to live for the universe of the spiritual, the hidden things of the heart. In the English the translation reads: "Whose adorning let it not be the outward adorning of plaiting the hair, and of wearing of gold, or of putting on of apparel" (I Peter 3:3). There have been some who have interpreted this passage as a prohibition against the wearing of any golden ornaments of any kind. That it is not a prohibition is readily seen by applying the ban to braiding the hair or to wearing clothing. The thought of being unkempt or nude is not in the passage. But when we realize that the word that is translated "adorning" is the same as that rendered "world" in more than a hundred passages, the verse is not only explained but becomes powerful in its appeal for separation from the world. "Whose world, let it not be the world of the beauty shop, the jeweler or the dressmaker, but let it be the hidden man of the heart, in that which is not corruptible, even the world of the meek and quiet spirit, which is in the sight of God of great price" (I Peter 3:4).

In like manner, we can understand the numberless "worlds" that attract men of different temperaments and woo them away from God. Several years ago during a series of meetings in Boston a young man, then an instructor at Harvard, came to talk with me at the request of a Christian relative. The young man simply was not interested in the

Gospel, and his eagerness to terminate the appointment which had been made for him by loving zeal was most apparent. He was not interested in the Gospel, he said, and I took him to the Word to show him why this was true. We read together, "And this is the condemnation, that light is come into the world, and men loved darkness rather than light, because their deeds were evil" (John 3:19). He was roused to a display of anger and spoke against those of us who were always looking for evil in the lives of other people. I stopped him, saying, "Do not misunderstand. I am not accusing you of having killed anybody, or of having spent the weekend in immorality or of having plagiarized another man's thesis. Your evil deed may consist in sitting in the stacks of the Widener Library thrilling with joy because you have discovered the answer to some problem about Shakespeare's plays which has puzzled scholars. If it keeps you away from God, the world of books is as evil as the world of banditry or the world of lust." He was mollified, quite willing to be kept from God by the world of learning, and somewhat proud that he belonged to that world, and glad that it could be recognized that he did not belong to worlds of moral evil. He was a good man with a world between him and God.

LOVE NOT THE WORLD

It makes no difference what the nature of your world is. If it keeps you from God, it is evil. The relationship between a career that is held in fief from God and one that is held by the soul of and for itself, is the same as that between marriage and adultery. The doctor, for example, holding as a gift from God his skill in which he wishes the Lord to be exalted has a career that is as honorable as marriage. The doctor who holds his work as his own attainment and which he loves for himself and for itself, has a career that is as dishonorable as adultery. He loves the world and has been engulfed by it. Perhaps, with this, we can comprehend why the Lord said, "Love not the world, neither the things that are in the world. If any man love the world, the love of the Father is not in him. For all that is in the world, the lust of the flesh, and the lust of the eyes, and the pride of life, is not of the Father, but is of the world. And the world passeth away, and the lust thereof: but he that doeth the will of God abideth for ever" (I John 2:15-17).

There is a definite way for the Christian to deal with the world, quite different from the way he must deal with temptations from the flesh or from the devil. After the whole man has been surrendered to God in that acknowledgment of His lordship as a general principle, and after we can say with Paul, "God forbid that I should glory, save in the cross of our Lord Jesus Christ, by whom the world is crucified unto me, and I unto the world" (Galatians 6:14), there must be a definite turning away from conformity to the world. "He hath set eternity in the heart" (Ecclesiastes 3:11, RSV). Knowing this, we have victory. "This is the victory that overcometh the world, even our faith" (I John 5:4). As we continue in faith we shall be more and more conformed to the image of God's Son, and thus we will learn the meaning of "be not conformed to this world" (Romans 12:2). The watchword against the world is: faith.

THE DEVIL

There remains to be considered the special nature of the temptations that come to us directly from the devil. We can treat this point more briefly here, as this whole work is on the general subject and the perusal of the whole will lend clarity to this point. In previous chapters, we have shown the nature of Satan's sin, and some of the devices he exercises to deceive the hearts of men. In a future chapter, we shall speak of his motives and what we might call his religion, so prevalent in our day and yet so ignored for what it really is. We do not need to define or illustrate further. All that will be needed here is to summarize the facts that we have seen: namely, that the sphere of the devil's great interest is the spirit of man, that he wishes to keep the debased and fallen spirit of man from looking to God as the true source of guidance and light, and that he wishes man to turn and adore him. Some men do give themselves to him, and these become those terrible blind leaders of the blind, the children of the devil (John 8:44). They will have a much worse eternal punishment for the Lord said that some would be beaten with many stripes. Most men, however, will be beaten with fewer stripes (Luke 12:48) than these. They have not truly followed the devil to become his children. They have fallen before the lesser sins of conformity to the world or the still lesser sins of the body. The very least of sins is, of course, very heinous, for men who live in such sins are children of wrath. But "He knoweth our frame; he remembereth that we are dust" (Psalm 103:14). This is why all manner of sins and blasphemy can be forgiven a man who is a child of wrath. But the blasphemy against the Holy Spirit, which is the sin of a child of the devil, is the denial of the working of God in the heart and life, and the ascription of that work to a base source. This is unpardonable; it is a most devilish sin and places a man beyond hope. (Anyone concerned that he might have been guilty of this sin may take hope in the fact that spiritual concern comes from the Holy Spirit, and its presence in the life is proof enough that God is still at work within.)

The Good Fight of Faith

There is a definite way for the Christian to deal with the Satanic temptations, quite different from the way he must deal with temptations from the flesh or from the world. After the whole man has been surrendered to God in that acknowledgment of His lordship as a general principle, and after we have given ourselves over to Him for what the Bible calls the crucifixion of self, there must be a definite fight against the power of the enemy. We are told to put on the whole armor of God that we may be able to stand against the wiles of the devil (Ephesians 6:11); and again, to "fight the good fight of faith" (I Timothy 6:12). Still another passage orders: "Resist the devil and he will flee from you" (James 4:7). The watchword against temptations from the devil is: fight.

In connection with this last verse, we may well explain why we have been so careful to note in each instance that none of these temptations could be met until there had been a preliminary surrender of self for crucifixion death. Years ago, in my first attempts to walk in the Christian life I had an older friend who guided me in the way of many victories. This man told me that there were times when it was necessary to lay hold upon the Word of God and just battle through to a victory. He said that there were times when he literally put his finger on a verse in the Bible and said, "O God, there is Thy promise. Thou art not a liar. Thou must answer. Thou must furnish deliverance." Months later I had some struggle in my own life, and I kept crying out to God that He had told us to resist the devil and that he would flee from us, but that as I resisted, it seemed as though the enemy "fled at me." Finally, I took the Bible and put my finger on this passage in James. There seemed to be no relief from the strain of the battle and I cried out to God incessantly. Finally, in a way that any experienced Christian knows is true, the Lord definitely spoke and said, "Read the whole verse." It was then that I saw that I had been quoting only half the verse. When the whole of the truth was read the perspective was quite different. Before we are told to resist the devil there is the preceding line, which is a prerequisite truth: "Submit yourselves therefore to God."

Flight, Faith and Fight

Three watchwords, then, are the banners of victory in the life of the believer We are to abstain; we are to believe and not conform, and we are to resist. In single words, flight, faith and fight. If we fail to comprehend the differences, we shall be like searchers running around on land looking for a submarine, or a pilot chasing saboteurs.

We believe that practical Christian living is a fundamental doctrine, and that it is taught in the Word of God, for after a long list of the sins of the flesh, Paul adds "and if there be any other thing that is contrary to sound doctrine" (I Timothy 1:10). It is true that the borderline between one phase of temptation and another may be quite fluid, and marked on the spiritual map with uncertainty like those unsurveyed areas which the catographers mark with dotted lines. There are certain identical acts which may be fleshly in one person and worldly or devilish in another. Sins cannot always be neatly classified. There might be a combination of circumstances that would make the same temptation apply to different fields of attack. I was told, for instance, of the purchase of a two-thousand dollar gown by a woman of fortune in society. If the woman were merely lustful and purchased the gown as a part of a campaign to seduce a desired lover, it would be a sin of the flesh. If the purchase were made by a woman, chaste in nature, but who desired to conform to the social set in which she moved, it would be a sin of the world. If the purchase was made by a parvenue, swelling with pride because she had attracted a man able to pay her *coutouriere,* and who wished to use the gown as a weapon to put her betters in their place, it would be a devilish sin, Satan's sin, the original sin of pride.

Drunkenness may be a sin of the flesh when indulged in for the sheer pleasure of seeking oblivion. It may be worldliness when the friendly glass is accepted in order to be thought well of by people who establish the standards of social custom. Adultery would be of the flesh were it for nothing but carnal indulgence; it would be intensely devilish if it were used to bring the partner under the domination of a proud and haughty spirit that wished to exercise creature control over another human being for the inflation of self-pride.

Here may lie the explanation of many office liaisons between older employers and young employees who are certainly not seduced by the glamor of their aged and paunchy partners. In the first case, there is the simple satisfaction of lust; in the second case, there is the attainment of worldly desires by extra money earned or the devilish satisfaction of proving that she is just as attractive as the woman who got the man in the first place. And if the wife wants to break up the home because she thinks that there is any love involved in the affair, she is failing to comprehend. Her precipitate action may well be a devilish sin of outraged pride where true love would have patiently awaited the passing of the fever of sin.

Letting a child have his own way might be a carnal sin of softness and weakness and indecision. It might be a worldly sin of conformity to a neighborhood, doing something because "everybody's doing it." It might be a devilish sin of towering pride if the child were indulged for the sake of self-glory. From observations made in my ministry I would judge that this is one of the commonest of sins, and one seldom named or thought of.

The results are so far-reaching in the life of the child that an illustrative incident might serve as warning. I know of a woman who, some thirty years ago, had a bitter disappointment in her first year of college life. She was "rushed" by three sororities. In her own mind she wished to join a certain one. She therefore refused immediately the invitation from the least desirable, and after great anxiety, also refused the second, gambling on the chance that she would be invited by the one she wanted to join. To her great chagrin, the invitation did not come. She passed the remaining years of her college life outside the social pale of that particular institution, where membership in one of the sororities was the stamp of social success. Several years later this woman married and had a child, a daughter. Those who knew her well could observe that the daughter was being reared according to a certain pattern that was far from the Christian atmosphere that had surrounded the mother in her childhood. As the daughter grew to adolescence, the mother moved to a certain community where she made friends with mothers who had been members of the idealized sorority in their various colleges. Almost all friendships were formed after ascertaining that there had been this connection. The daughter was sent to a small college where most of these friends were sending their daughters, who were generally sure of being pledged to the sorority because their mothers had been members. To her enormous delight, which seemed almost obscene to spiritually-minded observers, the daughter became a member of the coveted group. This was not all. At the end of the first year the mother, who was by now a widow and seemed to live but for the one thing, moved to her own old college town, and her daughter, a sure member by transfer from the first college, now lived in the sorority which had snubbed her mother a generation before. The latter watched from her nearby apartment and seemed to live her own life over again, gloating over the position of her daughter constantly referring to the fact that her daughter was a Kappa.

Psychiatrists may call such a pattern of life by terms of "fixation" and "complex," but the Biblical fact remains that if the motives were what they appeared to be, such a life was just plain sin, and it was devilish sin.

Because the human heart is a stage on which the individual walks the boards in lone grandeur, speaking nothing but soliloquies, human motive is a difficult thing to determine. "Man looketh upon the outward appearance (Hebrew, the eyes), but the Lord looketh on the heart" (I Samuel 16:7). This is why we can never judge, and the Lord says we may not judge, the motives of others. Indeed, we are strictly forbidden to judge in matters of conduct (Matthew 7:1). While we are ordered to judge in matters of primary doctrine such as the Person and work of Christ (I John 4:1-3), we are just as surely ordered not to judge in matters of secondary doctrine, such as that of matters of diet or the keeping of a certain day above the others rather than every day alike (Romans 14:1-10). God says that the Christian is a trustee, and that the requirement in one who bears such a relationship to God is faithfulness (I Corinthians 4:2). Since this is so, all men are freed from the burden of worry about the judgments of others by the counterpart of the teaching that forbids us to judge others. Paul says, "But with me it is a very small thing that I should be judged of you, or of man's day (Greek): yea, I judge not mine own self. For I know nothing by myself; yet am I not hereby justified: but he that judgeth me is the Lord. Therefore judge nothing before the time, until the Lord come, who both will bring to light the hidden things of darkness, and will make manifest the counsels of the hearts" (I Corinthians 4:3-5).

The heart, in Scripture, does not refer to the cardiac pump which circulates the blood through the arterial system; it is the symbol of the soul of man, the center of his being. Every attack of Satan is directed against this citadel, for it is here in the soul that the will resides and where each man decides his part in the invisible war.

In the unsaved, Satan is warring in order to keep this will centered in man, himself, so that it will not turn to the Saviour. He is willing that a man become a fleshly beast if that is what the man wants, in order to keep his allegiance away from Christ. He would rather have men good, noble, even religious, than to have them as beasts, for his only hope of winning them to his own cause is through their sins of the spirit. In those who are born again, Satan knows well that the new life has been planted within the being, that the influence of the new spirit is permeating the whole being, and that there will be a continuous progress be it ever so small. God has told His own that "He which hath begun a good work in you will perform it until the day of Jesus Christ" (Philippians 1:6). Satan's tactics are centered on keeping the Christian man's spiritual life poor and his witness nullified. The attacks from the flesh are for the purpose of reaching into the center of the man's will, for "fleshly lusts," we are told, "war against the soul" (I Peter 2:11). The attacks from the world are for the purpose of turning us aside from first things so that second things, and sometimes seventy-second things, become first, for if the temporal can dominate our thinking the eternal takes the second place. The attacks from the devil are again directed downward to our will, for if our pride can be exalted so that we think that we are self-sufficient, it goes without saying that we will look to self for the plan of life and the orders of command instead of resting in quiet faith looking to the will of God. The spirit-sin of leaning upon one's own understanding results in the soul-sin of failing to trust in the Lord with all one's heart (Proverbs 3:5). If with all our renewed hearts we truly seek Him, we shall be victors in the invisible war.

23 : *Satan and History*

IN a previous chapter we set forth some of the results of the hatred that is in the heart of Satan against the people of God. While such hatred is recorded here and there on the pages of history, it does not hold a large place in the records of man, since history, for the most part, has been written by men who have not been interested, primarily, in spiritual things. Historians deal with the material facts and occurrences in the lives of men throughout the centuries and across the earth, and attempt to link them in what they call history, but at the best it is a very incomplete record. Frequently, they give us magnificent pictures of single lives, or restricted decades, but they seldom relate or are capable of relating their incidents to the universal scene or conveying the idea that the shifting kaleidoscope of human events is not the chance falling of crystals in a pattern of light but is rather a momentary revelation of the invisible drama, whose scenes are being played with frightful continuity. Human history, as it is found in the books, frequently contains, therefore, a great part of misinformation and sometimes even deception.

EVOLUTIONARY ATTITUDE

The reason for this lies in the fact that modern historians, for the most part, have adopted an evolutionary attitude toward history and see no interrelationship between events that transpired far from each other in time and space, but whose true meaning demands a frame of reference which has been neglected or despised and rejected by the writers of history. Human events are treated as purely human phenomena. Unwilling to believe that God has intervened in the affairs of men, and that He is still intervening — still more unwilling to believe that there is a personal devil who is the prince of this world and the god of this age — they are totally unable to see the spiritual and invisible causes that are above and beyond the earthly arena, and confuse Satan's puppets for God's real, live actors. Events which are really

189

consequent they treat as unrelated, and incidents which are truly inseparable they record as though the happenings were on different worlds.

What historian has connected the building of the first bridge across the Euphrates and the declaration by Cato in Rome that Carthage must be destroyed? Who has joined these two events with the fight between Sarah and Hagar after the birth of Ishmael, and all of them with the defeat of Pharaoh Necho at the battle of Carchemish? For good measure, let us add the very close relationship of this apparently unrelated series with such facts as the plagues in Egypt, one of the most frequently used titles of the Pope, and a slander against the Negroes which is of comparatively modern origin. We will admit that the juxtaposition of all these pieces seems impossible and their oneness incredible, but a little attention to a few verses in the Bible will bring the whole matter into a perspective that will reveal the common link between them all.

An Announced Program

Satan had attempted to corrupt the entire population of the earth during its early centuries, and God had answered with the destruction of all by the sudden cataclysm of the flood. Eight people had been saved alive, Noah, his wife, their three sons and their wives. In the new life that followed the flood, the three sons and their families became the progenitors of all of the races of the earth. But the differences between them were very great, and their history was charted in advance with an announcement by God of His program and the consequent efforts of Satan to frustrate the plan and to undo the will of God. It is in the light of this announced program that we must see some of the underlying causes, not only for the strange series mentioned above, but for all the great events of history, for the rise of certain personalities, for the movements of armies and even for the destruction of some civilizations.

After the flood Noah became drunk with wine and lay in his tent. His son Ham went into the tent and something horrible took place which is evidently hidden beneath the words of the Scripture account. It may not be alien to our thought to remind ourselves that Sodom and Gomorrah are included within the bounds of the territory of Ham (Genesis 10:19). He came out and talked about it to his brothers, Shem and Japheth, who took a garment and laid it on both of their shoulders, and backing into the tent, covered their father's nakedness. When Noah awoke, he knew what had taken place, and undoubtedly under the inspiration of the Holy Spirit, pronounced a curse and a blessing on his sons, which has had more influence on subsequent human history than have almost any other lines spoken in the course of that history.

STUBBORNNESS AND REBELLION

We know that the Word of God sets a very high premium on filial piety. The fourth of the ten commandments, the only commandment "with promise," is the one that demands honor for father and mother (Exodus 20:12). When Moses reviewed the law before the entrance of the children of Israel into the land of Canaan, the sin of disobedience to parents was considered so terrible that the death sentence was attached to it. "If a man have a stubborn and rebellious son, which will not obey the voice of his father, or the voice of his mother, and that, when they have chastened him, will not hearken unto them: then shall his father and his mother lay hold on him, and bring him out unto the elders of his city, and unto the gate of his place; and they shall say unto the elders of his city, This our son is stubborn and rebellious, he will not obey our voice . . . And all the men of his city shall stone him with stones, that he die: so shalt thou put evil away from among you; and all Israel shall hear, and fear" (Deuteronomy 21:18-21). Perhaps this sin of stubbornness and rebellion was then considered so terrible because the children of Israel were about to go into the land of Canaan, that is, the sons of Shem were about to enter into the land of Ham, for Canaan was the son of Ham, named with his father in the original curse against the family.

This same sin was accented once more in Moses' farewell address. He uttered the curse on him "that setteth light by his father or his mother" (Deuteronomy 27:16), "and all the people said, Amen." The Hebrew word which is here translated *to set light by* is the same that is elsewhere rendered *base, contempt, despise, esteem lightly,* and *seem vile.* It is worth noting, also, that one of the marks of the time of the end, the desperate days that precede the return of the Lord Jesus Christ, is that children will be "disobedient to parents" (II Timothy 3:2). In passing, let it be said that the parents who discipline their children properly not only teach them obedience to themselves as parents, but develop a pattern which enables them to obey God throughout their lives. Disciplined children have learned the great and important principle of the acknowledgment of and submission to authority, and this attitude is one which God demands of His creatures.

The curse which was pronounced by Noah was brief but very comprehensive. "Cursed be Canaan; a slave of slaves shall he be unto his brethren. And he said, Blessed be the Lord God of Shem; and Canaan shall be his slave. God shall enlarge Japheth, and he shall dwell in the tents of Shem; and Canaan shall be his slave" (Genesis 9:25-27).

BLESSING FROM THE CURSE

When God first pronounced a curse upon mankind in the garden of Eden, Adam and the woman both submitted to it and the result was great blessing. It is possible for God to take a second best (or a sixty-fourth best!) and make it into something very wonderful when it is accepted as being the present condition in which a man finds himself, and when he moves toward God from that condition. If you will take your situation, just as it is, and ask God to develop it to the fullness of its possibilities in blessing and submission to His will, there cannot fail to be great blessing. One of the glories of God in Christ is that He is able to make music from bruised reeds, and set smoking flax on fire (Matthew 12:20).

The Satan who had failed in his attempt to corrupt the entire human race before the flood would now work through Ham and his son Canaan who are filled with a wicked spirit of rebellion at God's curse upon their actions. They did not wish to take their place as slaves of their brothers, and the result was more than a thousand years of war which ended in the virtual extermination of some branches of the Hamitic family and in the greater degradation of other branches.

Satan has even attempted to obscure the history of the great defeat of the Hamitic peoples by circulating the slanderous scandal that the Negro race is the sole descendant of Ham, and that their color and slavery are the result of the curse by Noah. We believe that the genealogical tables of the tenth chapter of Genesis refute this teaching. There is no more evidence for it than there is for the common slander on a New Testament woman, Mary of Magdala, who has been called a harlot so often that the name of her town has become synonymous with prostitution, and a woman of ill-repute can be called a Magdalene. The Bible does not teach this or even suggest it.

We propose to show that as a result of the great sin of Ham and possibly his son Canaan, and as a result of the terrible curse pronounced by God upon them and all their descendants, Satan laid hold upon this branch of humanity and began to use it in his attempt to bring all humanity under his sway. Great wars resulted that lasted almost to the time of Christ, when the last of the Hamitic nations was destroyed by the Romans in Carthage.

THE SONS OF HAM

The sons of Ham are recorded as "Cush, Mizraim, and Phut, and Canaan" (Genesis 10:6). Some of these are easily and positively identified: beyond any question Mizraim is Egypt, and thus the RSV translates it, while Canaan is the father of the peoples who occupied what we now call the Holy Land, and its environs. Furthermore, the verse following states that the son of Cush was Nimrod. Most of our translations are so weak in the paragraph concerning Nimrod that the truth behind the story has not become as evident as the facts warrant. Never has there been a regular Sunday school lesson and rarely a sermon on this Satanic character, this grandson of Ham, who took up the curse of God as a challenge and warred against God, against the divine judgment and against the people who had been promised superiority over his family. The use of the word *hunter* to describe Nimrod has increased the confusion, for a good hunter is one to be admired, and the name has even been taken as a compliment for men who brought home a large bag of game. But a close study of the use of the word throughout the Old Testament reveals that Nimrod was a hunter of men and not a hunter of animals.

This is certainly made clear in the Jeremiah passage which speaks of the judgments that shall come upon scattered Israel, and of how God will seek them out and bring them back to their land. We read, "Behold, I will send for many fishers, saith the Lord, and they shall fish them; and after will I send for many hunters, and they shall hunt them from every mountain, and from every hill, and out of the holes of the rocks" (Jeremiah 16:16). These hunters of men are the Nimrods who have marked history in their hatred of God's chosen people. They have been the despots, the tyrants, the enslavers of souls, the subjugators, the arrogant, the proud, the defiant, who find their only authority in their own bosoms and despise the living and true God.

In the light of such a passage as this, we may well render the Nimrod passage as follows: "And Cush begat Nimrod; he began to be a mighty despot in the land. He was an arrogant tyrant, defiant before the face of the Lord; wherefore it is said, Even as Nimrod, the mighty despot, haughty before the face of the Lord. And the homeland of his empire was Babel, then Erech, and Accad, and Calneh, in the land of Shinar. From this base he invaded the kingdom of Asshur, and built Nineveh, and Rehoboth-Ir, and Calah, and Resen between Nineveh and Calah. These make up one great city" (Genesis 10:8-12). Note the changes which we have made from the King James Version. We have given to Nimrod the quality of a tyrant rather than that of a mere hunter; we have seen that his attitude was a presumptuous and arrogant one before the Lord; that he invaded Assyria, a Semitic country, since verse 22 records that Asshur was a child of Shem.

We will not here give space to the proof that in Nimrod was the beginning of Satanic religion. A monumental volume by Alexander Hyslop, *The Two Babylons,* is available for the demonstration of this fact. One illustration only is very pertinent to twentieth century history. The king of Babylon built a bridge across the Euphrates and gave himself the title of the great bridge builder. This title was transferred, centuries later, to a king of Asia Minor, was taken by the Caesars, and finally fell to the Popes who boast in it today, *Pontifex Maximus*. The survival of Hamitic practices in the Roman Church is astonishing to the one who meets it for the first time. It should not surprise us, however, to realize that Satan, the god of Ham, still defies the true people of God as he has done through all ages.

The great Jewish historian Josephus, writing shortly after the earthly life of Christ, has preserved for us in his *Antiquities of the Jews* the summary of Jewish tradition about Nimrod. If the translators of our modern versions had carried this in mind, they would not have given such a faulty paragraph concerning Nimrod.

After writing of the early prosperity of the sons of Ham, and their desire to stay together, disobeying the commandment of God to fill the earth, Josephus says (I.4): "They imagining the prosperity they enjoyed was not derived from the favor of God, but supposing that their own power was the proper cause of the plentiful condition they were in, did not obey Him. Nay, they added to this their disobedience to the divine will, the suspicion that they were therefore ordered to send out separate colonies, that, being divided asunder, they might the more easily be oppressed.

"Now it was Nimrod who excited them to such an affront and contempt of God. He was the grandson of Ham, the son of Noah, a bold man and of great strength of hand. He persuaded them not to ascribe it to God, as though it were through His means they were happy, but to believe that it was their own courage that procured that happiness. He also gradually changed the government into tyranny, seeing no other way of turning men from the fear of God, but to bring them into a constant dependence upon his power. He also said he would be revenged on God, if He should have a mind to drown the world again, and that he would avenge himself on God for destroying their forefathers.

"Now the multitude were very ready to follow the determination of Nimrod, and to esteem it a piece of cowardice to submit to God, and they built a tower, neither sparing any pains, nor being in any degree negligent about the work; and, by reason of the multitude of hands employed in it, it grew very high, sooner than any one could expect; but the thickness of it was so great, and it was so strongly built, that thereby its great height seemed, upon the view, to be less than it really was. It was built of burnt brick, cemented together with mortar, made of bitumen, that it might not be liable to admit water. When God saw that they acted so madly, He did not resolve to destroy them utterly, since they were not grown wiser by the destruction of the former sinners, but He caused a tumult among them, by producing in them diverse languages, and causing that through the multitude of those languages, they should not be able to understand one another. The place wherein they built their tower is now called *Babylon,* for the Hebrews mean by the word Babel, Confusion."

The military invasion of the land of Asshur by Nimrod was but the beginning of hundreds of years of Hamitic ascendancy. From our vantage point of the twentieth century of the Christian era and of an open Bible with its completed revelation of God's plans and their fulfillment, we are able to see the whole picture, in spite of the fact that every effort seems to have been made to hide the results from posterity. When Kipling wrote

> Lo, all the pomp of yesterday
> Is one with Nineveh and Tyre,

he was putting in poetry the obituary of the Hamitic peoples.

Satan even uses his defeats as an arm to attack the Bible. Among the sons of Ham are to be numbered the Hittites. So crushing was their defeat, so definite the end of their great empire that by the nineteenth century there were higher critics who were denying the inspiration of the Bible on the grounds that no such people as the Hittites ever existed. Early editions of the *Encyclopedia Britannica* to be found in the basements of most libraries, contain long articles on Biblical criticism in which the scorn of the scholars (spiritual Hamites) is turned against the Bible because of its references to the Hittites as a great and mighty people. But suddenly archaeological discoveries made the encyclopedia laughable and quite out of date. I have walked in the ruins of Boghazköy, the ancient Hattusa, the Hittite capital whose existence was denied, and have spent days with the relics of that civilization in the museum that has been built in Angora to house the findings. A hundred miles away on the walls of a rocky canyon are bas-reliefs that are among the greatest in the world showing the exploits of the Hittite kings. These Hittites, sons of Ham, held the Semites in subjection for centuries. How they and Satan must have gloated in the light of the fact that God had said that they were to be the slaves! And here they were the masters! But God does not count history by minutes.

The sons of Ham who lived near to Jerusalem were a constant thorn in the flesh of Israel because the latter did not obey the command of God to destroy them utterly upon entrance into the land. Let those who cavil against God because He ordered the destruction of men, women, and children by the host of Israel remember that He was commanding in the light of all-knowledge, and that the Canaanites had great traffic with demons. This is evidenced by the report of the spies who discovered that the "giants" were in the land — the *nephilim* who were demon-controlled if not demon-propagated.

Since we can treat in a phrase the last branch of the Hamitic people, those of Canaan's coasts who survived and fought against Shem and Japheth, let us realize that Tyre and Sidon were cities of Ham, and that their Phoenician sailors who roamed the Mediterranean founded Carthage, the great outpost city on the northern coast of Africa, from which they continued to battle against the divinely appointed nations until Carthage was destroyed. Cato in the Roman senate ended every debate, whether on taxes, food supplies, army movements, or what-not, with the famous phrase, "Carthage must be destroyed." Though he almost certainly was unaware of the divine impetus that was behind his words, there was the movement of God in the Punic wars. It is interesting to remember that as the name of God is to be found in the last syllable of Israel, the name of Baal is to be found in the last syllable of the name of the Carthagian leader, Hannibal. Only with the destruction of Carthage was the age of Japheth established upon the history of Europe and the world.

24 : *Satan and History*
(CONTINUED)

THE greatest symbol of Satan's enmity against the children of Israel is that of Egypt. The traveler goes today to that ancient land and is filled with wonder at what he sees. One may speedily become accustomed to the sights of other lands and take them in normal course, but Egypt still has the power to evoke a strange amazement at what remains of that stupendous civilization. The magnitude of the buildings, the hypostyle halls, the giant columns of the temples, the lanes of sphinxes, and supremely, the great pyramids, all remind us of the swelling force of a people who did all this work with nothing but their hands. And this people came from the loins of the accursed Ham. Even today in the language of the land, the name of the people and the country in which they dwell is that of the second son of Ham, Mizraim.

The Scriptures clearly say that Satan made a special alliance with this son of Ham and built in him the colossal pride that raced in the veins of this people and furnished them the physical force to tear at the rocks and mountains of their land as though to compensate for their curse. They were to be slaves, were they? Then they would enslave every people upon whom they could forge chains, and they would rearrange the cosmic disorder of barren, stony hills into intelligent mountains of pyramids and other monuments that would show the greatness of Ham.

THE LAUGHTER OF GOD

The first time I came to the pyramids was by the slow approach of the road and the slower gait of the camel. The weight of the evidence of the ability of puny man was astounding, and one stood with no uncertain awe before these remnants of the seething energy of the ancient people. On a later occasion I came to the pyramids in the cabin of a stratoliner, flying up the coast of the Red Sea, enthralled with the tumbling ranges of mountains. We swung inland at dusk and the first lights of Cairo were beginning to twinkle. The earth was flat before us and from our great altitude the pyramids could be discerned with difficulty. Then suddenly they could be clearly identified, tiny warts on the vast plain, excrescences upon the clean, sandy desert. I entered into the laughter of God. It seemed to me that the sons of Ham, crawling ants by the great river below, must have been the cause of the Holy Spirit's sad smile as He recorded the rage of the nations and the vain imagination of the people. "The kings of the earth set themselves, and the rulers take counsel together against the Lord, and against his anointed, saying, Let us break their bands asunder, and cast away their cords from us. He that sitteth in the heavens shall laugh; the Lord shall have them in derision. Then shall he speak to them in his wrath and vex them in his sore displeasure" (Psalm 2:2-5).

SATAN DISCOMFITED

The key to all that happened in Egypt is to be found in a verse buried in the book of Numbers. I say "buried," although nothing is buried in the Word of God except by the neglect of man. "Man shall not live by bread alone, but by every word that proceedeth out of the mouth of God" (Matthew 4:4). It is only when we comprehend this, and see, for example, the way that our Lord at His temptation discomfited Satan with three little phrases taken out of the book of Deuteronomy that we can see the true nature of the volume that lies in our hands.

In the thirty-third chapter of Numbers, there is a record of the journeys of the children of Israel after they left the land of Egypt. The force of the verse should bring us to our feet with every nerve awake and every vein pulsing. It comes in the midst of what might be called a humdrum account of the geographical movements of the tribes.

First we read, "These are the journeys of the children of Israel, which went forth out of the land of Egypt with their armies under the hand of Moses and Aaron. And Moses wrote their goings out according to their journeys by the commandment of the Lord: and these are their journeys according to their goings out. And they departed from Rameses in the first month, on the fifteenth day of the first month; on the morrow after the passover *the children of Israel went out with an high hand in the sight of all the Egyptians.*" It is only an ordinary chronicle until we realize the drama of the last clause which we have set down in italics to prepare us for the next verse which needs to have a part set down in capital letters. "For the Egyptians buried all their firstborn, which the Lord had smitten among them: UPON THEIR GODS ALSO THE LORD EXECUTED JUDGMENTS" (Numbers 33:1-4). The next line goes back to the ordinary account of travel: "And the children of Israel removed from Rameses and pitched in Succoth."

EGYPT'S PLAGUES

Here is the formal statement that the forces of Satan were in alliance with the sons of Ham, and that the plagues in Egypt were God's method of bringing things back to the course which He had determined. Here is the proof that it was not merely man acting against a decree of slavery but that it was Satan in all the force of his might in the invisible war engineering the movements of history for long periods of time while God patiently waited for what He has called "the fullness of time" (Galatians 4:4).

This verse alone would be sufficient to justify our position that the whole movement of the Hamitic peoples was engineered by Satan and was a part of his campaign of rebellion. In the New Testament, there is a direct revelation of the fact that the power behind the thrones of earth is always a Satanic power. We are told by the Holy Spirit that "we wrestle not against flesh and blood, but against principalities, against powers, against the rulers of this world darkness, against wicked spirits in the heavenly places" (Ephesians 6:12). We are told, therefore, to take unto us the whole armor of God that we may be able to stand against the wiles of the devil. Elsewhere it is revealed that "the weapons of our warfare are not carnal, but mighty through God to the pulling down of strongholds" (II Corinthians 10:5).

The devil was in Egypt. The devil was ruling Egypt. Behind Pharaoh there was Satan. When God sent Moses into the land, it was to lift the bondage of Ham from the children of Shem. It was also to lift the bondage of Satan and crush that sinister force which was in league with Ham and which is responsible for the wisdom of the Egyptians and the wonder of their civilization.

STANDARDS OF POWER

The Bible records that there are three standards of power exhibited by God in the course of history. The first of these standards of power is that which He exercised in breaking the yoke of the mighty men and the mightier demons of Egypt and in bringing the children of Israel out into freedom. The third of these standards of power, in point of time, is linked with the first in a comparison that takes it out of its chronological order.

A hundred times in the course of the Bible narrative we have the record of the appeal to the first standard of power displayed when the Lord broke the bow of Egypt and set the mighty of that land to naught. But when God told the children of Israel that they were to be cast out of the Promised Land because of their sin, and were to be dispersed through all the world in a slavery that would be worse than their bondage in Egypt, he announced their future deliverance, and linked it with a coming display of power that will dwarf all that happened on the shores of the Nile.

God speaks through Jeremiah, saying, "Therefore will I cast you out of this land into a land that ye know not, neither ye nor your fathers [surely they could not in their wildest imagination have thought of Manhattan and the Bronx, or the prison camps of Hitler!] and there shall ye serve other gods day and night; where I will not show you favour. Therefore, behold the days come, saith the Lord, that it shall no more be said, The Lord liveth, that brought up the children out of the land of Egypt; but, The Lord liveth, that brought up the children of Israel from the land of the north, and from all the lands whither he had driven them; and I will bring them again into their land that I gave unto their fathers" (Jeremiah 16:13-15).

Again, speaking through Micah, God describes the miraculous works which shall be performed by God in bringing the Jews — every last one of them — from their corners of the earth. "According to the days of thy coming out of the land of Egypt will I show unto him marvelous things. The nations shall see and be confounded at all their might; they shall lay their hand upon their mouth, their ears shall be deaf. They shall lick the dust like the serpent" (Micah 7:15-17).

WONDERS TO COME

The wonders that God will yet perform upon this earth will be of a measure to cause men to forget all that He did in the plagues of Egypt. "Dust shall be the serpent's meat," was spoken of the devil in the garden of Eden. Here it is stated that all who follow him shall know the same discomfiture. In the mouths of men shall be the dust of utter defeat, even as in Egypt He executed judgments on the gods of the land.

The second standard of power, the greatest of all, is that which the Lord has performed on our behalf in raising Christ from the dead, and with Him, counted as being raised and seated in the heavenly places, the whole host of those who have put their trust in His Word and have followed by faith the path of God which seemed to be the path of humiliation but which ends in the skies. For when Christ rose from the dead, the infinite company of the believers, chosen in Christ before the foundation of the world, were freed forever from the thralldom of the earth and Satan, and were joined to the risen Lord. The Greek vocabulary is ransacked to bring together the expressions of force and might and power that were displayed by God in that triumphant hour when He manifested "what is the exceeding greatness of his power toward us who believe, according to the working of his mighty power, which he wrought in Christ when he raised him from the dead . . . and you who were dead in trespasses and sins . . . and hath raised us up together and made us to sit together in the heavenly places in Christ" (Ephesians 1:19, 20; 2:1, 6).

JUDGMENT ON THE GODS

We are now concerned with the first of these standards of power in which it is expressly stated that the Lord executed judgments upon the gods of Egypt. In order to understand this passage, and the whole of the chapters in Exodus relating to the plagues, it is necessary for us to understand a little of the nature of the religion of Egypt.

The worship of the land along the Nile is the greatest illustration of the truth of the revelation in the first of Romans concerning the departure of man from God and his consequent degradation. The history of humanity's descent into devil worship is clear and detailed. "They are without excuse: because that, when they knew God, they glorified him not as God, neither were thankful; but became vain in their imaginations, and their foolish heart was darkened. Professing themselves to be wise, they became fools, and changed the glory of the uncorruptible God into an image made like to corruptible man, and to birds, and four footed beasts, and creeping things. Wherefore God also gave them up . . ." (Romans 1:20-24).

There is the perfect description of the religion of Egypt. The whole picture becomes comprehensive when we realize the extent of the identification of the demon gods with the land, the water, and the sky of Egypt. In order to realize this fully, it is necessary to understand some of the special features of life in Egypt. The country is like one of the small towns in America where the inhabitants have built only along the highway for several miles; the town is thus forty blocks long and one block wide. Multiply this and you have a picture of much of Egypt.

The Nile was the highway of the ancient land as it is today. The river came from the impenetrable south, and its source was lost in the mystery of legend. Cataracts barred the upper river from navigation and burning deserts came down to the water's edge in what we know as the Sudan, while beyond the division of the river lay giant mountain chains, impassable to the men of that day. Vague rumors concerning the Nile source had come down into the lower land, and had been garbled to such an extent that Herodotus reported merely that the river came from the mountains of the moon. It is quite understandable, then, that a people which had departed from the solid ground, the true

revelation of God, and had entered on the precipitous slopes of poly-
theism should have identified some of their divinities with the river.

At certain seasons of the year the river overflowed its banks, and,
when it retired to its accustomed bed, it left behind it an alluvial deposit
of rich topsoil which made it possible for the land to bring forth in
abundance. It was natural, therefore, that the Egyptians should have
associated other of their gods with the fruitful soil which gave such
abundance for such comparatively little labor. Finally, there was almost never any rain in Egypt, and the clear blue sky above, with its
cloudless sun, drew the gaze and soon the worship of the people who
had abandoned the Lord God and who did not like to retain Him
in their knowledge.

With the desert always at their backs, the people were in the happy
prison of the narrow strip of land along their river, and their trinity of
multiple deities were centered in the water, the land and the sky. Satan,
so hungry for worship, had brought his principalities and powers into
the land in great force and was collecting all of the adoration that both
the cultured and educated leaders and the simple farm folk were capable
of offering. It was against these gods that the Lord was about to execute
judgment. There is evidence that Satan himself came into Egypt to
direct his side of the warfare. The Hebrew word that is used for the
serpents of the magicians (Exodus 7:10, 12) is the word that is translated *dragon* whenever that word is found in the English Old Testament.
The last book in the Bible identifies the dragon with "that old serpent,
called the Devil, and Satan, which deceiveth the whole world" (Revelation 12:9).

The contest in Egypt was not a matter to leave to one of his minions,
no matter of how exalted a rank such might be. The presence of the
evil one in person is not astonishing in view of the importance of the
conflict. The entire band of the children of Abraham were slaves in the
grip of the Hamitic masters, themselves under the grip of Satan. If
they could be crushed and destroyed in Egypt, the promise of God
would be frustrated and the Lord defeated. It was a bold chance, but
the only chance, and Satan threw in all his reserves and came to lead
them in person. The discomfiture of his hosts is therefore all the more
marked. The God who announced that "against all the gods of Egypt
I will execute judgment; I, Jehovah" (Exodus 12:12), is the God who
announced through Moses in the passage which we have read from
Numbers, that He did execute judgment against these gods.

The first of the judgments was upon the waters of Egypt. Not only
the Nile, but the other waters of the land, even the water that was drawn
for use in the houses, and which was kept in wooden vessels and stone

jars, turned to blood, and for seven days the whole land was in this horror, with the fish dying and the river stinking (Exodus 7:19-25). In order to comprehend the loss of face that this plague must have been for the gods of Egypt, we must realize how important and numerous were the gods of the river. Osiris, one of the chief gods of Egypt, was first of all god of the Nile. He, together with his companion, the mother god, Isis, and their child, Horus, were human-headed gods, among the many that had heads of birds, beasts and reptiles. This trinity of gods was the most favored among the common people, the ordinary peasant who was predecessor of the *felaheen* who work the banks of the Nile today. There were other gods of the Nile: Hapimon in the north, and Tauret at Thebes in whose honor and worship the greatest festival of the year was centered, and who was known as the great one, the hippopotamus goddess of the river. There was also Nu, the god of life in the Nile.

To these gods, prayers had been addressed for centuries and countless offerings had been made to propitiate them. Now they are seen to be as nothing. With a single word, the Jew, Moses, speaking through his brother, Aaron, declares the wonder, and the river turns to blood. The Hebrew word translated *wonder* indicates something outside the knowledge of man. Even the children of Israel did not know what was going on, for in the Psalms, it is revealed that "our fathers understood not thy wonders in Egypt" (Psalm 106:7). If the chosen Semites could not understand the marvelous working of God, how much greater the ignorance of the Hamitic Egyptians!

There is much evidence in the Bible that men do not understand the language of grace, and that they comprehend little of the language of judgment. If they are forced into a corner, they retreat with hatred and their hearts are not changed for the better, but rather for the worse. It was thus with Pharaoh — his heart was hardened. There have been those who have attacked the Scriptures and the God of the Scriptures because of this phrase. Their argument is that Pharaoh could not do anything else if Almighty God hardened his heart, and could it be just to harden his heart and then hold him responsible? The King James Version says that the Lord hardened Pharaoh's heart, but the Revised Version is closer to the Hebrew where the name of the Lord is not mentioned. "Pharaoh's heart was hardened" is the true rendering, and if it be asked who hardened his heart, there is a double answer. As we pointed out in a previous chapter, God makes the rules under which sin shall be sinned, though He Himself is not the author of sin. It a man chooses to go in a path of rejection, the course of that path carries him inevitably to hardness of heart. With every step of his stubborn erring, he takes himself farther from the melting power of the grace of God, and is carried on his own way. But is there not an answer in the fact that Satan was in the land, that Pharaoh was his principal human representative, and that he was in possession of the man's soul? This does not, of course, lessen the responsibility of Pharaoh, for every man is fully responsible for his own choices and doings.

Pharaoh had the abundant evidence of the truth of God before him, but his throne had been maintained by reliances on the forces of Satan who was the real power behind that throne. In spite of the evidence, and in spite of the fact that the Lord had said in the beginning that He would make Pharaoh's heart strong (Exodus 7:3) — strong enough to resist Satan if he really desired to — that carnal mind was enmity against God and was not subject to His law (Romans 8:7). Pharaoh's heart was hardened by a combination of the facts that he hated God, that the devil wanted him to head his forces in the war with God, and that God had created the conditions under which men's hearts operate in sin.

The second of the wonders also proved the emptiness of the powers of the gods of Egypt. The land was covered with a plague of frogs in such abundance that they entered the houses of the Egyptians and were found in their very beds (Exodus 8:2-14). We spoke of the fact that the Osiris trinity was represented by idols with human heads. These were comparatively rare among the pantheon of Egypt. Although nearly all the gods were represented with human bodies, almost all of these were represented with heads of birds, beasts and reptiles. One of the principal goddesses of the land was Hekt, wife of the creator of the world, who was always shown with the head and the body of a frog.

What were the people to do? We have a living illustration of their predicament in the actions of some of the devotees of India who hold life so sacred that they will not kill even vermin. It is possible to see beggars in the market places of India carefully removing fleas and lice from their bodies and dropping them alive at arm's length, from which point they are soon back on the itching carcass of their host. So the Egyptians, possessed by similar ideas, could not make war on the frogs that infested their dwellings, climbed upon them with their cold and clammy bodies, and penetrated even into their ovens and into the kneading troughs where their bread was made. To make it worse, these frogs had all come out of their sacred Nile (Exodus 8:3). When the myriads of frogs died, their decaying bodies must have turned the fields and banks of the Nile into a stinking horror. With what loss of face to the gods these events must have been accompanied, but with the respite Pharaoh hardened his heart.

25 : *Satan and History*
(CONTINUED)

THE LORD AND THE EARTH-GOD

THE third of the judgments on Pharaoh and on the gods of Egypt came out of the soil of Egypt. The alluvial deposits from the annual inundations made this soil, and make it today, one of the richest soils in the world. Nowhere can there be more bountiful crops. The Hebrews remembered the leeks, the onions, the garlic, the melons of Egypt, and the traveler today can find an abundance of luscious fruit in Egypt at modest prices. Our English versions translate the plague as one of lice, but this leaves something to be desired. The margin of the revision shows the hesitancy of the translators who added *sand flies,* and *fleas* as possible renderings of the Hebrew word *ken* which comes from a root meaning *to dig.* It is probable that the insect was one of that variety which digs under the skin of men, still found today in many parts of the world in different forms.

But where was the great god of the earth, Geb, to whom the priests made offerings because of the bounty of the soil? The artifice of the priests failed them at this point. They could not duplicate such things with their magic as they had done before, and they were too busy with the inconveniences of the itching to carry on their mummery!

THE LORD AND THE SCARAB-GOD

Our version records the fourth of the plagues as being "swarms *of flies.*" The last words are in italics because they are not in the original. The plague consisted of swarms, and perhaps the word signifies that the swarms were insects of all kinds. This would be a great irony on God's part because of the position of the sacred scarab among the gods of Egypt. Archaeologists have discovered tens of thousands of beetles, many carved from the most precious stones and with intaglio inscriptions on their backs. The reason for the deification of the scarab beetle is typical and most interesting. The insect is about as big as a five-cent piece, but it feeds on dung in the fields in a most curious way. When the flocks and herds defecate, these insects swarm from their holes in the ground and collect their provender for their future meals. They take the stercoral matter and form it into a mathematically perfect sphere about the size of a golf ball and roll it across the fields to their subterranean dwelling. The Egyptians were not very good entomologists, but they could not help observing the thousands of perfectly formed balls being rolled across their fields. They soon made a connection in their minds between the spheres of dung and the sun in the sky and conceived the idea that a giant beetle rolled the sun from evening until morning through the underworld until the sunrise brought it back into the sky once more. They also had the false idea that the beetle deposited its larva in the sphere, but modern entomology has proven that this is not true. The sun as the seed of life, however, they found illustrated in the work of the scarab, and some of the giant ones were accorded the honor of mummification and entombment with the Pharaohs. Amon-Ra, who was counted to be the king of the gods, had the head of a beetle. We can well imagine the consternation that covered the land at the arrival of swarms of these sacred insects in the houses. Possessed as they are with mandibles that are so serrated on one side that they can saw through wood, their destructive qualities would exceed that of termites. At the same time, they were looked upon with a reverence which might be compared to that of a Roman Catholic priest toward the piece of bread which he has supposedly turned into the body of Christ. The plague of the swarms had one other aspect which was humiliating to the gods of Egypt. God the Lord had divided between Egypt and the land of Goshen where the Israelites were encamped. The swarms came upon the Hamites in Egypt, but the Semites were not touched. The presence of the swarms caused Pharaoh to call Moses and plead for a cessation of the plague and offer the first hint of compromise, even asking to be prayed for (Exodus 8:28). But God does not compromise, always demanding an unconditional surrender. This was not acceptable to Pharaoh, and the judgments continued.

The LORD and the Bull-God

The fifth plague was against the domestic animals of Egypt. The worship of Apis, the bull-god, and of the cow-headed Hathor, goddess of the deserts, was so widespread that the children of Israel had themselves become infected with this worship, and later, when they thought that Moses had disappeared, gave their gold to be made into a calf, the image of Apis, and cried, "These be thy gods, O Israel, which brought thee out of the land of Egypt" (Exodus 32:4). Truly they did not understand the wonders that God was performing. In India also the traveler sees the cow, most sacred of all the animals, walking down the main streets of cities, going freely into stores and shops, nosing its way along the counters, or obstructing traffic in the streets. In Egypt the domestic animals were sacred, and in every temple there was a pen into which only the priests and Pharaoh could penetrate. In such a pen in each temple a live bull was kept and worshiped as being the incarnation of one of the gods. The plague that now came upon the land was a "murrain," a contagious disease among cattle, and even the sacred bulls in the temple died (Exodus 9:3-7). The other domestic animals were sacred also, and the murrain struck the goats and rams, the images of whose heads adorned the bodies of many idols. Perhaps even Bubastis, the cat goddess of love, feminine matters and fashion, was scourged with the pestilence. At all events the judgments executed against the gods had come into the back yards of every farmer and into the sacred enclosures of every temple. Once more the sons of Shem were spared, and when the news of this came to Pharaoh he sent messengers to investigate. The report proved that there was indeed the division between the two peoples and that even the cattle of the Hebrews was not touched. Yet still Pharaoh hardened his heart.

Ashes of Cursing

The sixth wonder was manifested against the bodies of men. The plague was one of "boils" (Exodus 9:8-11), though this word may hide something even more terrible than we see at first glance. The Hebrew root means *burning,* and the concordance reveals that the same word is translated as leprosy (Leviticus 13:18-20), and as the Egyptian botch (Deuteronomy 28:27, 35) which is declared to be incurable. The account of the plague gives no indication that any Egyptians were cured, for such cures might have been ascribed to the gods of the land, to many of whom they attributed great powers of healing. Among these there were notably Thoth, the ibis-headed god of intelligence and medical learning, Apis and Serapis and Imhotep. The author of the article on Egyptian religion in the *Encyclopedia Britannica* confesses a confusion among scholars concerning the attributes of the Egyptian deities, and seem disturbed about it, but when we consider that there were local deities who took on various characteristics at home and were overlapped by national deities, the difficulty disappears. The polytheistic mind is liable to consider that any god has any attribute in time of need. We can study the same phenomenon today where various powers are ascribed to a certain statue of the Virgin Mary not possessed by other statues of the same person, and where, for example, the Virgin of

Lourdes and the Virgin of La Salette and the Virgin of Fatima vie for the faithfulness of different devotees in the same church building.

At all events this sixth plague brought the conflict to the individual, and the magicians did not escape. We are informed directly that they were tainted with the plague, and must, therefore, have been unable to carry on their priestly functions. People may have brought their gifts and offerings in feverish hands, but feverish priests received them, and gods that were impotent must have been impotently served. More and more it was being forced upon the leaders that their gods were vanity. To add insult to injury the priests may well have known the particular means used by Moses to launch this plague against them. There were human sacrifices in the Egyptian religion, and it was the custom to take the ashes of these sacrifices and cast them into the air. Borne by the wind they floated over the milling populace who counted it a token of sure blessing to have some of the ashes fall upon them. From this heathen custom there is derived the modern practice of putting ashes on the forehead on the first day of Lent. Now Moses steps to the furnace and casts ashes into the air. We are not given the identification of the furnace, and it is useless to speculate. But the Moses who had access to the inner court of Pharaoh must have had access to the sacred precincts of the royal temples. His rod that changed to a serpent and his hand that could become leprous or cured by thrusting it into his bosom must have cleared a way for him to any place he desired to go. It is possible that the ashes were from the same source as the Egyptian ashes of blessing, but at the touch of Moses these ashes were ashes of cursing. Terrible to record, once more we read that "Pharaoh's heart was hardened."

THE CRACKING OF PUBLIC OPINION

The coming of the seventh wonder must have brought quaking terror to the hearts of the people. A great tempest came upon the land (Exodus 9:18-33), terrifying because Egypt is the sunny land with almost no rain. Now there was not only rain — the account tells us twice that there was rain, as though to make doubly sure that we comprehend the phenomenal nature of the storm — but there was also hail and fire. The Egyptians worship red water and fire, and now these two things were to break out and curse them. Where was Shu, the wind god? And where was Nut, the sky goddess? Where was Horus the elder, the hawk-headed sky god of upper Egypt? Could they not protect the land from these dire outbreaks in the nature that was supposed to be subservient to them?

The first cracking of public opinion came with this wonder. It had been announced that the animals that were left in the field would be destroyed, but that the animals that were put under cover would be spared. There were some that believed, for we read, "He that feared the word of the Lord among the servants of Pharaoh made his servants and his cattle flee into the houses" (Exodus 9:20). Once again the hardened ruler sent for Moses and confessed his sin and the sin of his people, even using the Hebrew names for God. "I have sinned this time: the Lord [Jehovah] is righteous, and I and my people are wicked. Intreat the Lord [Jehovah] that there be no more mighty thunderings [voices of Elohim]" (Exodus 9:27, 28). But it is possible for a man to confess his sin and to ask for prayer and yet be a hardened sinner. The French have a phrase that needs to be circulated in English. They speak of those who use spiritual language but whose heart is far from God as using *le patois de Canaan,* the dialect of Canaan. Pharaoh had the heart of Ham, even though his mouth was filled with the names of God that had been revealed to the Semites. Thus the judgments had to continue.

There seems to have been a long interval between some of the earlier plagues, but the eighth followed hard on the seventh. Locusts were brought into the land. It would appear that this was a new thing for Egypt. Locusts had been known in other places, but now the dread scourge of western North Africa and of western Asia was to come into the land of the Nile where it had not been known before. Every grain and twig and leaf that had escaped the fire and the hail was now taken by the locusts. Where was Nepri, the grain god? Where was Ermutet, goddess of childbirth and crops? Where was Anubis, jackal-headed guardian of the fields? Above all, where was Osiris, great head of the Hamitic trinity, who was also an agricultural god? The people of Egypt lost all faith in their gods. Rebellion even reached the palace. For before the locusts had come, Pharaoh's courtiers had pleaded with him to let the Semites go. "Let the men go that they may serve the Lord, their God [Jehovah, the God]; knowest thou not yet that Egypt is destroyed?" (Exodus 10:7). But after much vacillation and attempted compromise, Pharaoh's heart was hardened and the plague had come. The devourers were swift and the land was devastated. Then the Lord took a mighty, strong west wind and swept all the locusts into the Red Sea. Once more Pharaoh's heart was hardened.

THE LORD AND THE SUN-GOD

The movement of events was increasing in tempo. Swiftly the ninth wonder came. Darkness fell upon the land, darkness that could be felt. Josephus writes (II, 14, 15): "But when Moses said that what

he [Pharaoh] desired was unjust, since they were obliged to offer sacrifices to God of those cattle, and the time being prolonged on this account, a thick darkness, without the least light, spread itself over the
Egyptians, whereby their sight being obstructed, and their breathing
hindered by the thickness of the air, they were under terror lest they
be swallowed up by the thick cloud. This darkness, after three days
and as many nights was dissipated."

Gross darkness could be a normal thing in the land of the midnight sun, but this was not Norway or Alaska, this was Egypt. This
was the land of perpetual sunshine. Three hundred and sixty-five days
in the year, the sun shines in Egypt. And three hundred and sixty-five
nights in the year, the skies are so alight with moon and stars that there
is little like it to be seen from earth. The planets seem nearer than the
lights of neighbors, and the stars hang in the sky, liquid in their trembling beauty. Through our fogs, the heavens may be millions of light
years away, but in Egypt they seem to be just out the window and just
beyond the tree tops.

Suddenly the sky and the light were eclipsed by a phenomenon
that fell upon the land. The verb is one that denotes swiftness as when
a lion falls upon an unsuspecting prey. Life came to a halt. The people
were forced to remain in their beds for three days. Josephus' phrase
that their breathing was hindered by the thickness of the air may mean
that there was so much moisture in the atmosphere, that there could be
no combustion for the open flames of their candles or torches. Provisions are not stored up in hot lands, and there was no refrigeration
in those days. The people were without food; they could not see each
other; they lived, choking and gasping, in their beds.

We have mentioned more than a score of the gods of Egypt in
recounting the execution of God's judgment against them, but the greatest comes at the last. For over all the gods of Egypt was the great Ra,
god of the sun. So great was Ra that in parts of Egypt some of the
people held a religious position that closely resembled monotheism. In
the school of On, or Heliopolis, city of the sun, Ra was the only god.
He and Aten, the sun's disc, were worshiped, and the *ankh,* symbol of
life from the sun, with these made another sort of trinity that was yet
a monotheistic trinity. Now Ra, the great Ra, has disappeared. Did
the sacred scarab lose him in the underworld of the dead while pushing
him from sunset to sunrise? Like some ball of dung has he been crushed
beneath some monster foot and destroyed? Where are you Ra? And
if Ra is gone, there is no need of speaking of the god of the sunrise,
Horus, or the god of the sunset, Tem, or the god of light, Shu, or the
deities of the moon and the planets.

Pharaoh calls for Moses as soon as it is light and offers to let the people go, men, women and children. Is this surrender? No. The compromising Pharaoh demands that they go without their cattle. The text above all others texts in the Bible that speaks against the possibility of compromise is Moses' ringing statement, "There shall not an hoof be left behind!"

Once more the division was made by God between the children of Ham and the children of Shem. Though there was darkness over all of Egypt, darkness that could be felt, yet the children of Israel had light in their dwellings. It is a wonderful figure of the difference that God has put between the true believer today and the unbeliever. One of the glories which the children of God have in the gross darkness of this present age of the prince of darkness is that we have light in our hearts that makes the world's darkness and light alike to us, even as the darkness and the light are both alike to God (Psalm 139:12). We have that light because the Son of God came in the great darkness of the cross, crying, "My God, my God, why hast thou forsaken me?" (Matthew 27:46). The Father forsook His Son in that darkness that He might not have to forsake us, and that He might bring us into the holiness of His eternal light.

What the Lord Jesus Christ was to be and to do was now illustrated in the Passover. Blood was put on the doors of the houses of the Israelites. The angel of death, messenger of judgment from Jehovah God, walked through the land. Where there was no blood on the door there was death. The gods of Egypt were exhibited as vain pretenders. In the announcement of the death of Egypt's first-born, there is also the inclusion of the judgment upon the devil gods of the land. "For I will pass through the land of Egypt this night, and will smite all the first-born in the land of Egypt, both man and beast; and against all the gods of Egypt I will execute judgment; I am the Lord" (Exodus 12:12).

But where there was blood on the door there was no death in the house. God in His judgment passed over them because the blood was there. Inside there may have been a trembling Hebrew boy, crying in terror for fear of the judgment that had been announced. In another house there may have been a lad full of faith and singing for joy. The angel of death passed over the first as readily as over the second. God had not said, "When I see you happy I will pass over you"; but "When I see the blood I will pass over you." Oh, the preciousness of the blood of the Son of God!

The plagues of Egypt delivered the people of God from the children of Ham. The power of the great land was broken. There would be other Pharaohs sitting on the throne of the ruler who had no tomb but the watery grave of the Red Sea, but Egypt would never be a material menace again. God would continue to warn the children of Israel against any spiritual turning to Egypt. He would never sanction any union with that land. As in the very first days when He refused to acknowledge Ishmael, since Hagar was an Egyptian and could never bear the child of promise, even though Abraham's strength begot the child, so to the very end of days God would warn His people against the evils that were dormant in Egypt and all that it stood for. Centuries later Pharaoh Necho would march an army hundreds of miles to the north to help the Hittites, other sons of Ham, against the power of Assyria. It would be a vain gesture. They would turn at Carchemish from other sons of Shem and would retreat ignominiously to their homeland, soon to be overrun by Greece and then Rome. Never again would they be anything but a base kingdom. God would say through Ezekiel: "Son of man, set thy face against Pharaoh, king of Egypt, and prophesy against him, and against all Egypt; Speak and say, Thus saith the Lord God; Behold I am against thee, Pharaoh, king of Egypt, the great dragon that lieth in the midst of his rivers, which hath said, My river is mine own, and I have made it for myself . . . I will bring thee up out of the midst of thy rivers . . . I will leave thee thrown into the wilderness . . . and all the inhabitants of Egypt shall know that I am the Lord . . . and the land of Egypt shall be desolate and waste, and they shall know that I am the Lord, because he hath said, The river is mine and I have made it . . . There they shall be a base kingdom. It shall be the basest of the kingdoms; neither shall it exalt itself any more above the nations; for I will diminish them, that they shall no more rule over the nations. And it shall be no more the confidence of the house of Israel, which bringeth their iniquity to remembrance, when they shall look after them: but they shall know that I am the Lord God" (Ezekiel 37). Thus it has come to pass.

Today it is the third brother, Japheth, who is dwelling in the tents of Shem, even as God announced (Genesis 9:27). As the many threads of the story of Ham's rebellion have made the strange ravelling which we have seen, so the threads of the story of Japheth have made an even greater tangle which will be cut across by a Gordian stroke in God's own time. The wonders of the Second Coming of Christ, greater by far than the wonders wrought in Egypt, will accompany the deliverance of Shem from the power of Japheth. That is another story. The vision is for an appointed time. He shall surely come and shall not tarry (Habakkuk 2:3; Hebrews 10:37).

26 : *The Battle of the Cross*

PERSPECTIVE ON THE BATTLE

I N one sense, of course, the cross was not a battle at all. In the same sense, the invisible war is not a war at all. Can we call it battle or war when one side has all the wisdom and all the power and all the might and all the dominion, and when that side knows before it all begins exactly what will happen, so that every detail is the simple fulfillment of an eternal plan?

But in the more limited sense it is a war, and in that sense the cross of Jesus Christ is the central and all-important battle in that war. It was at the cross that the great principles of God's ways were manifested. The matter of the ways of God is second in the Bible only to the doctrinal truths of God. In one great passage He says: "For my thoughts are not your thoughts, neither are your ways my ways" (Isaiah 55:8).

The cross of Jesus Christ is the supreme demonstration of the ways of God. Here, before men, angels and demons, the principles of the divine purpose and method shall be revealed so that all who follow shall be able to know and understand the good purpose of His will and shall be able to see the holiness of the working of that will.

There have been thousands of sermons preached on the cross, most of which have stressed the effect of the atonement on the believer as being the basic ground of his salvation from sin. But we shall see that there is something in the work of the cross much greater than the salvation of the sinner. A nation may fight a great war and thousands of its soldiers may be killed. In a remote village, a lonely mother's concern is primarily that her only son return safe and sound. To the nation, the important thing is that the war be won, even though a certain number of thousands of lives are expended in the conflict. My individual salvation is very important to me, but the honor and glory of God are much more important. The vindication of the divine righteousness and holiness far transcends any human interests in the great conflict.

213

THE SCOPE OF THE BATTLE

In this chapter we propose to show that (1) the redemptive work of Christ is applicable to us because God was using it to nullify the law that was against us; (2) in so doing He revealed to the universe that Satan is in reality a mere boastful pretender; (3) on the basis of the righteousness manifested by Christ in the manner in which He proceeded to the cross, our Lord was able to strip Satan of all his pretensions; (4) He gave to us, the believers, all the powers and offices which had once been given to Satan or which had been usurped by him. In doing these four things, God revealed the method of the operation of His holiness.

One of the key passages of this theme is to be found in the epistle to the Colossians. There we read, "And you, who were dead in trespasses and the uncircumcision of your flesh, God made alive together with him, having forgiven us all our trespasses; having canceled the bond which stood against us with it legal demands; this he set aside, nailing it to the cross. He disarmed the principalities and powers and made a public example of them, triumphing over them in it" (2:13-15).

THE LAW NULLIFIED

Proceeding now to the exposition of this passage, we have first the declaration that somehow the cross of Jesus Christ nullified the law that was against us. It has frequently been argued that God was not just, because He took the sins of believers and put them upon Christ, the Lamb without spot and without blemish. The answer is found in the nature of what Christ became before God put Him to death. When we have understood this, we can see how the provisions of the law that were against us have been completely nullified.

It is true that the Lord Jesus Christ was sinless and infinitely perfect. In every way possible His godhead and holiness were announced. At the time of His conception it was announced to His mother, the Virgin Mary, that her child should be called the Son of God because "The Holy Spirit will come upon you, and the power of the Most High will overshadow you; therefore the child to be born of you will be called holy, the Son of God" (Luke 1:35). It should be noted that this verse vitiates the Romanist doctrine that Mary was "the mother of God." What would have been an ordinary human child if born to her by natural generation was called the Son of God only because the Holy Spirit overshadowed her. When John the Baptist identified Him as the Lamb, God the Father would not permit the human testimony of John to describe the Lord Jesus. John could say only that the One coming was mightier than he and that he, the forerunner, was not worthy to stoop to tie the latches of His sandals. But at best that was the estimate of a man, looking upon outward appearances. It was God, who looks upon the heart, who spoke from heaven, "This is my beloved Son, in whom I am well pleased" (Matthew 3:17).

Throughout the gospels, every opportunity is taken to reveal the Lord Jesus as the Messiah, the Holy One of Israel. At the end of three years of ministry, the moment has now come for Him to go to the cross and be sacrificed. But is He still the Lamb without spot and blemish? For He has sat in taverns with publicans and sinners. The sneering have called Him a glutton and a winebibber (Matthew 11:19). Evil women have touched Him and looked Him in the eye. Is He still without sin? Man cannot discern, but God takes the Lord Jesus into the mount of transfiguration, and the holiness of heaven shines through Him, visible even to the sleeping disciples who stumble into the scene. The voice of God once more speaks from heaven, and God the Father, the all holy, takes the responsibility for declaring once more, "This is my beloved Son in whom I am well pleased" (Matthew 17:5).

THE SINLESS TRANSGRESSOR

How then can the Holy God put this Holy Son to death? The answer is in the mystery of His becoming sin for us. We read, "For God hath made Christ to be sin for us, he who knew no sin; that we might be made the righteousness of God in him" (II Corinthians 5:21). How could this be? The answer is to be found in another passage of Scripture: "Christ redeemed us from the curse of the law, having become a curse for us — for it is written, 'Cursed be every one who hangs on a tree'" (Galatians 3:13). The Lord Jesus, though sinless, became a transgressor of the law and thus drew down the curse of God upon Himself.

To understand this, we must realize that God the Father does not count transgression in the same way that man counts it. Human law never counts a man guilty until he has performed an actual deed of transgression. Not so with God. The police might arrest a man who is found in a dark alley beside an open window through which can be seen money and other valuables. If the policeman reached the scene in time, and there was no loot found on the man, he could be arrested only for vagrancy or trespassing or loitering. If he had reached his hand through the window and taken five or ten dollars, he would be tried in a police court and convicted of petty larceny. If he had taken five thousand dollars, he would be tried in another court and charged with grand larceny. If he had opened the window himself there would be a further degree of guilt. If the window had been locked and he had forced it open, the crime would be still greater. If he had been in possession of a weapon at the time, the charge and the penalty would reach a still higher level. Man's law operates on this basis; so whenever a man is arrested, his first thought is to get a good lawyer who can have him charged with something less than that which he has really done. A good lawyer may get a murderer free from hanging by persuading the prosecutor and the judge to accept a plea of manslaughter. Man's law says that a man is not a thief until he has stolen, not a murderer until he has, with premeditation, killed another. God says that the man steals because he is a thief and that he kills because he is a murderer at heart.

For this reason God does not recognize many and varying shades of guilt. Any human being who is morally less perfect than God is declared to be a sinner. "Whosoever keeps the whole law but fails in one point has become guilty of all of it" (James 2:10). Thus, no human being can escape the charge of being a sinner in the definition of the law of God. It makes no difference at what point the law has been transgressed; the guilt is the same in all cases.

This principle is amplified in another passage which recounts how the sinless Saviour became a technical violator of the law and thus guilty of all; therefore, subject to the wrath of a holy God against sin. We read, "For all who rely on works of the law are under a curse; for it is written: 'Cursed be every one who does not abide by all things written in the book of the law, and do them' " (Galatians 3:10). If we paraphrase that verse, it reads that there is a curse of God against anyone who is not absolutely perfect in the deepest and most absolute sense of holy perfection.

The next verses go on to tell how the Lord Jesus became the technical violator of that perfect law. Back in the book of Deuteronomy, the Lord God had seen to it that there was a pregnant phrase incorporated into the giving of the law. Men may never have understood the tremendous part that line was to take in the plan of God. There it was stated, and in our King James version it is presented in almost a casual form in a parenthesis, "And if a man have committed a sin worthy of death, and he be to be put to death, and thou hang him on a tree; His body shall not remain all night upon the tree, but thou shalt in any wise bury him that day; (for he that is hanged is accursed of God;) that thy land be not defiled, which the Lord thy God giveth thee for an inheritance" (Deuteronomy 21:22, 23). The New Testament passage makes this verse the secret whereby the righteous and holy Father God could curse His Son, the Lord Jesus, and turn away from Him when He was dying on the cross. We read, "Christ redeemed us from the curse of the law, having become a curse for us—for it is written [in that parenthesis in Deuteronomy]: 'Cursed is every one that hangeth on a tree' " (Galatians 3:13).

Now we can understand that the sufferings of the Lord at the hands of evil men in the guardroom or on the road to the cross were not sufferings for sin. The blood that was shed by pressing the crown of thorns into His brow was not blood shed for the atoning of sin. He was at that time the perfectly righteous, holy God. That was blood shed to show all the martyrs that should follow Him that He had suffered for righteousness sake at the hands of evil men. It was a suffering that He permits us to share with Him. But when the executioners took the nails and put them through His hands and feet and lifted the cross upright, He became in that moment a violator of the law of God. He was made sin. He was made the curse. God the Father was able to pour out on Him all the wrath which He had stored up against sin, already committed or to be committed, by an innumerable company of men. When the Lord Jesus thus hung upon the cross, He was accursed. God could do nothing other than turn away from Him. This is the ground of that terrible cry which rose from His lips in those dark hours, "My God, my God, why hast thou forsaken me?" (Matthew 27:46). Dr. Harry Emerson Fosdick once said that Christ was mistaken when He thus cried out upon the cross and that the Father was never more with Him than in that dark hour of His suffering. Such a denial shows a total failure to comprehend either the holiness of God, the sinfulness of sin, or the nature of the work that the Lord Jesus was performing by becoming sin for us.

WHO PUT CHRIST TO DEATH?

No man will ever comprehend the death of Jesus Christ until he realizes that the Lord was put to death by God the Father. The fact that the Jews delivered Him over to death is relatively unimportant, even if they did cry that His blood was to be upon them and upon their children. The fact that Gentiles did the actual hammering of the nails through the hands and feet of Christ is again relatively unimportant. The one thing that really matters is that God the Father put God the Son to death. This is what makes the atonement for sin. The substitute is taking the blow that should rightfully have been ours. It had been thus prophesied, "Yet it pleased Jehovah to bruise him; he hath put him to grief" (Isaiah 53:10). On the day of Pentecost Peter immediately proclaimed this fact in the first recorded Christian sermon — "Him, being delivered by the determinate counsel and foreknowledge of God" (Acts 2:23).

Thus the love of God in Christ presented Himself as the Substitute, paying the fine to the justice of God and satisfying the claims of the holiness of God. Thus the full vicarious, substitutionary payment was made. Thus we have the Saviour. It immediately follows that there can be no claim whatsoever left against the sinner whose guilt has been put upon the Saviour. He paid it all, and there cannot be anything left to collect from the transgressor. If God attempted to exact payment from a believer after He Himself had put all his guilt upon the sin-bearer, there would be unrighteousness with God. When we sing, "Jesus paid it all," we are stating the fact that God Himself has obligated Himself in such a way that He must look upon the believer as being free from debt, as Christ Himself was free when He had cried, "It is finished" (John 19:30). It is for this reason that the Holy Spirit can bring the wonderful promise to us, "There is therefore now no condemnation [no judgment] to them that are in Christ Jesus" (Romans 8:1). When we come to the study of the difference between the judgment of the believers and the judgment of the unbelievers, we must remember this point. God will take the believers to heaven without any judgment whatsoever as to their guilt for sin. That is in the past, and the believer will never face it again in time nor in eternity. The believer will be judged for his Christian life, so that his position and rewards in heaven shall be determined; but the question of his being in heaven has been settled on the cross, and the Lord God Almighty Himself cannot become guilty of bringing the believer into double jeopardy.

I remember hearing a simple story that illustrates the certainty of our position and that brings delight to the trusting soul. It is said that a young Scotch minister, newly out of school, went to visit a dear old saint of God who lay dying. She was filled with the glory that comes at the sunset of a rich life, passed in a close walk with the Saviour, and was praising God with great joy. The young man was long on theology and short on Bible and had never come so close to such rich fellowship before. He attempted to bring her back to an experience more nearly approximating his own. He told her that she should be careful to give diligence to make her calling and election sure; that she must remember that the one who thinketh he standeth should take heed lest he fall. The dear old lady was so much beyond this in spiritual experience that she was not disturbed for an instant. She said to the young minister, "Laddie, if I should nae be in heaven the guid Laird would lose much more than I." This frightened the minister and he began to expostulate even more until she broke in upon him, "Laddie, if I should nae be in heaven, the guid Laird would lose His honor. His word would be gone."

And, of course, she was absolutely right. "What more can He say than to you He hath said?"

The doctrine that we have here set forth explains a part of what we have seen in Colossians: "And you who were dead in trespasses and the uncircumcision of your flesh. God made alive together with him, having forgiven us all our trespasses: having canceled the bond which stood against us with its legal demands; this he set aside, nailing it to his cross." This brings us to the next phase of the truth: "He disarmed the principalities and powers, and made a public example of them, triumphing over them in it."

We find it easier to understand the spoiling of the principalities and powers when we have comprehended the great fact that in the triumph of the cross the Lord Jesus made a public example of them. The cross was the revelation of the truth of God's ways and the falsity of Satan's ways. When this is realized, the whole of our civilization will be seen in a new light. The mad rush of men to get to the pinnacle of their selfish desires by climbing — climbing even at the expense of those they ruthlessly brush aside in the race for what they call success — is seen for what it really is when we put it beside Satan's similar method to achieve power and worship, and when we put it beside the work of the Lord Jesus Christ.

27 : *The Battle of the Cross*
(Continued)

THE EXALTED HUMBLED

IT is well-known that the Lord Jesus repeated some of His sermons. A close study of the gospels reveals the fact that He set forth certain truths under widely differing circumstances, using the same illustrations over again, and at times drawing the same conclusion from widely differing incidents. This is especially seen in one sentence which He spoke on three different occasions, "Whosoever exalts himself will be humbled; and whoever humbles himself will be exalted." I believe that the thrice-repeated phrase can be understood only in the light of what He Himself did at the cross. Or to put it in another way, what He did at the cross was the final exemplification of the truth of His statement and, at the same time, the full proof of the hollowness of Satan's flimsy pretense. The first time we find this phrase is at the end of a passage of sharp criticism of the scribes and the Pharisees. The Lord told the people that they were to follow these leaders on their teaching out of Moses but were not to follow their doing, because they did their works to be seen of men. They wore wide signs on their foreheads and broad borders on their garments. They loved greetings in the market places and titles conferred upon them by the crowd. But, said Christ, "He who is greatest among you shall be your servant. And whosoever exalts himself will be humbled; and whoever humbles himself will be exalted" (Matthew 23:1-12).

On another occasion the Lord was invited to eat in the home of a Pharisee. There were many guests and He watched how they all crowded to the places of honor. The Lord said, "When you are invited by anyone to a marriage feast, do not sit down in a place of honor; lest a more eminent man than you be invited by him; and he who invited you both will come and say to you, Give place to this man; and then you will begin with shame to take the lowest place. But when you are invited, go and sit in the lowest place, so that when your host comes, he may say to you, 'Friend, go up higher'; then you will be honored in the presence of all who sit at table with you. For everyone who exalts himself will be humbled; and he who humbles himself will be exalted" (Luke 14:8-12).

On still another occasion he spoke what has become known as the parable of the Pharisee and the publican. The Pharisee looked within himself with the eyes of the flesh and thought that he had fulfilled the requirements of the moral law because he had fulfilled the ceremonial law. He thanked God that he had done all that was required and that he was not like the poor publican. The latter, however, understood the doctrine of salvation by grace. He accepted the bankruptcy of his own position before God. We can paraphrase what he did and said as follows: "O God, I have nothing of works to offer. I come not daring to look toward heaven. Do not deal with me on the basis of judgment, but, God, deal with me in pure grace." His literal words were "God be mercy-seated to me a sinner." There has been untold misunderstanding because of the translation, "God be merciful." God, of course, has been merciful, and there is nothing more that He can do for the sinner or that He need do for the sinner. "God be mercy-seated" means: deal with me on the basis of the blood sacrifice, the propitiation which the High Priest pours upon the mercy-seat on the great day of atonement. Christ added, "I tell you this man went down to his house justified rather than the other; for every one who exalts himself will be humbled: but he who humbles himself will be exalted" (Luke 18:10-14).

THE HUMBLE EXALTED

Here then is a divine principle which pervades the teachings of the Lord Jesus and the whole of the Scripture. It is found as early as the book of Job, "When men are cast down, then thou shalt say, There is lifting up; and he shall have the humble person" (Job 22:29). David, in the Psalms, sings, "Thou dost deliver a humble people; but the haughty eyes thou dost bring down" (Psalm 18:27). Solomon expressed it in the Proverbs: "A man's pride will bring him low; he who is lowly in spirit will obtain honor" (Proverbs 29:23). James wrote, "God opposes the proud, but gives grace to the humble" (James 4:6). Peter used the identical words that James used (I Peter 5:5) and added, "Humble yourselves therefore under the mighty hand of God, that in due time he may exalt you."

In spite of its constant use throughout the Bible and the special emphasis put upon it by our Lord's threefold use of it, the principle has never been accepted by the world; nor is it to be found in history, ancient or modern. The world has built its own proverbs which are absolutely contrary to the divine teaching: "Every man for himself and the devil take the hindmost"; "The Lord helps those who help themselves"; "Might makes right"; "Money talks"; "God is on the side of the strongest artillery." The proverbs are expressions of widely held attitudes. In our own day of high-pressure methods, advertising agencies and Hollywood publicity, it would seem that there is no possible chance of the world being wrong and the Lord being right. The formula of success in the world has simply nothing in common with the truth expressed by the Word of God.

It was the death of the Lord Jesus Christ, however, that revealed the bankruptcy of all that the world still clings to, and that provided the basis for the ultimate triumph of the divine principle which now is in total eclipse in the world dominated by Satan, prince of this world and god of this age.

Satan had spoken first. His idea had been set forth in his original declaration of independence. "I will ascend . . . I will exalt . . . I will sit . . . I will ascend . . . I will be like the Most High God" (Isaiah 14: 13, 14). To that great cry of pride the Lord Jehovah had answered, "Yet thou shalt be brought down to hell, to the sides of the pit" (verse 15).

The movement of the Lord Jesus had been in exactly the opposite direction. Satan had said, "I will ascend." The Lord Jesus Christ said in effect, "I will descend." The sevenfold descent is set forth: "Who though he was in the form of God, did not count equality with God a thing to be grasped; but emptied himself, taking the form of a servant, being born in the likeness of men. And being found in human form, he humbled himself, and became obedient unto death, even death on a cross" (Philippians 2:6-8).

THE BANKRUPTCY OF SATAN

The death of the Lord Jesus Christ demonstrated the bankruptcy of Satan's entire theory of success. It was in this that He made a public example of Satan and all his principalities and powers. Their embattled efforts to build a kingdom on earth would fail. They would seek to give man power through the place of pride; their kingdom would fall. It would take a little time for the full effect to be manifested, but the invisible war would come to its triumphant conclusion and all the force of Satan would be put down on the principles that were established when the Lord Jesus humbled Himself to the death, even death on a cross.

It was on the basis of this unmasking of Satan at Calvary that the

Lord God took from the pretender all of the offices which had been given him in his unfallen state and deprived him of all that he had seized in the rebellion. Lucifer was the original possessor of certain God-given rights, titles and offices. As Satan he proceeded to claim other privileges. The death of the Lord Jesus Christ spoiled him of all that he had been given and of all that he had seized. We must understand the phrase as a military metaphor. For example, at the end of the great battles around Stalingrad which resulted in the overthrow of German power in Russia, it was announced that a vast spoil had been taken from Hitler's forces. The lists were published: so many tanks were taken, so many trucks, so many pieces of heavy artillery, so many pieces of light artillery, so many machine guns, so many prisoners, all in the tens of thousands; so many millions of rounds of ammunition were seized, and so many hundreds of miles of territory were reclaimed. But after this came something more. The Germans had originally possessed Germany by right of inheritance. They had occupied other lands by force. Now they were to lose all that they had occupied, and ultimately they were to lose their own land and their original power and would be crushed to death.

The spoil which the Lord Jesus Christ took from Satan at the cross may be counted in even more categories and in even greater dimensions. At his creation Lucifer was given the office of prophet, to speak for God; the office of priest to take the worship of the universe of creatures to God; the office of king to rule for God. At the moment of his rebellion, he, of course, forfeited the right to all of these offices and the practice of some of them. In the very nature of his fall, he gave up the office of prophet. He no longer spoke for God, though he has never ceased to insist that his voice is the voice of God. In the very nature of his fall, he gave up the office of priest. He no longer took worship to God, though in a million ways he seeks such worship and deceives multitudes in giving to him the worship which should go to God alone. Carefully understood, it will be seen also that in the very nature of his fall he lost the office of king, though he still retained certain domains, the title of which even the Lord Jesus Christ admitted was valid. He is still prince of this world (John 12:31), still prince of the power of the air (Ephesians 2:2), still the head of the world-rulers of this darkness (Ephesians 6:12), still the god of this age (II Corinthians 4:4). The cross established the basis of the ultimate destitution of all of these offices. God did not seize the authority and offices which he had given Satan, when the rebellion first came to light. He could have done so, of course, for omnipotence is infinitely beyond any degree of finite power. God was waiting for the cross in order to begin the work of disarming Satan. The process might seem slow to men, living within the ticking moments of time, but in the sight of the eternal God and the spirit-beings who are beyond time, the process was inexorable and certain. From the moment Christ died, the watching universe would see that Satan and his hosts were sentenced and that the present and future manifestation of his impotence and his complete despoiling would be carried out in accordance with principles so true, so certain, so perfect, that there could never be a whisper raised — even in the lake of fire — against the fact or the method of the procedure.

THE DESCENT INTO HELL

Although the victory was fully won by the descent of the Lord from glory to the cross, there was to be one more descent of the Saviour, even into the realm of hell. The victory had been won by the principle of humiliation and death. The prize would be seized by one more triumphant plunge into descent. We recite it in the Apostle's Creed: "He descended into hell. . . ." The early Christians who formulated this creed had a clear understanding of the importance of doctrine, and they rightly included this phrase which has been omitted by some modern editors of the creed, because they do not understand the wonderful nature of the victory which the Lord Jesus won in His death.

Satan was in possession of a very great spoil. He had in one part of hell all the souls of all the believers from righteous Abel, who had been the first human being to die, down to the soul of the penitent thief, who was to linger on in life for a brief moment after Christ gave up His spirit, and who would die after the executioners broke his legs with blows. Such blows could never touch the Saviour because all of the price had now been paid, and it had been written that not a bone of Him should be broken (Exodus 12:46; Numbers 9:12; Psalm 34:20; John 19:36).

The triumph of Christ and the nature of the spoil is all the more wonderful when we understand just what had been the state of the dead before the time of the cross. The Bible teaches clearly that the bodies of all who die return to the dust from which they were made (Genesis 3:19). In the grave of the body, there was no knowledge and no return. The bodies of the dead knew not anything. All the verses in Scripture that speak of unconsciousness after death are referring to the sleep of the body. Longfellow grasped the truth well when he wrote:

> Dust thou art, to dust returnest
> Was not spoken of the soul.

But hell, whether we speak of it under the Hebrew word "sheol" or the Greek word "hades" or under our English translation, "hell," was the place of the conscious existence of the souls and spirits of all the dead, believers and unbelievers, who died before the time of the death of the Lord Jesus Christ. This hell was in two compartments, torment and paradise, and between the two there was a great gulf fixed. In the story, not parable — be sure you understand that it was not a parable — of the rich man and Lazarus, the Lord Jesus describes the difference between the death of a believer and an unbeliever while He Himself was yet alive on the earth (Luke 16:19-31). The beggar died and was carried by angels into "Abraham's bosom"; the rich man died and "in hell he lift up his eyes being in torments." Abraham and Lazarus were visible "afar off," and Abraham told the rich man that "between us and you there is a great gulf fixed."

It was to Paradise in hell that the Lord Jesus Christ went in His Spirit at the moment He dismissed it on the cross. It was a direct invasion of territory that Satan had considered as being his own. We are greatly tempted to let our imagination run to what must have happened when the Lord of glory made His appearance there. What must there have been in the hearts of all who had opposed Him in His righteous ones through all generations! What must have been in the hearts of those who had ventured all in faith, with nothing more than His promise, waiting for this moment! But since our God has not been pleased to reveal any of the details, we shall never go beyond that which is written.

The arrival of Christ in hell and His subsequent departure, taking with Him all the spirits and souls of all believers, emptying hell of the saints, casts great light on several passages of Scripture and reveals more of the nature of the spoil which He took from Satan by this work of atonement and its consequences. The triumph by humiliation had revealed the rightness of the divine methods as opposed to the false methods of pride and arrogance. Christ's descent into hell was to bring the immediate announcement of His victory to all the spirit world and to show the authority that He had now gained by conquest.

Up until this time, the devil had had the power of death (Hebrews 2:14), and he had also in charge the keys of death and hell (Revelation 1:18). When man sinned, the law of sin and death began its operation, and Satan had the power of enforcing this law within limits set by God. It would appear that all the unregenerate are within the devil's power at any time and are taken captive by him at his will (II Timothy 2:26). When he desires, he can make an unsaved man sick, or can make him well, or can take his body in death. Before the cross, he held the keys, or the authority, over the decay of the tomb and the entrance to hell, but there is no line to say that he had any power whatsoever in hell. We know from the book of Job that Satan exercised the power of death over the children of Job only when permitted by God, and that he could not touch Job's body until he had the divine permission. The New Testament reveals to us that he is still the agent forced by God to perform some actual task in connection with the physical death, even of a believer (I Corinthians 5:5). Perhaps here is a part of the explanation of the conflict between Michael, the archangel, and Satan concerning the body of Moses. God had designed that Moses should appear with Christ at the transfiguration (Luke 9:30), and that he shall be raised from the dead as one of the two witnesses of the Apocalypse (Revelation 11:3), and therefore, an exception was made in connection with his body at the time of his death. Even though Satan's task concerning death might have been a loathesome one, he was offended when Michael interfered. But whatever his work in connection with bodies, the spirits and souls of the believers were never, for an instant, in his power, and upon death they are taken in charge by the angels of God, who, before the time of the cross, carried them to Paradise (Luke 16:22).

The death of the Lord Jesus Christ destroyed – brought to nought – "him that had the power of death, that is, the devil" (Hebrews 2:14). The word "destroy" has no suspicion of any such meaning as annihilation but rather is that of rendering harmless, useless, worthless. Thus the Lord made a public example of Satan and immediately proved the decline of Satan's power by taking the keys with which Satan pretended to some authority over the righteous spirits and, entering among them until the three days and nights should be accomplished, announced the freeing of those who had been thus detained.

The fact that our Lord told the penitent thief that they would be together on that very day in Paradise also demonstrates that He did not have to go to torment in hell, where the unregenerate spirits had been confined. Herein lies the explanation of three passages in the Bible. First, here is the meaning of our Lord's prayer in the garden of Gethsemane: "O my Father, if it be possible, let this cup pass from me; nevertheless not as I will, but as thou wilt" (Matthew 26:39). Some have thought that He was flinching before the thought of the agony of the cross that was about to come. Such flinching would have been a spot and a blemish, which would have rendered Him ineligible to be the Lamb slain for sinners. Some have thought that Satan had come with a fierce attack that would have meant premature death, when He sweat great drops of blood and that the attempt was being made in order to prevent Him from going on to the cross to become the Saviour. Such an explanation would have Satan to possess power superior to that of the Son of God and would negate His own express statement, "No man [Greek, no one] taketh it [my life] from me, but I lay it down of myself. I have power to lay it down, and I have power to take it again" (John 10:18). The cup, as another passage clearly shows, was the wine of the wrath of God, the full wages of sin, the second death, separation from God in torment in hell, and ultimate eternity in the lake of fire. Thus the whole scene of the cup is described, "Who in the days of his flesh, when he had offered up prayers and supplications with strong crying and tears unto him that was able to save him from death, and was heard . . ." (Hebrews 5:7). That this is the true meaning of the passage is also proved by the nature of prayer. God *must* answer all prayer that is in His will (I John 5:14, 15). Christ, being of the deity, could not have prayed a prayer outside of the divine will; otherwise He would thereby have been a sinner. Therefore the prayer for the passing of the cup must have been heard and answered affirmatively. This is what the writer to the Hebrews clearly affirms: He prayed and was heard.

This, too, explains the triumphant cry of Peter on the day of Pentecost. He quotes the Psalmist: "For David says concerning him, I saw the Lord always before me, for he is at my right hand, that I may not be shaken; therefore my heart was glad, and my tongue rejoiced; moreover my flesh will dwell in hope, for thou wilt not abandon my soul to hades, nor let thy Holy One see corruption. Thou hast made known to me the ways of life; thou wilt make me full of gladness with thy presence. Men and brethren, I may say to you confidently of the patriarch David, that he both died and was buried, and his tomb is with us to this day. Being therefore a prophet, and knowing that God had sworn with an oath to him that of the fruit of his loins, according to the flesh, he would raise up Christ to sit on his throne; he foresaw and spoke of the resurrection of the Christ, that his soul was not abandoned to Hades, nor did his flesh see corruption" (Acts 2:25-31).

So Christ descended into Paradise and on the third day the Lord God brought Him forth and with Him emptied hell of the spirits and souls of all the vast company of the redeemed. What a spoil! What a prey! Now before all of the angels of the universe, fallen and unfallen, could the plan of God begin to be seen in all its righteous perspective. The spirits and souls of all the redeemed were taken to heaven on that day of His Resurrection, For it was on the day of the Resurrection that this happened. He appeared to Mary and told her not to touch Him because He had not yet ascended to His Father (John 20:17), yet a few hours later He was back in the midst of the disciples, saying, "Handle me, and see" (Luke 24:39).

Not only had our Lord thus used the keys of hell to empty it of all the spirits and souls of believers, but He had locked that compartment so that none of His own, forever, would ever be forced to pass even one moment away from Himself. Here was the fulfillment of His announcement concerning His Church, that the gates of hell should never prevail against it (Matthew 16:18). How often has the force of Satan prevailed against the Church on earth! The proof lies in even a casual glance at Rome, Corinth, Galatia, Ephesus, Philippi, Colosse and Thessalonica. But "when he ascended on high, he led captivity captive" (Ephesians 4:8). Henceforth death would usher all believers directly into the presence of the Lord. To be absent from the body would mean to be present with the Lord (II Corinthians 5:8); to depart would mean to be with Christ which is far better (Philippians 1:23).

Moreover, in order to reveal to the universe that the victory over death was complete, He invaded the very dust of the earth at His Resurrection and took out the bodies of a select company and gave them resurrection bodies. "The graves were opened; and many of the bodies of the saints which slept arose, and came out of the graves after his resurrection, and went into the holy city, and appeared unto many" (Matthew 27:52, 53). We have no idea whatsoever as to whom these were or as to their number. We simply know that here was the fulfillment of the great feast of the first fruits which had been practiced yearly by Israel. On the day of the harvest, they took one sheaf from the field and laid it up before the Lord (Leviticus 23:10). On the day of the Resurrection, our Lord thrust His sickle into the cemeteries of earth and drew one sheaf to Himself. The eternal bodies are there in heaven, one first handful of all the billions who are to follow. Is it any wonder that He cried to John, "Fear not, I am the first and the last, I am the living one; I died and behold I am alive for evermore, Amen, and have the keys of death and of Hades" (Revelation 1:17, 18).

All that was done was by the condescension of love and grace. The Son of God came from heaven alone and went to the cross alone. But when He came forth from death, He brought with Him not only the hosts of the believers who had awaited this moment of triumph in Paradise, but He brought with Him, in foreview, all of those who would ever believe in Him as their Saviour. "For it became him, for whom are all things, and by whom are all things, in bringing many sons unto glory, to make the pioneer (the originator and the one who carries through) of their salvation perfect through suffering" (Hebrews 2:10). As God had said, "It is not good that the man should be alone" (Genesis 2:18), so it was not good that the Son of God should be alone.

He was to be made perfect by placing at His side the redeemed who should be as a bride with a bridegroom. Out of the side of Adam, God had taken a rib from which He made the woman for the man. Out of the wounded side of the Saviour, the Lord God would bring the church, "the fullness of him that filleth all in all" (Ephesians 1:23).

That company of believers, called in the Scriptures by so many names — bride, body, friends, the chosen, the *ekklesia,* the church, the called-out ones — have been given the authority to become sons of God (John 1:12). Anyone calling himself a child of God without having been born again, is really a child of Satan, the no-god. But those who have, by the work of the cross, been made partakers of the divine nature (II Peter 1:4), are sons of God by divine begetting through His own will (James 1:18), by means of the divine and incorruptible sperma, the Word (I Peter 1:23), and are therefore possessors of the very life of God, a life that is above and beyond anything with respect to physical life, a life that came by the divine inbreathing (Genesis 2:7), a life that was lost as a result of the fall.

One of the greatest of the divine purposes in calling out this great company of believers was in order that they might replace Satan and all his hosts. Thus it would be seen that a company of beings, made lower than the angels, but who were willing to count themselves as one with Christ in His humiliating death for sin, could take over all of the functions that had been given to Satan or usurped by him and his followers. These would perfectly perform, through humble submission to the divine principles of total dependence upon God, all that could be required in the divine government. Thus we read that God's purpose is "that through the church the manifold wisdom of God might now (since the cross) be made known to the principalities and powers in the heavenlies" (Ephesians 3:9,10). *Through the Church!* Not the organization, of course, but the organism. The living, vital body of believers, redeemed by His blood and accepting the principles that underlie the redemption that is in Christ, knowing self to be nothing and Christ to be all in all, are destined, with Christ, to judge the world (I Corinthians 6:2), to judge the angels (verse 3), to sit upon the very throne of the Saviour (Revelation 3:21). How God's manifold wisdom should be known through the Church, to all the hosts of the varied ranks of the angelic world, we shall now see.

28 : Satan's Great Frustration

A PROBLEM FACING SATAN

IN an earlier chapter, we spoke of the fact that some of the sins of man result in the defeat of Satan's larger purposes: that Satan is frustrated in his attempt to regiment the human race because man wishes to follow his own propensities for carnality and worldliness rather than accede to Satan's desire to have a perfect kingdom which Satan can then show to God as proof of his own ability to organize and govern. In the days of his first sin, Satan had been left with a scrambled world which he was unable to organize, but which lay, a wreck and a ruin, beneath the darkness of God's judgment. It took the Word of God to bring light and life to the dead planet. Now bankrupt, Satan stands spiritually as he stood materially in the time before God said, "Let there be light." Then he could do nothing with physical elements. Today he stands before the world of men, without form and void, with darkness covering the face of the depths of their hearts, and he can do nothing with these spiritual elements. His problem is far greater, the frustration is more humiliating, and the dust will be even more bitter than any he has been forced to eat in the past. His task is to organize that which cannot be organized, and to bring into conformity with his will the billions of wills which will not be conformed. For since the moment when God said, "I will put enmity between thee and the woman, and between thy seed and her seed" (Genesis 3:15), it might be said paraphrasing man's rebellious attitude toward God, that the carnal mind is enmity against Satan, it is not subject to the law of Satan. There is this difference, that while the carnal mind cannot move upward to the plane of the will of God, it can by an act of the will slip downward onto the plane of Satan's will. Thus a man ceases to be what he is by nature, a child of disobedience, a child of wrath (Ephesians 2:2, 3), and becomes a child of the devil (John 8:44). Satan must lay hold of all

230

the wills that fly out on the orbits of the centrifugal force of self and bring them to quiescence within himself. He who is restlessness must find a way to say to man, "Come unto me and I will give you rest." The negative pole that repels must find some way to become the positive pole that attracts.

A KINGDOM DIVIDED

The matter is all the more difficult because he is no longer in the first phases of his war. In the beginning, the principalities and powers that followed him in his mad cause were near to him. As the ages have passed, the early loyalties have been dissipated. He who was once Lucifer, sun of the morning, with the brightness of his created beauty, has become a graying ember, no longer able to maintain the first flame of the enthusiasm of his satellites. By the time of the incarnation of the Lord Jesus Christ, the civil war was apparent. The Lord Jesus when accused by the Pharisees of using Satanic power replied that "if Satan cast out Satan, he is divided against himself"; and asked, "How then shall his kingdom stand?" (Matthew 12:26). Here in this statement and question is hidden a truth that anwers many questions and explains many facts. Satan is still able to divide, but he is not able to unite. In his frenzied rushings to and fro, he is powerless because he cannot count on the loyalty of his troops.

THE IMMINENT COLLAPSE

Satan in his fall was followed by many angels of various ranks. They saw Lucifer's beauty and wisdom and chose to give their allegiance to him instead of to the Creator, Possessor, and Sustainer of the universe. They did not know that an evil choice carries within itself the divine law of disintegration and decay. Their love of Lucifer inevitably had to erode, and their love of self inevitably had to grow. The constancy of their submission to their chosen master thus having dissolved, Satan's force has become more and more divided against itself. Understanding this, the Christian is able to comprehend the failure through the ages of Satan's efforts and foresees the imminent collapse of his empire. The structure of his power is made up of alien wills, and his kingdom will fall apart completely the moment God chooses to blow upon it. From the instant of his departure from God, Satan was doomed to win little battles but to lose all wars. He would toil through the ages toward his objective but at every sunset find himself on the brink of a bottomless pit that lay between him and his desire. He grasped the sword of power with both hands, but he took it by the blade and so wounded himself on its sharp edges that he could not with his hands take up his food and henceforth has lapped it from the earth, and dust has been the flavor of all that he has ever tasted.

The father of lies can beget nothing but deceit. Ironically, though he is the archdeceiver, he can himself be deceived, and is being deceived by the conspiracies of his partisans. We can perhaps see the point more clearly by comparing Satan's whole struggle with an incident that took place during World War II. The great Japanese fleet lay just over the horizon from the American fleet. After the first contacts were made, the Japanese in superior force started their movement against us. United States Naval fliers, however, came down out of the air and in the first moments of the battle destroyed the bridge on the ship of the commanding admiral. The radio communications with the rest of the Japanese fleet were destroyed in an instant, and from that moment the captain of each ship was more or less on his own. In the darkness of the night that followed, some of the Japanese ships fired on each other, and the defeat became a rout.

THE CHAOS OF HISTORY

Now if Satan is unable to unify his own spiritual forces behind himself, how shall he organize the world of mankind with its multiple desires and clashing wills? The resulting disorder is the chaos of history. Any attempt to understand history apart from this, will end in failure. Spengler and Toynbee have created great philosophies of history that see the disintegration without seeing the cause. They have not comprehended the fact of God and the fact of the rebellion of Satan. They have not realized that God had and still has all power and has answered the rebellion against His will by simply allowing the rebels to run everything within prescribed limits, and letting the resulting chaos witness against them. Events must continue until it has been made evident before men, angels, and demons that no will apart from the will of God is capable of bringing order, peace and righteousness. When this truth is seen, the world's present confusion will be not only understood, but expected, and the ultimate collapse of all man's efforts toward union and unity, peace and stability will be anticipated. Faith, of course, will go beyond and see the ultimate rehabilitation of all things by the intervention of God in the return of the Messiah, "by whom all things were created, that are in heaven, and that are in earth, visible and invisible, whether they be thrones, or dominions, or principalities, or powers; all things were created by him and for him; and he is before all things, and by him all things consist . . . that in all things he might have the preeminence" (Colossians 1:16-18).

Satan's great frustration, then, can be seen only against the background of God's announced purpose. Satan made his claim and his boast: God took His hands off and announced what would happen. The revelation of God's purpose furnishes us the only frame of reference that will give us an understanding of either past, present or future. With the sin of Satan and the sin of man, a flood of chaos rolled out over the world, and that flood covered every phase of life: spiritual, physical, political, economic, social, cultural and all else that could be imagined. It is Satan's task to stem the flood and bring it into bounds, to organize the race and bring calm and order to its life. It is God's announced purpose to let the flood of chaos roll on, and to save some individuals out of the wreck of humanity and its civilization, and then to return in Christ to restore order by the force of His power and majesty.

From the human point of view, the conflict is seen on the level of our own experiences here in this life. The opposing parties are the forces of evil and the body of Christ, the believers. In the Scripture these two forces are described as "the world" and "the Church." Let us examine these two in order to have the problem clearly before us.

THE WORLD AND THE CHURCH

There is some confusion possible through the fact that the English word *world* translates several different Greek words. Thus, in the Gloria, we sing, "As it was in the beginning, is now, and ever shall be; world without end. Amen." Having sung about a world without end, we then have a Scripture reading which speaks of "the end of the world" (Matthew 13:39, 40; 24:3; 28:20; etc.). Both of these *worlds* refer to a time word, *aion,* meaning an *era,* an *age,* an *aeon.* The end of the *aion* will be the end of this present evil age (Galatians 1:4), but there will be the eternal age that will have no end. There is quite another word, *oikumene,* which is translated *world,* in the sense of the civilized world and from which is derived *ecumenical.* We say, in our blurred thinking, that the whole world knows something, when we mean, of course, those with radios and newspapers — a small fraction of the human race. One of the lexicons even gives to *oikumene* the specific definition of *the Roman empire.* Oikumene is the sphere where the Gospel is to be preached to all for a witness before the end shall come (Matthew 24:14); it is the sphere covered by the decree of Caesar Augustus that all the world — the Roman empire — should be taxed (Luke 2:1).

The most important word for *world,* however, and the one that Christ used to refer to that element which is opposed to those who are His own, is the word *kosmos.* Originally it meant *order* and *beauty,* but Satan took the cosmos and fouled it with his embrace. "The whole world lieth in the evil one" (I John 5:19). The importance of the meaning of the word is found in its usage by the Lord Jesus Christ. The word is found nine times in Matthew, three times each in Mark and Luke, but seventy-nine times in John of which forty-one usages (not to mention the pronouns substituted for it) were spoken on the evening of the Last Supper, in His experiences with the disciples in the Upper Room, and in the garden of Gethsemane. Beyond any question the word is chosen by Christ to represent the sphere of Satan's activities in this earth: this is the world of which Satan is called the prince (John 14:30), and which God so loved that He gave His only begotten Son (John 3:16). This is the world of which Jesus is called the Saviour (John 4:42), and of which He called Himself the Light (John 8:12).

THE WORLD HATES THE BELIEVER

What Christ was about to do would divide mankind into two irreconcilable camps. Satan was the prince of one host, and He, the Lord Himself, was the Prince of the other. It can be seen by even the casual reader that the thought that was uppermost in the mind of Christ, as He came to the last evening of His life and faced the cross, was the terrible struggle that would face His loved ones when He left them alone as His representatives in the alien province of earth. In understanding this we can gain the true meaning of the first phrase of the account, "When Jesus knew that his hour was come that he should depart out of this world unto the Father, having loved his own which were in the world, he loved them unto the end" (John 13:1). It is not astonishing, therefore, that Christ said, "The world cannot hate you (at the time He spoke), but me it hateth, because I testify of it, that the works thereof are evil" (John 7:7). Announcing the course of this age, He further testified, "If the world hate you, ye know that it hated me before it hated you. If ye were of the world, the world would love his own: but because ye are not of the world, but I have chosen you out of the world, therefore the world hateth you" (John 15:18, 19).

This world, of course, is composed of human beings, and in the mass has been abandoned by God (Romans 1:24-28), sentenced to judgment (Psalm 2:8, 9) and left to be the scene of the Christian's conflict and victory (I Corinthians 1:20-27; I John 5:4). In spite of the fact that God has said that "the world passeth away and the lusts thereof" (I John 2:17), Satan has sponsored the idea that the world is to become a beautiful kingdom, called the kingdom of God. The message is clear and plain in the Bible, but Satan has confused the thinking of many people by religious teaching that is false. The Satanic teaching has become so commonplace that many people look in startled wonder at the Bible teacher who brushes away the encrustations of falsehood and returns to the clean rock of truth. The Lord God today is not saving the world. The Lord Jesus Christ announced that all its works were evil and refused to pray for it (John 17:9).

In refusing to pray for the world, the Lord did not refuse to pray for a portion of the people in the midst of the world. He prayed for those who were given to Him by the Father (John 17:9). All of the Lord's work today is in relation to this group, which He has called *the Church*. The Greek word is *ekklesia,* and comes from a preposition *ek,* "out of," and a verb *kaleo,* "to call." God is not saving the world, and at no time, since the creation or before, did He ever have the idea of saving the whole world. God is not saving any nation in its entirety, although all the members of one nation living at a certain future time will be saved at that time. God is not saving all the members of any one church denomination. What God is doing is to take out a people for His name. This fact was clearly set forth in the first of the church councils. The Lord had told the disciples that whatsoever they should bind on earth would be bound in heaven, and that whatsoever they should loose on earth would be loosed in heaven. There was the maze of the ceremonial law which neither they nor their fathers had been able to bear. The apostles were to meet and make the decisions as to which of these practices would be binding on the Church, which not, from which they could be loosed. After Christ's Ascension, the leaders of the Church came together in Jerusalem in response to this order of their Lord and discussed the relationship of the ordinances of the Jewish law to the life of liberty of the believers under the new covenant. James, the presiding officer (it is interesting to note that Peter spoke but did not preside) set forth the divine purpose in a remarkable sentence: "Simon hath declared unto you how God at the first did visit the Gentiles to take out of them a people for His name" (Acts 15:14). The people that are being taken out of the rebellious, unregenerate world is the true Church. It is one true flock, though in many folds, or even outside of any fold. Mark well that Christ announced that He had other sheep of His one flock that were not in the Jewish fold, and that there would be one flock — the revised versions are correct — and one Shepherd (John 10:16). The Lord is not dealing primarily with the world today; He is in the process of calling out His flock. The world which has long abandoned God has been abandoned by Him (Romans 1:24, 26, 28), and His one concern during this age is the out-calling and care of His flock of believers.

Now that we have identified the two bodies of individuals in the earth, the Church and the world, let us turn to the time element in the problem and see the course of the age in which we live and the ripening process that develops within the two bodies. At the present time the chosen people of God, the true Church, who are taken out of the world spiritually, are left in the world physically, and are so thoroughly mingled with the unsaved world that only God can tell which individual belongs to which group. The parables of the thirteenth chapter of Matthew set forth the twofold movement in the earth in a remarkable way. Whether we stand with Christ and look at the interpretation of the parables as lying in the future, as an outline of history written in advance, or whether we plunge into present history and go back through the years to what He announced in that day, the result is the same. The parables are a pageant of the unfolding of the history in the two peoples that inhabit this earth, namely, the Church and the world.

In the first of these parables, we are told that this age was to be a seed-sowing age. There would be a company of men who would proclaim the divine truth with results that would vary sharply, depending on whether or not the message was mixed with faith in the hearts of those who heard it (Hebrews 4:2); depending upon whether they received it as the word of men, or, as it is in truth, the Word of God (I Thessalonians 2:13). Some of the seed, the Lord said, would fall on hard ground, and the devil's birds would snatch it away. Some would fall on thorny ground, and the cares of this world and the deceitfulness of riches would choke it as it grew. Some would fall on stony ground and would be burned out because of the shallowness of its rooting. This would happen, the Lord said, when persecution would arise "because of the Word." It is interesting to note that the real divisions within Christianity today may all be traced to a different attitude toward the Bible. Whether it is Rome that puts tradition and ecclesiastical authority above the Bible, or whether it is a liberal Protestantism that puts the human critical faculties above the Bible, it is always the inspired Book that is the touchstone of truth. But some seed, and only some, would fall on good ground and would grow to maturity, producing a hundredfold, sixtyfold and thirtyfold. This is the Lord's own teaching and the Lord's own interpretation.

In the second parable, the Lord announced that in the midst of His own planting of wheat, the enemy would come with a planting of imitation wheat. This would grow in such a mingling confusion that no man could tell the true from the false. Moreover, He commanded His disciples —and through them His followers in all the centuries since—not to attempt any separation during this present age. Any such attempt to winnow the true wheat from the imitation wheat during this present age would only endanger some of His true wheat, some of which evidently looks so much like the devil's planting that even spiritual men are unable to tell them apart. The disciples were to go on sowing the seed. They were not to be concerned about the mingling of the true with the false. The harvest would come in the end of the age; the Lord Himself would send the angels as reapers; and they would infallibly separate the wheat from the tares, taking the former into the house of the Lord and carrying the latter to destruction (Matthew 13:36-43). This, too, is the Lord's own teaching and the Lord's own interpretation.

Further evidence on the same line comes from our Lord's description of the inhabitants of the earth at the time of His own return. Were the truth other than it is, how easily the Lord could have found examples to describe a situation of love, light and brotherhood. If such characteristics were to have come to dominate the hearts of all men, He certainly would have said so. He could have said, for example, "As it was in the days of Enoch so shall it be when the Son of Man cometh; everyone will be walking with God." But He chose no such event for His comparison. With the whole of the Old Testament lying before Him, He chose the incidents that set forth the deepest iniquity and rebellion of man as the description of the state most like that which shall again prevail upon the earth at the end of this present age. "As the days of Noah were, so shall also the coming of the Son of Man be. For as in the days that were before the flood they were eating and drinking, marrying and giving in marriage, until the day that Noah entered into the ark, and knew not until the flood came, and took them all away; so shall also the coming of the Son of Man be" (Matthew 24:37-39). And again, "Likewise also as it was in the days of Lot; they did eat, they drank, they bought, they sold, they planted, they builded; but the same day that Lot went out of Sodom it rained fire and brimstone from heaven, and destroyed them all. Even thus shall it be in the day when the Son of Man is revealed" (Luke 17:28-30).

To sum up, then, we find that the Bible teaches that the world hates Christ, is embraced by Satan, and is at enmity with the true people of God. God sees the course of this age, that it is evil, and, far from doing anything about it, God has definitely abandoned the race to its rush toward judgment. That judgment will surely come, and it will be at a time when there is a mixture of good and evil, which God shall separate by supernatural means through the personal intervention of the Lord Jesus Christ and His angels. God is at work today choosing individuals out of the wreck before He plunges the whole mass into the terrible judgments that are comparable only to the destruction of Sodom by fire and the destruction of the earth by the flood.

Naturally, Satan hates this picture, which shows so definitely his own impotence and reveals the failure of all his efforts to organize the *kosmos* into a kingdom which shall own his rule. He remembers the bitterness of that period when the physical universe lay wrecked and ruined, with darkness covering the face of the deep, and where he was totally powerless to do anything about it. He remembers the blinding moment when the judgment of chaos on the material creation was revealed to all the universe, when God took away the blanket of darkness with His fiat, "Let there be light" (Genesis 1:4). He does not like to make a comparison of that long past era of darkness, when his impotence was suddenly revealed, with the present darkness and its promise of another catastrophic moment when Christ shall come from heaven and expose all with the brightness of His coming. He would like to think that what he was unable to do with inert matter he might be able to do with the wills of men. But his frustration is just as great today as it was in the past, and his failure to succeed is as clearly written in the prophecies of the Word of God as his failure in the past is written in its pages of history. The world of men is without form and void, and darkness covers the face of their hearts. Satan cries, "Let there be organization!" And there is chaos. He calls out, "Let there be United Nations!" And there are vetoes and wars. He raises the pitch of his voice, "Let there be peace of mind!" And there are more psychiatric cases. He commands, "Let there be brotherhood!" And there are race riots. In the provinces of earth that have been almost totally his own, he is unable to produce a civilization in which the children can grow up to be lost. The best he can do in China and India sees eight out of ten babies die before they are five, and thus go to God. His demands become ravings, and will become increasingly so as the age draws to its close.

But God, the Holy Spirit, says to some hearts, "Let there be light!" And the command of God is instantly fulfilled. Thus the entrance of His word gives light (Psalm 119:130). Those to whom He speaks are immediately delivered from the power of darkness, and are translated into the kingdom of His dear Son (Colossians 1:13).

In spite of the clear teaching of the Word of God, the evil one — malignant being that he is — goes on his desperate, his hopeless way. The twenty centuries since the cross of Christ are marked with his constant efforts to organize humanity into one great kingdom and are strewn with his failures.

29 : *Satan's Great Frustration*
(CONTINUED)

IN the prophecy of Daniel, God had announced a succession of world empires. He had told Nebuchadnezzar that he was the head of gold represented by the great statue in the dream which Daniel had recovered and interpreted for him. Following Nebuchadnezzar, there was to be the silver empire of the Medes and the Persians, succeeded by the brazen kingdom of the Greeks, and ultimately by the iron empire of Rome (Daniel 7). Although God has said that the kingdoms of the world shall not last, but shall be brought down in crushing defeat before the might of the returning Lord Jesus, Satan has done everything in his power to bolster up the earthly empires that he might have some human force to use in his fight against the plans of God.

We have seen how he gave power to the nations that came out of Ham for more than a thousand years. When it became evident that Japheth was indeed going to dominate, Satan shifted his hopes to this third son of Noah and the nations that came out of him. God had said that Japheth would dwell in the tents of Shem, and this has been the case for about two thousand years. Satan knows that the promises are to the sons of Shem, so it pleases him to support Japheth. Look for a moment at one or two characteristics of the history of the "Christian" era. The power of the Roman Empire was great, but it had the forces of decay within and was doomed to be eclipsed. Time and again Satan sought to give life to its ghost. Charlemagne was the first effort. The Holy Roman Empire (which, as Lord Bryce pointed out, was neither holy, Roman nor an empire) put its dwarfish self into the giant toga of the Caesars, but the misfit was obvious, and it had more trouble lifting Caesar's sword than David had with that of Goliath. Charles V of Spain, Napoleon, Kaiser Wilhelm, Hitler — various puppets of Satan moved in the same direction but never with ultimate success. The kings adopted the name of the Caesars, and its distorted grandeur echoed in Europe until our own generation, when its German form, *kaiser,* disappeared with World War I, and its last syllable, *czar,* was lost in the Russian revolution.

The fact should be evident. Satan cannot unite the political world. If such an attempt at world union as the League of Nations or the United Nations should really come to fruition, Satan could point to his success in uniting mankind and bringing peace on earth by a combination of his efforts with those of men, and there would be no necessity for the further intervention of God. In pointing out the folly of human character efforts to bring salvation to an individual, God has said, "If righteousness come by the law, then Christ is dead in vain" (Galatians 2:21). It is just as true that if righteousness could come by the conglomerate efforts of the kingdom-builders the return of Christ would be unnecessary.

SATAN TRIES RELIGIOUS UNION

While Satan has been working at his efforts to unite political man politically, he has not overlooked the possibility of uniting religious man religiously. As decided an effort as that to build an empire through kings and armies has been his effort to build a religious kingdom through the papacy. But there can be no doubt of the fact that God's promises to the believers are spiritual, not temporal promises during this present age. Thus we do not read that the believers shall be loved by the world, but that "they that live godly in Christ Jesus shall suffer persecution" (II Timothy 3:12). We do not read that the world will accept our leadership, but "the world knoweth us not because it knew Him not" (I John 3:1). Our Lord said, "My kingdom is not of this world, else would my servants fight" (John 18:36). If we have battles, they are to be in the spiritual realm. If we have enemies, they are not of flesh and blood, but among the principalities and powers, the rulers of this world's darkness, the spiritual hosts of wickedness in the heavenly places (Ephesians 6:12). It is in this warfare that we may triumph. Clothed in the armor which He has provided for us (Ephesians 6:13), we may expect victory, for the weapons of our warfare are not carnal but mighty through God to the pulling down of strongholds (II Corinthians 10:4).

The devil has worked in at least two ways to overcome the announced plan of God to bring righteousness upon the earth through the return of the Lord Jesus Christ and through the superimposition of the kingdom of God by the direct act of the Lord Himself. The one effort has been to build a temporal religious kingdom and claim all the promises for it; the other has been to deny the material reality of the future kingdom and look for the gradual coming of some kingdom of sweetness and light by the efforts of man. The one has been largely Roman Catholic, the other has been largely Protestant.

ROME — THE TEMPORAL RELIGIOUS KINGDOM

The first of these efforts finds it fulcrum on the hill of the Vatican. We look back into the Scriptures and see that the true Church was to be composed of those who were born again, called out of the world and hated by it. The body of believers was to be a company of witnesses to the truth in the midst of a Christ-rejecting world, despised and rejected by that world even as Christ had been rejected of men (Isaiah 53:3). There was to be an organization, yes, but it was to be a simple thing — twelve disciples, seven deacons, and elders ordained in every community.

Suddenly there came a great and abnormal growth. The Lord had described it in advance in the third of the parables of Matthew 13. He did not give the interpretation of this parable of the mustard seed, and the imagination of men has run riot seeking an interpretation that would please the carnal mind, instead of realizing the absolute necessity of adopting the interpretation that does not make a mockery of the parables which our Lord Himself explained. Men have fancied that the tiny mustard seed was the beginning of a great world religious organization, that its foliage would fill the whole earth, and that all would rest in its branches or lodge in its shadow. Ultimately the Church would triumph, and man would have done it all — with slight aid here and there from God.

The true meaning, of course, is the one which harmonizes perfectly with what the Lord taught elsewhere. The key is found in the abnormality of the herb that grew up to be a tree. We could paraphrase it by speaking of a rosebush that had buds when you left your garden, but when you returned it had become a California redwood tree, piercing the sky. Rosebushes do not become redwood trees while their gardeners are having lunch, and mustard seeds do not produce trees. It is abnormal. The Lord planted the tiny seed and meant the church organization to be, like the small plant, only large enough to cover its simple administrational needs, for the Church was to be directed spiritually by the true vicar of Christ, the Holy Spirit, sent from heaven. The tiny seed, which should have produced merely the herb of the mustard plant, suddenly was seized with a cancerous disorder which in one church could be called megalomania. The church organization became like the dog in Aesop's fable who dropped its bone in order to snatch at a reflection in the water. There were rich promises and possibilities which belonged to the Church, and she could have remained spiritually powerful and persecuted. But she dropped the wonderful reality of her true position to grasp at the phantom of temporal power which she saw in the crumbling empire, and thus lost both. There came the lust for temporal power, a lust that still burns in the veins of Rome like the fires that burn in a senile harlot who reaches for the ghost of her youth. But all who are clutched to her foul bosom shall die with her. It is written, "I will show unto thee the judgment of the great whore that sitteth upon many waters: with whom the kings of the earth have committed fornication. . . . Behold I will cast her into a bed, and them that commit adultery with her into great tribulation" (Revelation 17:1, 2; 2:22). Thank God, it is written.

SATAN AND THE BROTHERHOOD OF MAN

The second effort of Satan is, for the most part, within the midst of Protestantism. It has been more subtle because its motives seemed to be unselfish, and its methods seemed to be pure. Theologians agreed that the kingdom would come on earth but developed the idea that instead of its coming at the return of Christ, brought by Him full-grown from heaven, it would come slowly by the religious efforts of the Church. The Church, not temporal, but spiritual, would slowly expand until all the earth was included in its embrace, until all the sons of Adam had developed their potential goodness to the point where their evil would be swallowed up in their good. Men would learn to love one another, and gradually truth and righteousness would triumph; the sweet atmosphere of brotherhood would settle down over all. Such an idea is so prevalent, such a dream haunts the minds of so many men, that one of the outstanding voices of American Protestantism, speaking before many thousands of people in a mass meeting in one of our great cities, said, "I will admit that I am confused. For I see the kingdom of God being built upon the earth. I see the advance of the leavening standards of righteousness. I see the breaking down of racial intolerance and the lifting of the common men. I see the establishment of a regime which desires peace based on brotherhood. I see it as the coming kingdom of God, but what confuses me is that I see it being built in Russia by professed atheists."

The poor deluded man had simply failed to see that it was a great Satanic counterfeit, born of Satan the father, carried on by the power of antichrists, and in the unholy spirit of opposition to the revealed will of God. If man is to bring the kingdom of God on earth, either by the preaching of the Gospel, or by his efforts at social reform and environmental improvement, then much of the Bible will have to be rewritten to suit the pride of man. The parables of our Lord that He

Himself explained will have to be done over. For example, we would have to find something like the following. "The kingdom of heaven is like unto an evil man who sowed tares in a field. But the Lord came along and dropped twelve grains of wheat in the field, and thus there began the slow development process of the kingdom of God on earth. Little by little, the wheat rubbed against the tares and changed some of the tares into wheat. More and more wheat rubbed against more and more tares until parts of the field began to take on an aspect of pure wheat. There were disappointing seasons and good seasons, but in the long run the wheat prevailed, and when the final harvest came there was nothing in the field but wheat." It sounds pretty, but it makes Jesus Christ a false prophet.

FUSION OR CONFUSION?

In the light of these objectives of Satan, we can see developing in the world a combination of the two movements. A Protestant imitation of Rome. How else can we look upon the ecumenical movement that seeks to tie in the Greek Orthodox Church (with its veneration of Mary and its prayers for the dead), with the American church organizations (with their unitarianizing liberalism), and the state churches of Europe (with their cold and dead formalism)? A leading French theologian, the late Doyen Emile Doumergue, once pointed out that fusion without a true theological basis was nothing but confusion.

THE SHADOW AND THE SUBSTANCE

When men desire to erect a great building in an old part of a city, they must first of all clear away the building site, sometimes necessitating the demolition of a substantial structure that might have some use, but which clutters the ground as far as the larger development is concerned. This is the spiritual case of men who wish to rear the edifice of truth in their cluttered minds. The process of demolition of old ideas that may have rich memories and may have been most dearly cherished is possibly painful, but absolutely essential. The Lord faced this situation in the minds of the Jews of His day who had their thoughts centered on earthly grandeur. They had made the Word of God of none effect through their tradition (Mark 7:13). Before any Jew could accept the Lord Jesus Christ as the Messiah, it was necessary for him to discard the shadows which God had given in order to accept the substance that was in Christ. Instead of the animal sacrifice, there was the death of the Saviour. Instead of the Aaronic priesthood with its robes and ritual, there was the simple worship in spirit and in truth. Instead of the ceremonial law of Moses, there was the naked glory of the grace of God apart from human doing. True, there were some who were willing to look upon the temple, the lambs, the priesthood, and all the rest as rubble which had to make way for the eternal, glorious structure which God was about to erect on the foundation of Christ. But there were others who clung to the form and ceremony and who lost their souls in so doing.

In our day, the tradition of the elders is as great an enemy as it was in the days of Christ. If men are to come to reality, they must hack through the accumulation of false doctrines that have come from Satan and build upon the clean rock of the Word of God. We repeat, though the process be painful, it is absolutely essential.

One of the old ideas that needs to go down is the idea that we are building the kingdom of God on earth. It is, if we analyze it closely, a distortion of the idea that Satan introduced into the Church at the time the mustard plant burgeoned into an abnormal tree: temporal ecclesiasticism. Of that Church God had said in advance, "I know thy works, that thou hast a name that thou livest, and art dead" (Revelation 3:1). When Luther and Calvin came out of the Medieval Church they were like Lazarus coming out of the tomb at the command of Christ. There was life in Lazarus, but he was bound hand and foot in the grave clothes and had to be loosed. There was life in the Reformation leaders, but they were bound hand and foot with the grave clothes that had been wound around the corpse of the Church. It was necessary for the Lord to give the command, "Loose him and let him go" (John 11:44). The same command must be given to those who seek to build the kingdom of God upon this cursed earth in the midst of the alien world that crucified Christ.

There is nothing more liberating than to be loosed from the blindness that makes men grope in the darkness of kingdom-building. With each increase in their organization, those who lead in his false direction imagine themselves that much closer to a fancied millennium. The fact that they do not keep up in any measure with the growth of population seems to mean nothing to them. They lord it over God's heritage (I Peter 5:3) and think that their motion is progress. They would be the last to see their image in the Scripture where they are called "spots in your feasts of charity . . . clouds without water, carried about of winds; trees whose fruit withereth, without fruit, twice dead, plucked up by the roots . . . their mouth speaketh great swelling words, having men's persons in admiration because of advantage" (Jude 12, 16).

When one is released from this, he enters into the true task of the Church — so to proclaim the Gospel that we become a savor of life unto life in them that believe and a savor of death in those who reject the truth. J. Wilbur Chapman has told in his introduction to Blackstone's *Jesus Is Coming* the story of his release from kingdom-building. He relates how he had been the pastor of a wealthy city church, going round and round in parish tasks. Then God opened his eyes to the truth of God's plan and purpose in this present age. The force of the new knowledge took him out of his complacent charge and made him a flaming evangelist who soon drew many thousands to Christ.

What pessimism to realize that the middle of the twentieth century is well-past; and still the world is in the state which any observer can see is one of corruption, misery and unbelief. What optimism to believe what the Word of God teaches — that at any moment the intervention of God, so definitely promised, may take place, and the quick retreat of the enemy forces from the vanguard to the rearguard shall come to pass before the wondering eyes of mankind. The true Church is left here, not to perfume the dung heap of a fallen humanity, but to save as many individuals out of the wreck as is possible before the final destructive crash comes.

The Lord taught this truth to the Jews at a moment when their mental and spiritual outlook was distorted by their political position. They were living, slaves of Rome, in occupied territory. They were looking for any leader who would take the foot of Rome from their prostrate neck and raise them so that they in turn could put their foot on the prostrate neck of their enemy. The Scripture says, "They thought that the kingdom of God should immediately appear" (Luke 19:11). Jesus answered and said unto them, "A certain nobleman went into a far country to receive for himself a kingdom, and to return." The orders were given to his servants, "Occupy till I come."

From the way that much of the Church has acted during the past two thousand years, one would think that the Lord had said, "Fritter until I come." There seem to be clerics in this and other countries who seriously believe that it is possible to reform society without the regenerating power of the Lord Jesus Christ in the life of the individual. There seem to be those who seriously believe that the greed of the economic system can be mitigated by taking possessions away from those who have acquired or inherited them and spreading them out, rather thinly perhaps, among those who have been less fortunate. Too often those who thus act to destroy our present system wish to hold the power of distribution in their own hands, and sometimes they wish to hold the actual possessions for themselves.

One would think that it was the folly of madness which clouded the minds of such men were it not for the fact that the Bible reveals to us that they are under the dark shadow of the sinister influence of Satan. It is not that all who cling to such ideas are given over to following Satan, but that many have allowed too close an association with Satan's world of ideas to color all their thinking with a dye that ultimately eats into the design and pattern of the fabric of truth.

There is a fourth distortion of the kingdom idea: the belief that the kingdom of heaven has no outward manifestation at all, but that it is something entirely within man. There have been many who have taken the ambiguous seventeenth century English translation of a statement made by our Lord and have used the error of a single proposition to build a new doctrine that would destroy the doctrine of the fall and the doctrine of redemption. "The kingdom of God is within you" says the King James Version (Luke 17:21). The devil and his theologians picked up the preposition like an opposing football player snapping up a fumble and have attempted to run through all truth to make their goal. "Ah! yes!" they say, talking very fast, "the kingdom of God is within you. There is a spark of the divine in all men. You are not to think that the fall left men in a hopeless position. There is much good in man. There is even some good in man that can satisfy God. Surely God must be pleased with all the desire for good that man brings out of his heart. There is a spirit of kindliness, of charity, of unselfishness in man that is glorious. If only you will understand these potentialities that are within. If you will hold the thought of the good, the true, the beautiful, all life will become good and true and beautiful. Nothing is anything but thinking makes it so." And these people wrap a smirk across their faces and go about in a perpetual haze of do-goodism, quite sure that everything is all right in this best of all possible worlds. They assure us that, if we will only think peace, we can change the nature of Russia and make the atomic bomb an unreality.

If Christ had spoken to the apostles, saying, "The kingdom of heaven is within you," there might have been some ground for teaching that the kingdom of God was within the heart and being of men. But the record shows that the words were spoken to the enemies that dogged His footsteps, setting traps for Him, and seeking to find something in His speech with which they might betray Him. In this instance, they asked Him when the kingdom of God should come. There can be no doubt at all that the entire Old Testament announces that the rule of God shall one day come upon this earth, the very stage where the rebellion began, and that here the warfare shall be terminated, and the power of God established forever. They were quite right in expecting that there should be a literal kingdom. Any other thought makes nonsense of the Bible.

In answering them, the Lord Jesus said, "The kingdom of God cometh not with outward show; neither shall they say, Lo here! or lo there! for behold, the kingdom of God is *entos* you." What did He mean? First, that they in their day were not to see any outward manifestation of the kingdom. The Jews had, little by little, established a blueprint and specifications of what they thought the Messiah was to be and what He was to do. Their one sigh, and groan, and cry was that the Messiah should free them from their bondage to the Roman Empire. It was for this liberation that the nation waited, and it was this false idea that blinded them from seeing the truth. When the Jews rejected Jesus, it was partly because He told them that the kingdom would not come to them with outward show.

True there would be outward manifestation enough in the time of God's fulfillment. He will make that abundantly clear in a moment when He turns to address Himself to the disciples. Then He will speak of the kingdom coming like a lightning stroke, being visible to every eye, and to all the wailing tribes of earth who would be destroyed before its shining power. But now He is speaking to the Pharisees. They were not to run around looking for a Messiah who would do a work that would go no deeper than the alleviation of their material position. They had sent their committees to John the Baptist and then to Jesus, asking a list of questions that in God's sight were pointless because of their false expectations. Christ would have them understand that they should not run hither and yon, looking in one place and then another for some candidate to measure by the standard of their own devising. Would they really desire to know the truth? If so, it was there for them to see: "The kingdom of God is *entos* you." This does not and cannot mean that the kingdom is inside their hearts. It means that the kingdom of God is *among* them, *in their midst*. It is thus that the Revised Standard Version translates it. In other words, Christ was standing there, surrounded by them, and all the time He was the King, and therefore the kingdom, for His kingdom, above all others, centers in Himself. If a Louis XIV who called himself the sun-king, could say, *"L'Etat, c'est moi"* — "I am the State," how much more could the King of kings and Lord of lords say, "I am the kingdom of God"?

This statement, "The kingdom of God is in the midst of you," must be considered along with His other majestic claims. The Lord Jesus said, "The queen of the south shall rise up in the judgment with this generation, and shall condemn it; for she came from the uttermost parts of the earth to hear the wisdom of Solomon; and, behold, a greater than Solomon is here" (Matthew 12:42). He chose His example from the greatest and most splendid of all the kings of Israel and boldly stated that He was greater than Solomon. When He was accused by the Pharisees of breaking the Sabbath, the Lord emphatically answered that He Himself was Lord of the Sabbath (Matthew 12:8). The priests, He said, went about their appointed courses in the temple on the Sabbath, but He stood there as One greater than the temple (Matthew 12:6). He calmly announced that He antedated Abraham as the eternal Jehovah (John 8:58). He claimed that He was One with the Father (John 10:30). They wanted to stone Him because He made Himself God (John 10:33). Can we not understand, therefore, that when He said, "The kingdom of God is *entos* you," He claimed to be the kingdom of God? He was greater than their greatest king; greater than their holiest day; greater than their most sacred place; older than their oldest patriarch; One with their God! He had no other opinion of Himself, and so to their false ideas of the kingdom the Lord opposed His person. I the great King, am the kingdom, and I stand in your midst.

The Lord Jesus Christ declared that the Scriptures cannot be broken (John 10:35), but the Holy Spirit, through Peter, declared that they could be twisted (II Peter 3:16). How this Scripture has been wrested by the unlearned and the unstable, even to their own destruction! This false idea is one of the foundation principles of such cults as Christian Science and Unity, and it has been adopted into much of modernistic Protestantism. What is in man? The Bible answers that there is nothing but the fallen, Adamic nature. The carnal mind is enmity against God (Romans 8:7); the heart is deceitful above all things and incurably sick (Jeremiah 17:9, Hebrew); and the will of the natural man receiveth not the things of the Spirit, they are foolishness unto him (I Corinthians 2:14). Oh, no! says the cultist or the liberal, you are mistaken. There is within you sweetness and light, and the kingdom of God. Cultivate it, and it will produce brotherhood and peace. The Word of God gives the lie to such an idea, and the crashing of our civilization in the doom that is to come will show what man is capable of, as man brings himself to the only result that is consistent with his fallen nature.

So the Word of God reveals Satan's frustration. He has not been able to organize a kingdom politically or religiously, he has been frustrated at every turn by the defection of his angels in the spiritual realm and the determined will of man in every earthly realm. So it must be to the end of the age.

30 : *The Sky and the Weather*

THE END OF THE WAR IS FOREORDAINED

T HE wars of men are won by might, not by wishful thinking. Both sides have the desire to win, but only one side has the power to win. Even in cases where a smaller nation has defeated a larger one, it has been because some superior strategy or advantage of position has forced the seemingly stronger country to abandon, through attrition, the conflict that it had desired to pursue to victory. Whenever it is possible in a human struggle to bring a war to a victorious end, the contender who possesses that might does not delay. In the invisible war the situation is quite different. First of all, it is not a war in the strict sense of the word, but a rebellion. Moreover, it is a rebellion that was foreknown and permitted, and a rebellion which was never at any moment out of God's hand. God's might could have terminated the conflict at any stage of its existence. It has not yet been the will of God to end the conflict, but when that moment in God's will comes, the struggle will end. The history of the end of the conflict has been written down in advance, and the culmination of the events will follow the prepared path even as the flood waters that come occasionally in desert country, surge through the dry river bed that has been long prepared for it.

It is not the purpose of this present volume to present a scheme of prophetic development. Too often, Christians have been and even now are sadly divided by relatively unimportant differences of opinion on future events. Sometimes, even churches have rejected vital ministries simply because they knew that a certain teacher held prophetic views differing from theirs, and this though they knew that his passing ministry with them would not be concerned with prophetic matters. Fellowship on earth should be on the basis of the redemption that has been provided in Christ Jesus. It is unfortunate and unprofitable when men who agree in the main points of sin and salvation, who truly adore the same Lord Jesus and believe in Him fully, should become separated because of disagreement over details of the prophetic outline.

THE STORY IS YET INCOMPLETE

It should be understood by now that the sweep of events from eternity to eternity which we have described from the Word of God are in a sequence which demands a continuation and a fulfillment. If we should suspend our narrative, even with the death and Resurrection of Christ, it would be an incomplete story. For though Christ defeated Satan at the tomb, yet for this little while Satan continues in command of much of the field, and he could claim a semblance of victory. Christ must reign until He hath put all enemies under His feet (I Corinthians 15:25), but now we see not yet all things put under Him (Hebrews 2:8). Those who wish to confine their preaching to the past work of Christ or to the present daily struggle with the forces of evil have an incomplete Gospel. The mathematical figure of a pyramid, if sliced through horizontally, leaves a mass that has no other name than a truncated pyramid, while the top part, the vertex, is in itself a true pyramid. Slice that pyramid again, and the top part is always a true pyramid. It is the point that completes the figure of any pyramid and gives satisfaction to the eye of the artist who contemplates it or to the engineer who constructs it. Thus it is with the pyramid of truth. All that we have studied thus far is the base of the pyramid of truth. Each chapter has built more and more toward the culminating point: the purpose of the redemption and the present conflict, namely, that God may be all in all (I Corinthians 15:28). In order to reach this end, it is necessary that the whole prophetic fulfillment, announced by God, should be brought to pass. The glory of God demands it, and the creation groans for it. "For we know that the whole creation groaneth and travaileth in pain together until now. And not only they, but ourselves also, which have the firstfruits of the Spirit, even we ourselves groan within ourselves, waiting for the adoption, that is, the redemption of our body. For we are saved in this hope" (Romans 8:22-24). Henry Alford ends his great hymn with a verse that expresses the longing for this climax of all the revelation of God:

> Bring near Thy great salvation,
>   Thou Lamb for sinners slain;
> Fill up the roll of Thine elect,
>   Then take Thy power and reign;
> Appear, Desire of nations —
>   Thine exiles long for home;
> Show in the Heaven Thy promised sign;
>   Thou Prince and Saviour, come.

This is the thought that must have been in the mind of the Apostle John when he wrote the inspired conclusion of the Apocalypse. The risen Lord Jesus Christ, author of the divine revelation, set His seal to the truth and reality of all that is in the Word by saying, "Surely I come quickly." And the heart of the beloved Apostle answered, "Even so, come, Lord Jesus" (Revelation 22:20). It is this that all of the events of history demand. It is this that all Scripture demands. It is this that the nature of God Himself demands. It is this that will surely come to pass.

Because various parts of the prophetic truth have been mistaken for the whole, much confusion has resulted. There have been some who have even attempted to deny certain of the prophecies because such portions seemed to contradict others. They ask, for example, puzzled by time periods, How can certain things be? If the return of the Lord is as unexpected as a thief's visit and as sudden as a stroke of lightning, how, then, can it be the establishment of a prolonged kingdom? The answer is, of course, that the various seemingly conflicting descriptions are illustrating different phases of the Lord's return.

No Contradiction in Prophecies

How long a time was involved in the first coming of Christ? The answer is that the first coming of Christ covered more than thirty years. The first coming of Christ included the birth of a baby and the death of a man. The first coming of Christ included a man who was called the meek and lowly Jesus, going about as a servant, despised and rejected, pushed about by men and brought to an ignominious end. At the same time, this first coming of Christ included a man so bold that the leaders of His day fell back affrighted at the strength and power of His words. Yet clearly there is no contradiction here.

In the same way, there are many aspects of the return of the Lord Jesus. One phase of the Second Coming of our Lord has to do with the true Church, which He has purchased with His own blood and has redeemed that He might call it by His own name. Another phase of the Second Coming of Christ has to do with the apostate church, the counterfeit church which has usurped the functions of the true Church and appropriates the glory for man. Still another phase of the Second Coming of Christ has reference to the nation of Israel, which God has chosen and prepared for the future manifestation of His glory in the earth. Yet another phase of the Second Coming of Christ has to do with the Gentile peoples, or what men might call today, the United Nations. Beyond this there is a phase of the Second Coming of Christ with reference to the material creation, which was brought into bondage through the entrance of sin: the very dirt of the ground, the crops which the topsoil brings to growth and fruition, and the animal world which groans and travails together until now, waiting for the fulfillment of the first event in the series that shall bring all others in its train. There is a phase of the Second Coming of Christ with reference to the devil and all his hosts that joined him in his rebellion. Finally, there is a phase of the Second Coming of Christ which has to do mainly with the person of God Himself. If we miss any one of these aspects, we have fallen short of the fullest meaning of the truth of the Lord's Second Coming, and of all that the nature of God demands.

Two Extremes Interpret Truths

Unhappily almost every truth of God finds, on the one hand, those who deny it and, on the other, those who make extravagant claims about it. This is true, for instance, of the doctrine of the Holy Spirit. There are some who deny the Godhead and personality of the Holy Spirit, and who speak of Him as an *It*. They would not wish to sing "God in three persons, blessed Trinity." At the other extreme are those who make a fetish of the Holy Spirit and who believe that possession by Him consists in physical contortions and speaking in tongues. Between the denial and the fanaticism, there is the truth of God, namely: that the Holy Spirit is indeed the third person of the Godhead, and that He wishes to dominate the lives of those who believe in Christ, and that He will order and control the lives of those who are surrendered to God in Christ, bringing peace and joy into those lives and a condition of power that is always subject to the individual who yields to God (I Corinthians 14:32, 33).

In the same way, there are widely opposing views concerning the doctrine of the return of the Lord Jesus Christ. There are those who do not believe that Christ will return in person to this earth, and, on the other hand, there are those who believe it and go to violent extremes of setting dates. We are not astonished to find a secular publication denying the reality of the return of our Lord and are not surprised to find the *Atlantic Monthly* permitting one of its writers to speak of "the lunatic fringe that believes in the Second Coming of Christ." There are not wanting ministers, and even whole denominations, who deny the reality of the physical, bodily return of the Lord Jesus. Thank God, there are millions of true believers who belong in what the natural mind calls the "lunatic fringe," and who do believe in the creed which Christendom recites, that the Lord shall "come to judge the quick and the dead," although it would appear that multitudes who pay lip-service to the doctrine seem to deny it by their failure to order their lives in the light of the truth that they must give an accounting to the returning Lord at any moment. Of the date setters there are wild groups, such as the Jehovah's Witnesses, who, being unitarian in their Christology, do not believe in the Godhead of Jesus Christ and must therefore be classed as heretical. These believe that the order of prophetic events has long since begun, and that we are already well into the judgment period. Others, like the British-Israelites, though maintaining the truth about Christ's person, are in error concerning His redemptive work, and have erected a scheme of prophecy that includes references to our present calendar. Even within the ranks of Christians who do not maintain any false views of Christ's person or of His atonement, there are some extremists who either have set dates for some of the prophetic events, or who have looked upon persons or events as being the fulfillment of prophecies which yet belong in the future. These err because they fail to distinguish between the *cycles or trends of history,* which move in ever accelerating tempo as time unfolds, and *the climax and fulfillment of these tendencies,* in which God will bring to pass the end of this present age of grace and the beginning of the restoration of all things.

THEY LONG FOR THE MESSIAH

As the ministry of Christ unfolded when He was here on earth the first time, the Jews, to whom He directed the first phases of His teaching, were confused because they misunderstood the prophecies of the Old Testament which related to the two comings of the Messiah. They easily grasped the purport of the prophecies which spoke of the glory of the Messiah, and of their glory with Him, and these blinded their eyes to the other prophecies, more drab for their carnal natures than the ones which described Israel as triumphant over all the nations. Isaiah and the other prophets, had looked forward and seen the future like a range of hills leading upward to a high mountain. Their eyes saw summit after summit, but they could not discern what lay in the valleys between. Most of the Jews of Christ's day had gazed at the topmost glorious peak, with its promises of an earthly kingdom in which Israel would be the principal agent of the government of God. They longed for the Messiah, provided He should fulfill all that their souls desired for the aggrandizement of their nation and the satisfaction of their pride. They were not interested in such simple matters as redemption from sin. They were quite willing to retain their sin provided that they could dominate in the world. Even some who were close to the Lord failed to comprehend the necessity of death before glory. After the Resurrection, two sad disciples on the road to Emmaus were joined by Christ who discussed His own death with them while He still hid His identity from them. When they talked of the cross, they showed their disappointment saying, "But we trusted that it had been he which should have redeemed Israel" (Luke 24:21). Christ might well have interjected that

He had done precisely that which they said they were anticipating. They would have answered that the Romans were still around, to which He would have replied that He had redeemed them from sin. We can almost see the blank look that would have come to their faces as they would have replied, "Oh! that! We were thinking of something important, like redemption from Caesar."

Israel longed for the Messiah, for they were lying beneath the heel of Rome. They wanted their foot on the neck of the empire, not for any glory of God but for their own selfish advantage. Little by little, as their eyes stared at the highest peak in prophecy, their vision was distorted. When the slow passing of time found them in the plan of God on the hilltop of Calvary, they did not realize the progress that they had made, but saw merely that the longed-for glory was still in the remote future. They rejected Christ because, when He appeared, He did not come up to the plan and specification which was announced in the Old Testament for the *Second* Coming of Christ. Because he failed to adjust his view to the true perspective of prophecy, even John the Baptist was momentarily confused. While in prison he sent his disciples to the Lord Jesus with a question that showed the turmoil of his soul: "Art thou he that should come, or look we for another?" (Matthew 11:3). The Lord Jesus answered, "Go and show John again those things which ye do hear and see: The blind receive their sight, and the lame walk, the lepers are cleansed, and the deaf hear, the dead are raised up, and the poor have the gospel preached unto them. *And blessed is he, whosoever shall not be offended in me"* (Matthew 11:4, 5). This last sentence is very revealing. It might be paraphrased, "Blessed is he who shall not get My first coming as Saviour mixed up with My second coming as Messiah." Even John the Baptist did not realize that there could not be a crown without the cross.

The Church of our day is made up of the people of God who live in the valley between the mountain of Calvary and the higher mountain of the Lord's return in glory. The communion table stands in that valley for the symbol of the nourishment of God's people, and as oft as we eat that bread and drink that cup we look back to the first mountain, showing forth the Lord's death, and then we turn our gaze to the peak of glory and say, "Till He come" (I Corinthians 11:26).

When Will He Come?

How far away is the time of glory? Is there any way whereby we can fix the time of the Lord's coming? The answer is a categorical, No.

Christ said, "Of that day and hour knoweth no man, no, not the angels of heaven, but my Father only" (Matthew 24:36). On the day when our Lord walked with His disciples to the Mount of Olives in order to let them see His final Ascension into heaven, they questioned Him about the future, saying, "Lord, wilt thou at this time restore again the kingdom unto Israel?" (Acts 1:6). Those people today who believ that there is to be no future restoration of the kingdom to Israel, certainly by implication, accuse their Lord of deception through avoidance because here He had a magnificent opportunity to clarify the matter and to tell His disciples that their minds were confused. Instead, He strengthened their belief (and ours) in the literal fulfillment of the promises that are found throughout the Bible by saying, "It is not for you to know the times or the seasons, which the Father hath put in his own power" (Acts 1:7). This is tantamount to saying, "The kingdom shall be indeed restored to Israel one day, but you are not to be concerned with the time element." What, then, is the proper attitude of the believer toward the future and the certain return of Christ? Is it not that he should live as though Christ would come in the next moment, but plan his life and work as though the Lord would not come in his lifetime?

There are two serious errors that must be avoided in thinking about the prophecies of the Bible. The one is the error of the historicist who looks upon the Bible prophecies as having been accomplished throughout the past two thousand years, and the other is the error of those futurists who look upon current events as being the first launching of the avalanche that shall sweep all to final accomplishment. Hundreds of books have been written which exhibit these two errors. Books published shortly after the Reformation took the prophecies of the Apocalypse and tied them neatly to events of the first fifteen centuries in such a way that there could be no other conclusion than that the Lord was about through with the age of grace and that all the prophecies had been accounted for. A century later the whole thing had to be done over again, for there had been new events which must be fitted into the scheme. Like an accordion player who pulls out his bellows farther and farther, getting one more wheezy tone from his instrument, the preterist of each generation keeps pulling the prophecies out to cover the most recent events. They already have the seals torn loose, the trumps blown, and the vials poured out. Nero, Mohammed, the Pope, the Reformation, Napoleon, and many others have been blocked into the prophetic picture, only to be pushed back to make place for the world wars. We have not yet seen the volume that will lug the catastrophes of nuclear fission and the third world war into the picture, but it is probably in the mind of some theologian with a blind spot.

Just as mistaken are those who hold that the prophetic events are in the future but that the Antichrist is now getting ready to be manifested. Once it was Mussolini, or Hitler. Some obscure prince in Syria was said to exist, and he would soon emerge to take over the reins of government. Stalin did not quite fit the picture. The mid-century return of the Jews to Palestine has been mistaken by many for that future return which shall be fully accomplished by the intervention of God in a manner that is to transcend the marvels which were displayed in the days of Moses and Pharaoh.

What is the line of demarcation between our present age and the age to come? If we would draw a time-graph of the events it would be as follows. At the left of the page a cross would be placed to represent the time of Christ. Draw a solid line toward the right, representing the passage of the centuries. When your pencil reaches the middle of the page, representing the second half of the twentieth century where we now live, the line must become a series of dots instead of a solid line. Then the line may be drawn solidly once more representing the events that shall transpire after the Lord comes again. The line of the past is solid because history tells us what has happened up to our own time. The line of the future from the coming of Christ to the end of the world is solid, as prophecy fills in the events that will most surely come to pass. But the line from the point at which we live down to the point at which the prophetic events shall begin to unfold, is a broken line. No man in this world is capable of knowing the length of time that is represented by that little series of dots. If we are honest with the Bible, we must say that the Lord may come back today, but we must also be willing to say that the Lord may not come back again for a hundred years, or even longer. Some look askance at that last statement, for they are so sure (and only because they want to be sure) that the events of the end are surely upon us, but it must stand as truth. What would Christians of the middle of the first century have said if they had been told that the coming was nineteen centuries away!

There is a most important passage in the book of the Acts which speaks of the ending of this present age and the beginning of that which is to follow. The Lord had told His disciples that whatsoever they should bind on earth would be bound in heaven and whatsoever they should loose on earth would be loosed in heaven (Matthew 16:19). In Acts 15, the account is given of the disciples meeting in Jerusalem to perform this work of binding and loosing. The law had prescriptions that were very onerous. Certain foods could not be eaten; certain ceremonies of washings had to be observed; certain materials could not be used together in making a garment; certain animals could not be yoked together for plowing. The ceremonial law of the Old Testament had been turned into a quagmire by the leaders of Israel, and the whole nation had bogged down. They had made the word of God of none effect through their tradition (Mark 7:13). The life of an Israelite was circumscribed in such a manner that Peter, at the church council, called the law "a yoke which neither our fathers nor we were able to bear" (Acts 15:10). James, the presiding officer (note that it was not Peter), summed up the discussion and in so doing gave us the only criterion in the Bible for marking the end of the age of the Church and the beginning of the age of judgment. He said, "Simon hath declared how God at the first did visit the Gentiles [i.e., in the house of Cornelius, Acts 10], to take out of them a people for his name: [here is a perfect description of the true Church, the *ecclesia*, a people taken out for the name of God] and to this agree the words of the prophets; as it is written, After this I will return. . . ." After what? After the taking out of a people for His name. How long will it be before the Lord has finished this calling out of His own? Who can know? Though we cannot, the context of this verse in Acts says plainly that *God* knows. How very glad we can be that the Lord did not come in the middle of the nineteenth century, for then we would not have been born, and would not be in the company of the redeemed to share the glories of eternity. So this passage continues to climb the mountain steadily to the end of the church age then goes over the ridge into the kingdom age on the other side: "After this I will return, and will build again the tabernacle of David which is fallen down." When God completes the present calling out of His chosen ones, He is definitely going to do something for the Jews. After telling the purpose of God's future dealings with Israel, James concludes, "Known unto God are all his works from the beginning of the world" (verse 18).

31 : *The Sky and the Weather*
(CONTINUED)

DO NOT WAIT ONLY, BUT WATCH

EXPECTANCY and watchfulness should be the attitude of our lives as we look forward to the days of the future program of God. The Lord told us not only to wait for Him but to watch for Him; and He has pronounced a special blessing on those who watch. The difference between waiting and watching is illustrated in a story told of a Scotch fishing village. After days at sea, the skipper of a fishing boat was bringing his craft back home. As the boat neared the shore, the men gazed eagerly toward the dock where a group of their loved ones were waiting for them. The skipper, looking through his glass, identified some of the women, saying, "I see Bill's Mary, and there is Tom's Margaret, and David's Anne." One man was very anxious because his wife was not there. He left the boat with heavy heart and pressed his steps up the hill where he saw a light in his cottage. As he opened the door, his wife ran to meet him, saying, "I have been waiting for you!" He replied, with a proper rebuke, "Yes, but the other men's wives were watching for them." It is this attitude of watchfulness which our Lord wishes us to have as we work and wait for Him.

THE LORD REVEALS HIS PLANS

Although we are not told *when* the Lord will come, the Bible gives us a rather complete picture of the state of affairs and the march of events that will take place *after* He sets in motion the various phases of the work of His coming. He does not leave His loved ones in ignorance of His plans. He is the same Lord who said that He would do nothing without revealing His secret to His servants, the prophets. It was in this spirit that He indicated that His followers would not be taken by surprise at the turn of any events, for if they looked carefully at the revelation of the plan which He proposes to execute upon His return, and if they looked carefully at the events of their own contemporary history, they would find in the latter the trends that would ultimately flower into complete fulfillment of all that He had announced. When the Pharisees and the Sadducees came to Christ asking Him for a sign from heaven, He answered, "When it is evening, ye say, It will be fair weather: for the sky is red. And in the morning, It will be foul weather to day: for the sky is red and lowring. O ye hypocrites, ye can discern the face of the sky; but can ye not discern the signs of the times?" (Matthew 16:2, 3).

To discern "the signs of the times" was the purpose of the series of studies of current events in the light of the Bible that I wrote for publication some years ago. Strictly avoiding the identification of any contemporary character or event with a Bible prophecy, the articles pointed out again and again (sometimes using large type for emphasis) that all we could look for in these events were tendencies which pointed in the direction of the prophetic Scriptures, noting where we might expect these trends to bring us. Some of these studies were astonishing in the way they foreshadowed events that have since come to pass.

TENDENCIES INDICATED IN GOD'S WORD

Now, after more than thirty years, it may be fruitful to put down here some of the paragraphs which were first published in article form. In the first issue (January, 1931) appeared the following:

"What right does the Word of God give us to look at any problem of the future? We know that God tells the end from the beginning. This is one of the proofs that He adduces as to His deity (Isaiah 46: 9-13) . . . What shall we attempt to do, then, in this page each month? *We shall be on the lookout for* TENDENCIES *that are indicated in the Word of God.*

"The Bible tells us that Israel is being kept in the world for a purpose. . . . Many passages of Scripture tell us of Israel's glorious future. We may, therefore, look for the *tendency* in current events that points to the regathering of Israel in the land. Since the Bible tells us that this regathering will be in unbelief at first, and that it will be, not merely a quiet colonization, but an upheaval that will be attended by 'new marvels' (Micah 7:15) that will rival those of the deliverance from the Egyptian bondage, we must look for all such tendencies the world over. . . .

THE UNITED STATES OF EUROPE

"The United States of Europe is an absolute certainty. . . . The idea is not new to us. Prophetic students have pointed this out for generations and the whole development may be found in the Scriptures themselves. We shall look for events that trace this *tendency,* and the hegemony of Italy within the Federation.

"Another great prophetic truth is that Russia and Germany will be united in the last days and will be the core of what we might call 'The Great Northern Confederacy.' We shall look for developments that *tend* toward this.

"The reason that we are repeating this idea of *tendency* and the word itself, is that we want to make it clearly understood that that is all the true student of Bible prophecy can do with current events. . . .

"We shall seek to develop the Bible teaching that indicates that we are to look for:

"The parallel development of absolutism, whether in the form of Fascism or in some other form [this was written and published two years before Nazism was created] and of democracy, with its varied manifestations even to the extreme of Communism.

"The increase of lawlessness.

"The alliance of the Roman Catholic Church with the strong temporal power of a lay government, and any indications that show an underlying animosity against that Church on the part of the government which would prepare us for the ultimate absorption of the church organization by the Empire, after, of course, the removal of all truly spiritual elements in the church organization at the coming of the Lord for the true Church.

THE TREND TOWARD ECUMENISM

"The trend toward the fusion of other organizations of Christendom with the organization of Rome. [The idea behind this thought could better have been expressed by the phrase: The trend toward ecumenism.]

"The increase in Satanic manifestations through so-called spiritualistic mediums.

"The increased concentration of business in the hands of a small group that some day is to be dominated by one man.

"The growth of apostasy within all churches, and the parallel deepening of the spiritual minority who grow in revival prayer desire and in hope of the Lord's return.

"The development of that new religion whose worship shall center in 'the god of forces' (Daniel 11:38).

"The economic phenomena which shall make possible the prevalence of luxuries (for the few) and the rarity of necessities (for the many).

"The popular exaltation of passing idols which shall develop into actual worship of great leaders and ultimately that of the Antichrist.

"The great growth of population.

"War and an increase in the deadliness of war's implements.

"Growing talk of peace, and movements toward peace.

"Natural catastrophes.

"The prolonging of the human life span.

"The rapid perfecting of means of inter-communication and travel.

"The growth of immorality with the special phenomenon of the woman as the aggressor.

NO DATES SET

"To this list we will add as time goes on. Once more, let it be understood that in speaking of these 'signs of the times' we are not linking them to anything that would give anyone the right to say, because these things are at present working in the world and are visible to any careful student of world events, that we are setting dates or in any way limiting the purport of those great declarations of our Lord, 'It is not for you to know the times or the seasons' (Acts 1:7) and 'Of that day and hour knoweth no man, no not the angels of heaven, but my Father only' (Matthew 24:36)."

The years that have passed have strengthened faith in the Word of God, and thus it is possible in the midst of a seething, shifting world, to be at peace with the One who is God of history and the Lord of detailed circumstance. As one pours jelly into a mold, the liquid may swirl around, but it will seek its own level and fit the form of the mold. Day by day history is being poured into the mold of God. The world sees the swirling succession of events, but the mold is invisible to their eyes; and they cannot understand how the churning circumstances will settle down. But we who can see the shape of the invisible know how it is all going to "set." The events of our day will seek the level that has been set forth in the Word of God.

This truth can be set forth in many ways. In the May, 1935, issue of *Revelation* the following incident, which had taken place just a few weeks before when I was traveling across South India, is related:

"It was night. There was a storm outside in the tropical darkness. Not a light was visible, not a star. Suddenly there was a flash of lightning. The whole black square of the scene outside the window became a picture. My eyes, like a photographic plate that is exposed for the fraction of a second, retained the etched image of the scene after the darkness had closed in again. There were clouds; there were high hills in the distance; there was a river; there were trees. I knew what kind of country we were approaching."

I then went on to tell that we were entering the Nilgiri Hills. I had seen it on the map, even when I was in America, but now the lightning flash revealed the contours of the hills in the distance. What I had once known on the map by faith, I could now glimpse in the far distance. I was sure that I was journeying toward a reality which had long been charted and which would be surely experienced.

"I began to think of the Word of God, especially of the prophetic Scriptures. They reveal very clearly to us the future of this world. We have only to take the whole light of the Word of God to know where time is carrying us. We wait with calm assurance the development of all events, for the One Who has proved Himself to be overruling in history is also Lord of what we call the future. 'He revealeth the deep and secret things; He knoweth what is in the darkness, and the light dwelleth with him' (Daniel 2:22). We are riding toward the future with increasing rapidity. Those who look are seeing that the world to-day is filled with events that are flashes of lightning, all confirming the hidden outlines which Scripture has long since told us we shall see. . . . Mark well, we are not saying that we have fully reached our destination. God has told us most surely what we shall see when we arrive, but He has given us no timetable that will tell us the hour of our destination. He has told us merely to be ready. Traveling through Java toward Batavia we were expecting a Chinese pastor to meet us when we reached a certain district, but we did not know at which station he might appear and call us to leave the train. Everything had to be in readiness and suddenly, as the train pulled into a certain station, our friend appeared on the platform and said, 'This is the place,' and in a moment we were out of the train. This is the attitude with which we wait for the coming of the Lord. We have His word. We know the future. He has told us to glance from time to time at the events of history, just as men keep their eyes upon the wind and the sun to anticipate the weather they will have (Luke 12:55; Matthew 16:2, 3)."

When the Scriptural attitude toward the Bible prophecies becomes a part of the life of a believer, there will never be any wild association of fancied Biblical parallels with the events that come up in the news. During World War II, one of the leading columnists in a New York daily newspaper stated that all England was reading a certain chapter in the book of Daniel, because the movements of Hitler were so clearly foreshadowed there. That type of extravagance can do nothing but bring ill-repute on the Scriptures in the minds of the Scripturally ignorant. The novelty seeker seizes upon the Bible avidly because it will tell him a little about the future, but soon he loses interest and throws it aside. In this connection we must never forget the story of John and the angel in the book of Revelation. The Biblical account tells of a mighty angel who came down from heaven with "a little book" in his hand. When John was about to write the things which he had seen, a voice from heaven ordered the angel to seal up the things that had been uttered by the seven thunders that had accompanied the giving of the book. Finally, the angel ordered John to 'Take it and eat it up; and it shall make thy belly bitter, but it shall be in thy mouth sweet as honey" (Revelation 10:9).

The honey of prophecy draws those who think it would be nice to be on the inside of events and to have one's curiosity satisfied. The vogue of the keyhole columnist who announce coming births, marriages, and divorces arises from the carnal appetite for the honey of foreknowledge. This also explains the success of spiritistic mediums, astrologers, and other fortune tellers. This carnal taste is revealed even in some who should know much better. For there are so-called teachers of the Scripture who are ever advertising in headline type their latest identification of the Antichrist or their latest program of dates for the appearance of the Lord. All such prophecies must necessarily be false.

The true man of God who approaches the Scripture of prophecy will discover that it may have a first taste of honey, but it will be a bitter taste when it is digested. For the doom of all the false hopes of the human race are clearly set forth in the prophetic Word. Man cannot do anything for himself. He has been completely ruined through sin, and it will take the intervention of God to bring righteousness and peace on the earth. Man can only spend his millions in peace conferences that eventuate in further seeds of war. He can create his leagues of nations and his united nations, which leave wonderful buildings in Geneva and New York like the tower of Babel, monuments to the folly of man's attempts to do that which can be done only by God. This is bitter to the belly of any humane man until he is willing to be totally surrendered to the plan of God and to accept the fact that, while there is much good in man that can help some men, or even help all men for a brief time, there is no good in man that can satisfy God. The Creator of the universe must proceed with His plan to stain the pride of all glory and to bring into contempt all the honorable of the earth (Isaiah 23:9) by demonstrating the total incapacity of man to do any lasting good for himself or his fellows. How bitter this is to the natural heart, and how alien to all the thoughts of progress which have been joined to the human dream of the ages. Yet this bitterness must be, inevitably, the after-taste of those who take the honey of prophecy.

The Bible is not an index to the Neros and Napoleons, to the Hitlers and Mussolinis of history. These men and their civilizations will pass and be "one with Nineveh and Tyre." Such an erroneous notion about prophecy can only lead to foolishness. During World War II, a "conservative" Bible teacher – conservative at least in his opinions of the person and work of Christ and the inspiration of the Scripture – allowed himself to write, and a "fundamental" magazine – at least fundamental in its attitudes on the more vital questions – permitted to be published, an article in which he stated that World War II was the war spoken of by Christ in Matthew 24. Having drawn that conclusion, he went on to state that the famine in Russia fulfilled the famine prophecy of the same chapter, the influenza epidemic of twenty years before was the pestilence, and the great earthquakes of China in the last decades were the earthquakes, so that all prophecy was tightly sewed up in a neat little package and his followers could expect the Lord to return the next week or, at the most, the week after next, at 2:17 o'clock of a certain Tuesday.

Following what we believed to be the Scriptural discerning of the signs of the times, looking upon these events only as tendencies, we wrote about the middle of June, 1940, an article, published in our August issue, mailed in the middle of July, when the evacuation of Dunkirk was in progress. We had just read the above-mentioned thesis which identified the events of our day as being the final events of Scripture leading to the immediate return of Christ. We then wrote the following: "Now we are quite ready to believe that the war that is being found today is the greatest war so far fought in history, but it is not the war spoken of by Christ. We are convinced that the greatest famine, the greatest pestilence, and the greatest earthquake known to human history have all taken place during the lifetime of the generation now living. But, nevertheless, they are not the calamities spoken of in the Bible. Men who teach in a way that leads people to think that we are living in prophetic days can do nothing but bring ill-repute on the whole field of prophetic truth.

"On what, then, do we base all our studies on current events in the light of the Bible? The answer can be found in a certain analogy. A width of cloth comes from a great machine where an ever-changing pattern is being stamped in clear design upon the fabric. This may illustrate the passage of time. We can look back at the great bolts of material that have come from the machine, and we may call our study of what has gone before by the name of history. We may examine the material as it comes from the machine and call our study current events. We have no way of knowing what is coming from the machine in the next moment, except as we look at the ever-changing pattern and can say that probably or possibly certain things will come to pass. As we write near the middle of June we can say that probably Paris will fall before the German hordes within a few days and that possibly England will be strongly attacked within the next weeks. But this is merely human observation. We have historians, journalists, statesmen, radio commentators, and others in like positions whose business it is to study and to guess.

"The work which we have laid out for ourselves here in these pages is an entirely different matter. We read the works of the historians and the writings of the journalists, we listen to the statesmen and the commentators, but we are not engaged in the same guess-work that occupies them.

"We have in the Bible a full-width sample of the cloth that is to come from the machine at a certain time. We do not know when that moment is to be. Whether the machine will pour out its product for a full mile before our sample is matched, or whether the next few inches will bring the complete design that will show the beginning of our sample, is a matter that is unknown to us. In other words, we have a complete description of the events that are to take place on this earth under the reign of the Antichrist during his rise and the culminating Great Tribulation. That covers a period seven years long, at least. In that sample period we see the rise of the revived Roman Empire which is to be a federation of ten kingdoms. One of these kings, according to Daniel's prophecies, is to take the leadership over three of the kingdoms and then is to become the head of the ten kingdoms. He is to make a covenant, a treaty, with the Jews to give them Palestine for a seven year period, and at the end of half of that time is to demand that his own statue be worshiped in the rebuilt temple at Jerusalem. He will have come to power with the aid of the great, unified church that will contain all that is left of all branches of Christendom after the true believers are removed at the outset of the period. There is to be a growing antagonism between this dictator and the church organization. Finally, he is to destroy the church organization in a day. During this same time the great northern confederacy is to head up under Russia and is to include Germany, Persia, Arabia and Ethiopia, with the great probability that the peoples of the Orient are also to be under its sway. The Jews will be converted to Christ and will furnish missionaries who will take the Gospel out to every creature on earth, accompanied by all the supernatural, Pentecostal signs. The hatred of the Antichrist will come upon all who refuse to follow him, and the judgment of God will fall upon all those who do follow him. Judgment follows judgment in swifter and swifter tempo, until the threefold civilization (commerce, government and religion) which has for so long been against the God of truth, will be utterly destroyed. The forces of Rome and the forces of the North join in a great battle at Armageddon, but, seeing the Lord coming forth with the armies of heaven, unite against Him and are destroyed with the brightness of His coming.

"This is the sample that we have in the Word. We look at the swiftly flowing design of current events and we see a growing likeness to the design which we hold in our hands. It must be remembered, however, that the full matching of current events with the design of the prophetic period will never take place while the true Church of Jesus Christ is on this earth. We are not the organization, but we are the organism. We are necessarily in organization — even those who think they have come out — for even the smallest assembly has its Diotrophes and all the other roots which make up the whole picture of ultimate apostasy. But out from among all organization or organizations, the Lord will call His own — the dead in Christ rising while the dead out of Christ remain in their graves for their ultimate judgment. It is then that the living believers are transformed, being made into the likeness of our Lord. After this has been accomplished, in a moment, in the twinkling of an eye, the events that are plainly described in our sample, will begin to come out of the machine of current events as actual history."

From the foregoing we see how foolish are those who seek to identify current events with the positive and actual fulfillment of Bible prophecy. All we may do is to show the direction of the flow, and note the tendency of movements in the light of the full outline which we hold in our hands.

32 : *The Phases of His Coming*

THE SECOND COMING A SERIES OF EVENTS

We have pointed out that the Second Coming of Christ is a series of events, even as the first coming of Christ was a series of events. Volumes could be written — and have been — on the unfolding of the ages, but we do not propose to do more than sketch a bare outline of the work prophesied in Scripture, which our Lord proposes to do as He comes forth in glory to set in motion the events which He has announced.

The transition from our age to that which is to come may be likened to a phenomenon which amateur movie makers know. When the reel of film is placed in the projector, a lever, when depressed, will keep the film from turning and only one small frame of the series can be seen. The light in the projector passes through this one picture, enabling the operator to focus the image sharply. This one frame is seen on the screen as though it were a stereoptican slide. Suddenly, when the lever is released, the film is engaged, and the motion starts, the figures in the still picture spring into action, and the film revolves toward its completion. The whole reel of prophetic events is in God's projector, and we can look forward to see the still, flat image of the first scene that will one day inevitably begin to unwind. The one difficulty — and it is undoubtedly an advantage rather than a difficulty — is that we do not know the hour at which the program is to begin. We have the scenario, however, and when God releases the lever, the various phases of the Lord's coming will unfold exactly as it has been written.

THE ORDER KNOWN

Granted that we do not know *the time* of His coming, we do know the order of events. What would happen if this series began developing today?

267

The first event in the fulfillment of these prophecies is the taking out of the true believers, who are variously called the elect, the body of Christ, the saints or the Church.

The Church, today, is divided into two groups: those who have completed their span of life on this earth, and those of us who are still living here. When Paul lived among the Christians of Thessalonica, he taught them that Jesus Christ was coming again, and that He would take the believers to heaven at His coming. As the days passed, this hope was the joy of all true believers. When the morning came, they thought that the new day might be the one that would see them joined to their Lord in glory. When the sun set, they thought that that night might be the one that would break into light with the splendor of His presence. Then death came into the circle of Christians, and some of the saints departed into heaven, while their bodies entered the long sleep of death. There was some consternation among those who remained. They looked upon the passing of their loved ones with feelings akin to those who would learn of the death of a bride on the morning of her wedding day. They felt that their loved ones had somehow been deprived of sharing in the glory of the coming of the Lord and of their union with Him for which they had so devoutly waited. When Paul heard of their difficulty, he answered immediately. The Holy Spirit said through him, "I would not have you to be ignorant, brethren, concerning them that are asleep, that ye sorrow not, even as others which have no hope. For if we believe that Jesus died and rose again, even so them also which sleep in Jesus will God bring with him" (I Thessalonians 4:13, 14). The direction of the verbs must be noted here. Christ, of course, is in the highest heaven, seated at the right hand of God, far above all principalities and powers (Ephesians 1:20, 21). The souls and spirits of all departed believers are consciously with Him there in heaven (II Corinthians 5:1-8; Philippians 1:21, 23). The bodies of these saints have returned to dust in accordance with the curse that was pronounced on the race at the time of the fall (Genesis 3:19). It is this separation of the conscious soul and spirit from the sleeping body that marks the present condition of the blessed dead, and it is the union of the separated elements that constitutes the Resurrection which is to take place at the first phase of the coming of the Lord.

THE DEAD PRECEDE THE LIVING

The passage continues, "For this we say unto you by the word of the Lord, that we which are alive and remain unto the coming of the Lord shall not precede them which are asleep. For the Lord himself shall descend [note the downward direction of the movement] from

heaven with a shout [bringing with Him the souls and spirits], with
the voice of the archangel, and with the trump of God; and the dead
in Christ shall rise first [note the upward direction of the movement]:
Then we which are alive and remain shall be caught up together with
them in the clouds, to meet the Lord in the air; and so shall we ever
be with the Lord. Wherefore comfort one another with these words"
(I Thessalonians 4:15-18).

Other passages of Scripture describe the nature of the transformation that shall take place in each individual believer: The resurrection
body of Jesus Christ is the model according to which all of the bodies
of the saints shall be raised. "Our citizenship is in heaven; from whence
also we look for the Saviour, the Lord Jesus Christ: Who shall change
our body of humiliation that it may be fashioned like unto His body of
glory, according to the working whereby he is able even to subdue all
things unto himself" (Philippians 3:20, 21). "And it doth not yet
appear what we shall be: but we know that, when he shall appear, we
shall be like him for we shall see him as he is" (I John 3:2). "I will
behold thy face in righteousness: I shall be satisfied, when I awake,
with thy likeness" (Psalm 17:15).

The same transformation that comes to those who are alive on
earth at the moment of the Lord's return is not delayed for those who
have gone to glory through death. For we read, "In a moment, in the
twinkling of an eye, at the last trump: for the trumpet shall sound, and
the dead shall be raised incorruptible, and we shall be changed. For
this corruptible must put on incorruption, and this mortal must put
on immortality. So when this corruptible shall have put on incorruption, and this mortal shall have put on immortality, then shall be brought
to pass the saying that is written, Death is swallowed up in victory"
(I Corinthians 15:52-54).

The great power of a magnet that will pick up tons of iron is a
feeble illustration of that which will be exercised by the Lord in the
spiritual field when He shall call all of His chosen ones from the dust
of the earth, and transform the living believers into His own likeness
in the twinkling of an eye. One of the things that fascinated me most
in a visit through a great automobile manufacturing plant in Detroit
many years ago was the action of the great electro-magnetic crane.
Friends arranged for an official to take me through the factory from the
place where the materials come pouring in at one end, down to the
place where the finished cars are driven off the assembly line. Near
the beginning of the process, whole trainloads of scrap iron were
shunted to the tracks over which the crane operated on elevated rails.
With a flick of the switch, the operator in a cab on the crane brought

the magnet over a carload of scrap and turned on the power. Instantly the entire contents of the car flew into the air to the magnet which then transported it to the maw of a furnace where the operator turned off the power and the material dropped into the melting pot. I remarked to my guide that one or two small pieces fell back to the ground when the rest of the carload was drawn to the magnet. He replied, "You can bet your last dollar that the pieces which fell back are not iron." He then took me over to a car that was about to be emptied and we watched as two small pieces fell back to the earth. When we examined them we found that one was a broomstick and the other a piece of copper tubing.

CHRIST'S VICTORY MADE MANIFEST

Such a division will be made at the coming of the Lord. The long age of Satan's seeming triumph comes to an instantaneous close. In the twinkling of an eye, the victory which Christ purchased for all His chosen ones is manifest before the universe, and the note of victory swells before heaven. As there is hidden in the iron that which answers to the magnet, so there is in the believer that which answers to Christ. For "if the Spirit of him that raised up Jesus from the dead dwell in you, he that raised up Christ from the dead shall also quicken your mortal bodies by his Spirit that dwelleth in you" (Romans 8:11). There is no movement whatsoever in the graveyards of the lost or in the bodies of the unbelievers who exist on earth at that time. How well, then, can the triumph of the believers be understood: "O death, where is thy sting? O grave, where is thy victory?" (I Corinthians 15:55). The moment is somewhat akin to that stabbing instant when the light of God penetrated the chaos of judgment which had lain like a shroud across the primordial world.

Some true Christian students of the Bible will probably disagree with the order of events given below that shall follow on this removal of all believers from the earth, whether from death or life. I am not going to quarrel with them too much. As I grow older in the faith, I know that the main strength of our warfare must be directed against the enemy, and not expended on fellow Christians. During World War II, there was the story told of a group of American soldiers, sailors, and marines in a café who were arguing vehemently about the skill and valor of their respective air arms. The quarrel was just taking on serious proportions, when military personnel of an allied nation came into the café, and (as there had been some friction with them before) the differences between Americans were immediately forgotten, and they at once united against the new faction. However, if there had come at that moment a paratroop invasion of soldiers of the actual enemy, even the allies of different nations would have immediately united against the common enemy. In somewhat the same light, various divisions within evangelical Christianity must be considered. There may be discussions and even arguments between those who are really close together, in fundamental truths, but these arguing parties would unite immediately against a third who holds a position where there is a more serious difference, and all of these in turn would instantly unite against the Satanic doctrines of stark unbelief. For example, Calvinistic Baptists and Presbyterians may argue about the question of water baptism, but they will unite with each other immediately to confront the Arminian theologians, and all these in turn will join together against the Unitarian who displays his Satanism by the denial of the person of Christ (I John 4:3).

In the discussions concerning the prophetic order of events, I will never spend a moment in discussing whether the seals, trumps, and vials are overlapping or consecutive. I believe that they do not overlap, but I also believe that I am going to live in heaven forever with many people who now think that they do, and I am certainly not going to draw the circle of my Christian fellowship to include only those who cross their prophetic "t's" at the same angle at which I cross mine.

CHRIST'S KINGDOM REALIZED

That there is some variation in opinion as to the order of events does not negate the fact that all who have been born again through faith in the blood of Jesus Christ are agreed that the Bible teaches, definitely, that the kingdoms of this world shall one day become the kingdom of our Lord and of His Christ, and that He shall reign forever (Revelation 11:15). It is not incomprehensible that Handel chose this verse as the theme of the Hallelujah Chorus in his *Messiah*.

The Bible teaches that after the phase of the return of the Lord Jesus Christ that sees the entire Church — the dead and the living — removed from this earth, there is to be a phase of His judgment connected with the false church, the apostate church. We have seen that the course of this age includes the general apostasy within the religious organizations of Christendom. The tares will grow together with the wheat until the day when He sends His angels to do the winnowing (Matthew 13:36-43). Throughout the Bible, the two movements are characterized as two women. The holy bride represents the true Church, and "that woman Jezebel, which calleth herself a prophetess" and who teaches and seduces the servants of God to commit the fornication of going after strange gods (Revelation 2:20), represents the apostate church.

The marriage of the Lamb is brought into view, and the Lamb's wife has made herself ready, arrayed in fine linen, clean and white (Revelation 19:7, 8). At the same time the evangelist is given a vision of "the judgment of the great whore that sitteth upon many waters . . . a woman seated upon a scarlet colored beast, full of names of blasphemy . . . having a golden cup in her hand full of abominations and filthiness of her fornication" (Revelation 17:1-4).

Just as the bride and the bridegroom are joined at the beginning of the prophetic fulfillment, so the judgment of those who have had religion without Christ is a sure and certain thing. It is not necessary for us to expand the details. It will suffice to note that the woman — the personification of false religion — comes to power riding upon the beast — the personification of political power in the hands of the Antichrist who shall rise as Satan's last great human ally in the invisible war. Throughout the Bible, the separation of church and state, or of religion and the state, is a well-defined Scriptural principle. In the Old Testament, a man was not permitted to be both priest and king. In the New Testament, the Christian is called to such a position of witness against the world that it is hard to conceive that the world could ever voluntarily exalt to a place of leadership one whose whole calling is to stand as a witness against the course of this world and its prince, the devil. It can readily be understood that Satan seeks power through the transgression of this principle. He is primarily interested in the souls of men that he may gain their spiritual and political allegiance.

We rejoice in everything that is good in the ecumenical movement. Beyond question there have been divisions among believers which are scandalous, and which need to be healed. We are thankful to God for everything that can draw believers together and heal the breaches that have existed between them. But there are also men in the ecumenical movement whose thrust is a bid for power. They are not interested in theology as much as they are interested in fusion of organizations. This is one of the reasons why Christians who are deeply committed to the Lordship of Jesus Christ have been suspicious of those whose theology is little more than "mother, home and country," without any sharp line to rule out the unitarianizers. It can well be understood that when the Lord comes to remove from the earth all of His own, the truly believing elements, the merely religious elements which remain will soon be able to come together in one great amalgamation. The spirit of ecumenism without the deity of Christ is, of course, a Satanic spirit in the light of all that we have seen in these studies. It should be realized that the very word *ecumenism* comes from one of the Greek words for *world,* and that as directed by those whose interest lies away from the person of Christ the ecumenical movement might well be called the world movement. Several years ago, when one of the preliminary efforts at fusion was rising, it was given the name, "Inter-Church World Movement." A man with keen spiritual perception characterized it as the "enter-the-church-into-the-world movement." When all the truly Christian elements have been removed from the Papacy and from the various Protestant organizations, the remainder will flow together with great rapidity, and shall seek power in conjunction with the political unifying movement that is also rising in the world. When we read that the whore rides the beast, we can see that the religious power seeks to advance on the back of the political. But the Scripture shows us that the political shall turn with great suddenness and destroy the religious power. "And he said to me, The waters that you saw, where the harlot is seated, are peoples, and multitudes, and nations, and tongues. And the ten horns [identified in the context as ten kings] that you saw, they and the beast will hate the harlot; they will make her desolate and naked, and devour her flesh and burn her up with fire, for God has put it into their hearts to carry out His purpose by being of one mind and giving over their royal power to the beast, until the words of God shall be fulfilled" (Revelation 17:15-17).

So much for the phases of the coming of the Lord that have to do with the true Church and the apostate church. Let us now turn our attention to the coming of Christ with reference to the nations: first, to the nation of Israel and, then, to the nations of the Gentiles.

There was a time when there were no nations. All were of one language and one speech, as we have seen, and all were joined together against God. Nationality was created at the tower of Babel as a curse by God upon the rebellious peoples of the earth. It was at this moment that God called Abraham to do a special work for Him. Through Isaiah He revealed that He called Abraham "alone" (Isaiah 51:2). When the race failed as a group, God set up one man as the head of a nation through whom righteousness should come to the earth in the person of the Saviour, to whom all government should one day be committed. We have seen that here is the real cause of anti-Semitism. The devil knows that he himself is a pretender to earth power, and that the race of Abraham has been called to become a nation and ultimately make a mockery of Satan's pretended power. The first of the unconditional promises was, "I will make of thee a great nation" (Genesis 12:2). This promise has never been fulfilled, and it must be fulfilled or the Lord is found false. If there be those who think the promise was fulfilled in Solomon's time, we have only to point to the multiple repetitions of this same prophecy after Solomon had been long dead. This matter has been fully treated in Wilkinson's *Israel, My Glory,* and no one has any right to doubt the literal fulfillment of these prophecies if he has not fully considered the arguments set forth there and in similar works.

Let it suffice here to quote just one passage. "It shall come to pass in the latter days, that the mountain of the Lord's house shall be established as the highest of the mountains, and shall be raised above the hills; and all the nations shall flow to it, and many peoples shall come, and say; 'Come let us go up to the mountain of the Lord, to the house of the God of Jacob; that he may teach us his ways and that we may walk in his paths.' For out of Zion shall go forth the law, and the word of the Lord from Jerusalem. He shall judge between the nations, and shall decide for many peoples; and they shall beat their swords into plowshares, and their spears into pruning hooks; nation shall not lift up sword against nation, neither shall they learn war any more. O house of Jacob, come, let us walk in the light of the Lord" (Isaiah 2:2-5). It is my considered judgment that anyone who says that this prophecy has been fulfilled is not fit to be considered as a Bible interpreter. There have been those who have attempted to show that the Church is the fulfillment, but to say that the Church has brought peace on earth is pitiable nonsense.

When the Lord Jesus Christ begins the work of His return, He will do something for the Jews simultaneously with His work of the judgment of the apostate Church. When the believers are removed from the earth, two men will arrive in Jerusalem to begin a remarkable work of preaching. They are called "the two witnesses" (Revelation 11:3-11), and may be identified as Moses and Elijah, brought back to the earth in order to accomplish the final purpose of God for Israel. This identification is derived from a careful study of the words of the passage in which they are found. (Those who desire further details are referred to my published studies on the Book of Revelation.) The Book of Revelation (as all Scripture) is to be comprehended best by the use of a good concordance, for the Bible is a universe, with its own natural laws in the spiritual realm, its own vocabulary and lexicon, its own symbols and usages – the parts to be understood by their relation to the whole, and the whole looked upon as a sum of the parts. This is clearly set forth in the first chapter of Revelation where the method is established in a way that cannot be controverted. John receives a vision of a being with head and hair white like wool, as white as snow, and with eyes like a flame of fire. His feet are like fine brass, and His voice as the sound of many waters. A golden girdle is around His breast; out of His mouth goes a sharp two-edged sword, and His countenance is as the sun shining in its strength. He holds seven stars in His right hand and walks in the midst of seven golden lampstands. I have seen one painting of this subject by an Italian primitive artist, and the effect was like some horror out of a Believe-it-or-not column. God never meant that such a paragraph should be understood literally, as the slightest reference to a concordance will demonstrate. We consult the various passages in the cross references. We find that only once else in the Bible is there mention of a being with head and hair white like wool, as white as snow. This is Daniel's vision of God as the Ancient of Days, seated upon the throne of heaven (Daniel 7:9). We turn to the remaining references, and all but two take us back to other visions of God in the Old Testament. Who is this risen Lord Jesus? John sees clearly that He is none other than the Ancient of Days of Daniel's prophecy. He is the Jehovah of Ezekiel and the God of Jeremiah. All that was said of God in these great visions given before the birth of the infant Christ must be looked upon as illustrations of the person of our Lord. John's testimony is that the prayer of Christ has been answered, "Father, glorify thou me with the glory I had with thee before the world was" (John 17:5). To underline the validity of this method of interpretation, the two symbols which have no answering cross references are immediately explained in the context. The seven stars are the ministers of the churches, and the lampstands are the churches themselves. This method is the one that identifies the two witnesses of this passage. They are first likened to two olive trees. If this phrase is sought out in the concordance, it will be found that the fourth chapter of Zechariah describes two men as anointed ones — literally, sons of oil — that stand by the Lord of the whole earth. They are to measure the earth for destruction as a plumb line would be used by a mason in measuring a building for construction. The great mountain of world empire will flatten before the power which they proclaim.

The fact that these anointed ones have power to shut heaven that it rain not in the days of their prophecy (which is stated to be three and one half years), causes us to turn to the work of Elijah who likewise shut the heavens so that it rained not for three and a half years (I Kings 17:1; James 5:17). This identification also explains two verses of the Old Testament where God announced through Malachi, "Behold, I will send you Elijah the prophet before the coming of the great and dreadful day of the Lord; and he shall turn the heart of the fathers to the children, and the heart of the children to their fathers, lest I come and smite the earth with a curse" (Malachi 4:5, 6). It also explains why the scribes and the Pharisees approached both John the Baptist and the Lord Jesus, asking each if he were Elijah. It also explains a passage that has often been regarded as a contradiction in the teaching of the Lord Jesus. He made a bona fide offer of the kingdom to Israel, as I have shown extensively in my book, *His Own Received Him Not*. In making the offer, He spoke of John the Baptist, and said, "And if ye will receive it [i.e., the offer of the kingdom on His conditions], this is Elijah, which was for to come" (Matthew 11: 14). They did not receive it, however, and therefore God did not count John the Baptist as the fulfillment of the Old Testament prophecies concerning Elijah. Some time thereafter, Jesus took three of His disciples into a mountain and showed them a glimpse of Himself as He would be in the time of the future kingdom (Matthew 16:28–17:13; II Peter 1:15-21) and definitely stated that Elijah would first come (Matthew 17:11).

Returning to the passage in Revelation announcing the work of the two witnesses, we find that they have power over waters to turn them to blood and to smite the earth with all plagues as often as they will (Revelation 11:6). The concordance leads us infallibly to the book of Exodus where we find Moses turning the waters of the Nile to blood and smiting the earth with the plagues. We also find him mentioned by name in the transfiguration scene, along with Elijah (Matthew 17:3). Thus we conclude the identification as settled. These two witnesses begin their supernatural preaching in Jerusalem after the true Church is removed from the earth. Almost immediately there is a great movement among the Jews, and they comprehend that the Messiah for whom they wait is none other than the Jesus who has come once to die for sinners. By the many thousands they are saved, and soon the twelve thousand of each of the twelve tribes who had been sealed by God before the judgment winds began to blow (Revelation 7:1 ff.) will begin their witness throughout the whole world, bringing out of the Gentiles "a great multitude, which no man can number, of all nations, and kindreds, and people, and tongues" (Revelation 7:9).

In the midst of the Great Tribulation which follows, which is called by the Old Testament prophet "the time of Jacob's trouble" (Jeremiah 30:7), a nation is born in a day (Isaiah 66:8), for Israel turns in its entirety to look upon the One whom they had pierced (Zechariah 12:10). The Lord has set forth all this in detail, He tells us, in order that we shall not be wise in our own conceits and think that the church is to be the kingdom. "For I would not, brethren, that ye should be ignorant of this mystery, lest ye should be wise in your own conceits; that blindness in part is happened to Israel, until the fulness of the Gentiles be come in. And so all Israel shall be saved: as it is written, There shall come out of Sion the Deliverer, and shall turn away ungodliness from Jacob" (Romans 11:25, 26). At that time there will not be a Jew in the world who does not accept the Lord Jesus as Messiah. Thus the stage will be set for the final scene in which Israel shall be brought to the place of government of all the world as the colonial administrators of God.

33 : *The Phases of His Coming*
(CONTINUED)

GOD SHALL DEAL WITH THE GENTILES

A̲ᴛ the same time that the two witnesses shall begin their preaching in Jerusalem and the salvation of Israel shall be getting under way, God shall proceed to deal with the Gentile nations. Ham contended for power through many centuries, and then Japheth took over the rule under Greece and Rome. But the day of Japheth shall come to a close, and the promises to Shem shall be fulfilled. God is in His heaven, and His wrath is going forth day by day against all that is happening on this earth contrary to His holy will. But He does not yet pour forth His wrath in judgment. Like the water that is impounded behind a great dam, the wrath of God keeps mounting in pressure against His patience until His day is completely come. Today we are living well down the years of what our Lord called "the times of the Gentiles" (Luke 21:24), and they will surely end.

The study of small words in the Bible is very important, and one that will yield rich knowledge is the word "until." There are many verses in which God states that He will do one thing *until* He starts to do another. Thus when Jesus ascended into heaven, the Father said to Him, "Sit thou at my right hand *until* I make thine enemies thy footstool" (Psalm 110:1). Very evidently, then, He was to retain His place as intercessor (Hebrews 7:25) *until* the time of the triumphs and the judgments that begin at His return. He is to act as the meek and lowly Jesus *until* He sends forth judgment to victory (Matthew 12:20). Again, the Jews shall remain largely scattered throughout the earth, and Jerusalem will be occupied by Gentiles *until* the times of the Gentiles be fulfilled (Luke 21:24).

The Greeks said that whom the gods would destroy they first make mad. There is an element of truth in this old proverb. The mad folly of men will bring the outpouring of the judgment of God. In the second

278

Psalm there is a dramatic conversation between the members of the Godhead and the kings of the earth. In order to understand the full sweep of its meaning, it is necessary to arrange the verses of the Psalm as dialogue.

The Holy Spirit (with sorrow). "Why do the nations rage, and the people imagine a vain thing? The kings of the earth set themselves, and the rulers take counsel together, against the Lord, and against his anointed.

The Kings (with bravado). Let us break their bands asunder, and cast away their cords from us.

The Holy Spirit (with scorn). He that sitteth in the heavens shall laugh; the Lord shall have them in derision. Then shall he speak unto them in his wrath, and terrify them in his sore displeasure.

God the Father (with majesty). Yet I have set my king upon my holy hill of Zion.

Jesus Christ (unfolding a scroll and reading). I will declare the decree: the Lord hath said unto me,

Thou art my Son, this day have I begotten thee. Ask of me, and I shall give thee the nations for thine inheritance, and the uttermost parts of the earth for thy possession.

God the Father (with joy). Thou shalt break them with a rod of iron; thou shalt dash them in pieces like a potter's vessel.

The Holy Spirit (with pleading). Be wise now, therefore, O ye kings; be instructed O ye judges of the earth. Serve the Lord with fear, and rejoice with trembling. Embrace the Son, lest he be angry, and ye perish from the way, when his wrath is kindled but a little. Blessed are all they that put their trust in him."

GOD'S WRATH KINDLED

We know from the Bible and from history that not many of the rulers of the earth have turned to Christ. The nations still rage and imagine the vain things of their leagues and conferences and their attempts at peace without the God of peace and His Son, Jesus Christ. In our own time when His wrath is kindled but a little, there are increasing judgments. But the time will come when His wrath will be kindled very much. When He has removed His true Church from the world, the fullness of this wrath, so well-deserved by the Gentiles, shall reach its peak, and He shall pour it out upon the earth. "For then shall be great tribulation, such as has not been since the beginning of the world until this time, no, nor ever shall be. And except those days should be shortened, no human being would be saved; but for the elect's sake those days shall be shortened" (Matthew 24:21, 22).

It is at this moment of God's great wrath that the action against Satan takes a new turn. Until now God has dealt with him in patience. Throughout the ages, He had shown that there was no permanent good that could come from the efforts of Satan or the efforts of man. He allowed Satan to fight the battle of Job, and the battles of myriads of other souls. The enemy at every turn had dust for his pains and could never triumph over the soul who fled to put his trust in the Saviour, Christ the Lord. At the cross the Messiah died, making a show of Satan openly, and spoiling him and all the principalities and powers (Colossians 2:15). Still Satan continued to have possession of the lower heavens (Ephesians 6:12), where he wrestled against those who were true believers, at the same time doing what he pleased with the unregenerate (II Timothy 2:26).

Suddenly, as the tribulation on earth is reaching its climax, God the Father, in the highest heaven, gives an order to Michael, God's faithful archangel who is in charge of Jewish affairs (Daniel 12:1). The order is to proceed against Satan and all his forces and to throw them out of the lower heaven which they had invaded on that first day when Lucifer became Satan, declaring that he would ascend into heaven and be like the Most High God (Isaiah 14:13, 14). Now there comes to pass the prophetic moment which Jesus Christ had foreseen and announced, "I beheld Satan as lightning falling from heaven" (Luke 10:18). The judicial sentence that had been passed upon Satan in righteousness by the death of the Saviour would now be put into execution. Christ had said, "Now is the judgment of this world, now shall the prince of this world be cast out" (John 12:31), and the moment arrives in the midst of the Great Tribulation.

CAST FROM HEAVEN, SATAN RAGES ON EARTH

"Now war arose in heaven," we read, "Michael and his angels fighting against the dragon; and the dragon and his angels fought, but they were defeated; and there was no longer any place for them in heaven" (Revelation 12:7, 8). The inevitable had come to pass. The God of judgment, who may have given an impression of laxity because of His patience, is now seen to be what He had always been in His nature and being. "And the great dragon was cast out, that ancient serpent, who is called the Devil and Satan, the deceiver of the whole world; he was thrown down to the earth, and his angels were cast out with him" (verse 9). Thus for the first time since sin entered the universe, the lower heavens were cleared of its presence, and of the presence of all the foul spirits that had followed Lucifer in his fall. No wonder the heavens echo with the shout of joy. When John the evangelist saw this moment in his prophetic vision, he recorded, "And I heard a loud voice saying in heaven, Now is come salvation, and power, and the kingdom of our God, and the authority of his Christ; for the accuser of our brethren is cast down, which accused them before our God day and night. And they overcame him by the blood of the Lamb, and by the word of their testimony; and they loved not their lives unto the death. Therefore rejoice, ye heavens and ye that dwell in them" (verses 10-12).

Immediately the next phase of the battle takes place. All evil forces having been cast into the earth and heaven rid of them the struggle now rages on the new scene. I use the word struggle because I am bound by earth-thoughts, but from the divine point of view there is no struggle involved. It is the calm sending forth of power by the force of the divine Word. But Satan struggles, even though he knows in advance that his doom is sure. The prophecy continues, "Woe to the inhabiters of the earth, and of the sea! for the devil is come down unto you, having great wrath, because he knoweth that he hath but a short time" (verse 12).

The rest of this same chapter of the Apocalypse recounts how Satan flings himself against the Jews in one final paroxysm of fury. The woman that brought forth the child (verses 1-5) is Israel, in spite of the fact that many have sought to teach that she is the Virgin Mary. Then it is that God throws His protecting care around Israel and shortens the days of the tribulation so that the elect may be spared, even as He said (Matthew 24:22).

Now that the true Church has been taken to heaven, the apostate church destroyed by the political power, the Jews come to salvation, and Satan forced out of heaven, events on the earth reach a swift climax. The Lord Jesus Christ, physically absent from the earth and present at the right hand of God on the throne of heaven since the day of His Ascension, now fulfills the ancient promises and comes back to the earth.

It had been said, even in Old Testament times, that His feet would stand on the Mount of Olives (Zechariah 14:4), and lest anyone should seek to interpret this as referring to the moment when He stood there in order to return to heaven after His first coming, it was stated that there would be a gigantic geological phenomenon, which would accompany the accomplishment of the prophecy. Of that we shall speak later when we describe that phase of His coming which has to do with the material creation. At present we are dealing with His return in connection with the Gentile nations of the earth.

There is to be a meeting of the United Nations, not in Paris, Geneva, or New York, or as they once met, at a place ironically called Lake Success, but in the plain of Megiddo in the north of Palestine. There the representatives of the nations will hear the pronouncement of their doom or the proclamation of the continuance of their further day of grace. The first earthward act of the Lord Jesus at His physical manifestation as Lord of the earth will be the judgment of the nations.

MORE THAN ONE DAY OF JUDGMENT

Through the centuries Satan, the liar, has done all in his power to cloud the issues and to confuse the minds of men. The general idea, which has grown as it spread and which has received the sanction of poetry and drama as well as that of false theology, is that there is going to be some nebulous general day of judgment at which God will gather together all of the human race from Adam to the last man, and that He will set them in two camps, the sheep on His right hand and the goats on His left, and that He, God, will take all of the "sheep," while the devil will take all of the "goats." The basis of separation, it is vaguely hoped, or perhaps firmly believed, will be on some line of character. Such ideas, even though depicted in medieval art or hymned by Dante, Milton and Goethe, and proclaimed by false theologians is totally erroneous when judged by the Bible. "The great day that's comin'," when "the saints and the sinners will be parted right and left," is not to be found in the Word of God. We have already seen that the true believers are exalted to heaven at the first phase of the Lord's return. Years, to use a time word, will have passed before the completion of God's plans concerning the Jews, and His judgments upon the apostate church and the wandering nations. How then has such error become so widespread? The answer is partly that people have simply not read beyond the topmost surface of the Bible, and have been unwilling or unable to exercise the care that is necessary to make distinctions between things that differ.

Perhaps an illustration will clarify the point. You meet a man who tells you that he is on his way downtown to "the trial." You ask him what trial he is talking about, and where it is going to be held. His answer, impossible unless he were singularly confused or moronic, is that it is the trial for murder, arson, larceny, and parking one's car by a fire-plug, and that it is being held in the State, County, Federal-

Municipal-Police Court. You suggest gently that he must be in error and ask if he has not confused several trials one with another. He answers, vapidly, "Oh . . . is there more than one trial?"

To expect a general judgment in which all men shall be brought together at one time for the passing of their sentence is a similar confusion. There are some of us for whom judgment is forever past, and we can cry, "There is therefore now no condemnation — no judgment — for them who are in Christ Jesus" (Romans 8:1). But, nevertheless, there are some who still think that they are on their way to the trial of saints, angels, demons, which is going to take place either on earth, or heaven, or certainly "somewhere," and they go on confusedly awaiting such a judgment. It would be too much to hope that God would forget about the whole thing and just let everybody come into heaven!

Even a cursory study of the Scripture will reveal that there are several scenes of judgment differing sharply in many details. If the question be, "Who is judged?" the answer in one case points to the saints, another to the nations, another to the lost souls, and so on. If the question be, "Where does this judgment take place?" the answer leads us to the clouds of glory, to a place on earth, and to an awesome place where "Heaven and earth are fled away." If we ask "When?" we find that one will come to pass at the first phase of the Lord's return, another will be at least seven years later, another a thousand years later.

Continuing our study, we discover that the judgments differ also as to the nature of the sentence that is passed on those who are brought to the bar, as to the aspect of the Judge, and as to the conditions of judgment. The Bible student must be aware of these differences, and if these various questions are applied to any given paragraph that describes a judgment scene, the differences will be so strikingly apparent that the confusion will no longer be possible.

In one sense, the cross of Jesus Christ was a judgment scene: He Himself was made sin for us (II Corinthians 5:21) and, in consequence, bore the stroke of divine wrath. This took place almost twenty centuries ago, at a definite place, the mount of Calvary. The Judge was God the Father, who turned His face away from His Son and forsook Him in that hour in order that an eternity of wrath might be stilled and an infinite justice satisfied by the infinite payment of poured-out love. The result was the death of the Saviour, but it was also the justification of the believer.

In one sense the return of the Lord for His bride is a judgment scene, for then believers will receive the recompense for things done in the body (II Corinthians 5:10). Who shall be judged? Believers only. When? At the Second Coming of Christ. Where? At a place described as "the judgment seat of Christ" — in the Greek, the *Bema*. Who is the Judge? The Lord Jesus Christ! What is the basis of judgment? The way in which believers have lived after they have had the guilt of all their sins removed. What is the result of the judgment? Crowns of reward are given in heaven to those who have builded their lives with gold, silver, and precious stones, while the others, who have builded with wood, hay, and stubble, see their works burned away, though they themselves are, of course, received into heaven (I Corinthians 3:11-15).

There are some acts of God which are all penalty, crushing without the formality of a trial. Such, for example, is the destruction of the apostate church. Members of this group who have died throughout the centuries have gone to hell along with all other unbelievers. Those alive on the earth at the time of the visible dealing with this organization are merely sent to join their predecessors; their formal trial will come later, along with that of all the other lost, who had been so despised in the ethical eyes of these religious pretenders.

But now we arrive at that moment when Christ shall come back to the earth, physically, bodily, personally. "This same Jesus," the apostles were told at the Ascension (Acts 1:11), "shall so come, in like manner as ye have seen him go into heaven." The nations existing on the earth at His return are brought to judgment for their treatment of the ambassadors of Christ, and the sentence depends upon their attitude toward these messengers of Christ. The scene is described in the well-known passage in the last portion of the twenty-fifth chapter of Matthew. Who is the judge? The Lord Jesus Christ, accompanied by His holy angels. Where? The place described here is definitely an earth scene, and we know from other prophecies that it is in the valley of Megiddo. The Old Testament speaks of "Multitudes, multitudes in the valley of decision" (Joel 3:14). I once heard an evangelist use that text for a sermon. The valley was his tabernacle, the multitudes were his audience, and the decision was theirs. In the Bible, however, the valley is Megiddo; the multitudes are the nations; and the judicial decision is that of the Lord Jesus Christ. There are three groups present: the nations divided by the Lord into two groups — the one on His right hand and the other on His left hand — and the Jews, called by Him, "My brethren," within the shelter of His protection, and not as subjects of the judgment. To one division of the nations, those on His right, Christ says, "As you did it to one of the least of these my brethren, you did it to me." The last verse in the chapter states that these righteous ones go away into eternal life, but it is clear from a previous verse that they are first to pass some time upon this earth, inheriting the kingdom which had been prepared for them from the foundation of the world (verse 34). To the other group of nations, those on His left, the Lord announces, "As you did it not to one of the least of these, you did it not to me." These, in the final verse of the chapter, are said to go away into eternal punishment, and in a previous verse it is said that they were cursed, and were to depart from Christ into the eternal fire that was prepared for the devil and his angels (verse 41).

There are often passages in the Bible that give a general, over-all picture of some of God's dealings with men, while other passages give more details and further explanation. For example, the Lord Jesus said, "Do not marvel at this; for the hour is coming when all who are in the graves shall hear his voice and come forth; those who have done good, to the resurrection of life, and those who have done evil, to the resurrection of judgment" (John 5:28, 29). We must refer to many other passages to discern that the souls and spirits of the righteous are in heaven, and that they are brought down from heaven as their bodies are brought out of the graves, and that they are united in the first resurrection. We must refer to other passages to realize that the "hour" in which the dead rise is one that includes the first resurrection, that of the righteous, and the second resurrection a thousand years later of the unrighteous. In like manner we must understand that there are other teachings of the Word of God that must fit into this scene of the judgment of the nations. For, as we shall see in a later study, there will be a population on the earth during the millennial kingdom which will be composed, not only of these righteous ones who inherit the kingdom, but also vast masses of the unrighteous. I am forced to conclude, therefore, that the nations on the left in this judgment scene are only those nations which have mistreated Israel; the others, vast pagan hosts, are not dealt with until the time of the kingdom, as we shall see.

Having judged the nations living on the earth at that time, the Lord then turns His attention to Satan and the malignant beings of every rank who followed him in his great rebellion. We have already seen that a brief while before, Michael, the archangel had fought against all of the forces of Satan and that their place was found no more in heaven. We have noted that Satan had come down to earth "having great wrath because he knoweth that he hath but a short time." That short time has now ended and as Michael had fought against him in heaven, the Lord Jesus now proceeds against him on earth. One of the most ma-

jestic passages in the Bible describes the coming of the Lord against
Satan. The thrilling sweep of the narrative, and the vigor of the action,
and the power of the judgments are such that the great counterfeiter,
Satan, could not let this scene go by without mimicking it. We shall
first look at his tawdry triumph before coming to the description of the
Monarch and His glorious descent from heaven to earth.

In an early chapter of the Book of Revelation, four horsemen are
seen, riding on various colored horses (6:1-8). The first, on a white
horse, is followed by riders on the red horse of war, the black horse of
famine, and what the translators call the *pale* horse because they were
afraid to translate the Greek word *chloros* as a green horse, simply
because no one had ever seen a green horse. This rider on the *chloros*
horse destroys a fourth part of the earth. It is my opinion that God
who knew all things in advance, gave us indications in the very language of the Scriptures, of things that would develop before the end
of the age and of methods of warfare capable of such destruction. To
me, it is possible, to say the least, that *chloros,* which has given us the
word for the chemical which is at the base of all the most deadly gases
discovered for use in chemical warfare, has been used here to give us
a hint of some of the ways in which men shall proceed to bring destruction on such a vast number of the earth's population. The world no
longer mocks at the Bible for describing such judgments. The world
knows all too well that mankind now possesses powers of destruction
that are terrifying. A comedian on television said that there were now
three sizes of nuclear bombs: medium, large and "Where has everybody gone?"

We have identified the riders of the red horse of war, the black
horse of famine, and the green horse of death. But what is the identity
of the rider of the white horse? "And I saw, and behold a white horse;
and he that sat on him had a bow; and a crown was given unto him:
and he went forth conquering and to conquer" (6:2). There have been
commentators who have described him as Christ. A hymn has been
written using the words of this verse, as though the identification of
Christ were sure:

> Conquering now, and still to conquer,
>   Rideth a King in His might,
> Leading the hosts of all the faithful
>   Into the midst of the fight. . . .

It may be pretty, but it is false. The rider of the white horse is not
Christ but the Antichrist. Note that he does not have a sword, but a
bow, the instrument that shoots the fiery darts of the wicked one (Ephesians 6:16). He does not have the diadem of the Lord which, in Greek

is called the *diadema,* but rather the *stephanos,* the tiara of the pretender which glints from his brow. We should not be surprised at the similarity of the horses and the imitation of the posture. After all, the Antichrist is not seeking to win the world by displaying the opposite characteristics to those of Christ, but by counterfeiting the known glories of the Son of God. When He whose right it is to reign (I Corinthians 15:25) shall come forth from heaven, it will not be with a flimsy tiara, but with the diadem of God. He will draw no ineffectual bow, but will wield the sharp sword of the Word of God. The great moment has now come. The warring nations of the world have tensely awaited D-days in various struggles, but the whole groaning creation awaits the day that is now described in the Word of God. "And I saw heaven opened, and behold a white horse! He who sat upon it is called Faithful and True, and in righteousness he judges and makes war. His eyes are like a flame of fire, and on his head are many diadems; and he has a name inscribed, which no one knows but himself. And he is clad in a robe dipped in blood, and the name by which he is called is The Word of God. And the armies of heaven, clothed in fine linen, white and pure, followed him on white horses. From his mouth issues a sharp sword, with which to smite the nations; and he will rule them with a rod of iron; and he will tread the winepress of the fury of the wrath of God the Almighty. On his robe and on his thigh he has a name inscribed, King of Kings, and Lord of Lords" (Revelation 19:11-16). There is another hymn which includes the lines—

> O day for which creation
> And all its tribes were made . . .

This is nearer the truth. Long enough the usurper has made his fantastic claims. The buffoon has adjusted his crown of mockery for the last time. The dwarf in giant's clothing is about to lose his costume and be seen in his ugly nakedness.

The judgment scene shifts as Christ deals with the nations and with the powers of Satan: "And I saw the beast [the Antichrist] and the kings of the earth, with their armies, gathered together to make war against him who sits upon the horse and against his army. And the beast [the Antichrist] was captured, and with him the false prophet [the counterfeit Spirit] who in his presence had worked the signs by which he deceived those who had received the mark of the beast, and those who worshipped his image. These two were thrown alive into the lake of fire that burns with brimstone" (Revelation 19:19, 20). These are the first beings to reach the eternal lake of fire, but we shall see it filled up as the Son of God moves in for the final judgment. If anyone wishes to quarrel about the lake of fire, or to wonder whether it is real fire, we shall spend little time on the argument. I know the Word of God and the way of God well enough to realize that He often uses symbolical language, but that He never does so unless there is a thought to be conveyed that is partly beyond the reach of our present comprehension. Even as we might have to use symbols with a pygmy of the Eastern Congo to describe our subways, and skyscrapers, and the other baubles and gadgets of our civilization, thus, if I may so speak, God must deal with us. The lake of fire is either a lake of fire or something so much worse that there is no human language to approach the reality. I am convinced that the latter is the correct meaning. In his book, *The Great Divorce,* C. S. Lewis describes hell as a dingy town on a dismal day, with sad citizens wandering around in the murky mist performing their aimless and fruitless errands, with no smile seen and no kind word heard. Such a description may well be a valid one for the outer darkness of eternal fire. And since God tells us that "every knee shall bow" (Philippians 2:10), I would have added that each individual had clothing that was torn at the knees, showing deep scars and unhealable wounds, mute reminders that before they entered that awful place some mighty angel had seized them bodily and forced them to their knees in the presence of the Lord Jesus Christ before whose glorious Being they had never been willing to bow in humble submission.